ADIÓS
NIÑO

ADIÓS
NIÑO

THE GANGS OF
GUATEMALA CITY
AND THE
POLITICS OF DEATH

Deborah T. Levenson

Duke University Press

Durham and London   2013

© 2013 Duke University Press

All rights reserved

Printed in the United States of America on acid-free paper ∞

Typeset in Quadraat by Tseng Information Systems, Inc.

Library of Congress Cataloging-in-Publication Data
Levenson-Estrada, Deborah.
Adiós niño : the gangs of Guatemala City and the politics of
death / Deborah T. Levenson.
p. cm.
Includes bibliographical references and index.
ISBN 978-0-8223-5299-0 (cloth : alk. paper)
ISBN 978-0-8223-5315-7 (pbk. : alk. paper)
1. Gangs—Guatemala—Guatemala—History. 2. Gangs—
Political aspects—Guatemala—Guatemala. 3. Gang
members—Guatemala—Guatemala. 4. Juvenile
delinquency—Guatemala—Guatemala. 5. Problem youth—
Guatemala—Guatemala. 6. Guatemala (Guatemala)—Social
conditions—20th century. I. Title.
HV6439.G92G9199 2013
364.106′60972811—dc23   2012044748

Frontispiece: Young boys running alongside a funeral car
carrying to his burial a young man killed in El Hoyón Prison,
2005. Credit: Victor J. Blue.

To Life

FOR ANA AND JASMIN

CONTENTS

ACKNOWLEDGMENTS

I am deeply grateful to the people who are at the heart of this book: the girls and boys, young women and men, parents, street educators, social workers, and neighborhood residents in Guatemala City with whom I have spoken and spent time over many years. I particularly wish to acknowledge the Barrios Santos and the Estrada Sulecio families in Quinta Samayoa, Zone 7. In addition, talks with psychiatrist Rodolfo Kepfer as well as the observations of the late Padre Manolo Maquieira, SJ, have been fundamental, as my notes suggest. I especially give my appreciation to three passionate and thought-provoking researchers with whom I worked in the mid-1980s: Julio César Cano, Marta Yolanda Maldonado Castillo, and the late Nora Marina Figueroa.

I thank Guatemala City. Its sights, sounds, secrets, protests, jokesters, *gimnasios, calles,* corners, and *avenidas*—and most of all that rowdy queen of avenidas, La Sexta before it got all fixed up—have had a part in this. I could not have written a word or had one idea without my incessant imagining of interiors and exteriors and the forever-renewed coming and going of people and traffic, rain and sun.

I wish to thank Clara Arenas, Avi Chomsky, the Guatemalaquistas Diane Nelson, Jim Handy, Greg Grandin, and Carlotta McAllister, U.S. historian Lynn Johnson, and medievalist Robin Fleming for graciously reading and commenting on drafts of this manuscript and giving me excellent advice, most of which I took. Of course, the errors are all mine.

I also want to express my thanks to Mercedes Barrios, Álvaro Caballeros, Juan Carlos Martínez, Herbert Sánchez, Álely Pinto, Liz Oglesby, Paula Worby, Luis Solano, Aníbal López, José Santos García Noval, Gustavo Palma, Linda Green, Davarian Baldwin, Beth Rosen, Anneliza Tobar Estrada, Arturo Echeverría and the staff of Casa Alianza, Helvi Mendizábal, Juan Carlos Mazariegos, Alejandro Flores, José Manuel Mayorga, Danilo Roman, Julia González Durás, Leslie Lemus Barahona, Kimberley Baker Medina, Stefaan Deschrijver, Jennifer L. Burnell, Marcie Mersky, Julie Reuben, Wendy Lutrell, my sisters at the Bunting Institute, Esther Parada, who lights up heaven, Miyan Levenson, Paul Vigeveno, and, in a category all her own, my lovely and talented niece, Claire Levenson.

The entire fantastic community of the Asociación para el Avance de Ciencias Sociales en Guatemala—which will always include Myrna Mack Chang (1949–1990), assassinated for exposing not only military violence in the highlands but resistance to it, and Elsa Ábrego (1968–2012), taken so suddenly from us—has my gratitude and admiration.

At Boston College, and in addition to Robin and Lynn, Virginia Reinburg, Dana Sadj, and Cynthia Lyerly have been bearers of that essential daily cheer. Hundreds and hundreds of Boston College students, from Sarah Mary Miner and Alejandro Velásquez way back when, to Mercedes Villanueva, Joe Neese, and Eddie Shore, have kept me sharp and lively, as have Alex Noonan, Adam Rathge, Aniruddha Bose, Megan Myers, Darren McDonald, Lana Barber, and Laura Baines Walsh. David Quigley has been generous by making time and resources available to me.

For years of lucha and love, I salute my bon vivant and beloved Boston gang: Aaron and Annie Cohen, Martha and John Lazarus, Brinton Lykes, Cathy Mooney, Fran Rota, and especially Emily Berg, my buddy.

These years have been quite a ride. I cannot imagine my life without the vivacity, clarity, and creativity of Emily and of Clara Arenas. Clara's encouragement on this project and her friendship truly kept me going, and her house kept me housed.

At Duke University Press I give my gratitude to the anonymous readers of versions of this manuscript, book project editors Mark Mastromarino and Liz Smith, and copyeditor Sonya Manes. I could not have hoped for a better general editor than the calm Gisela Fosado. So many of us scholars love and honor the great Valerie Millholland, who keeps ships running with her insight, good humor, and love of a good evening. I only hope to reciprocate her kindness to me.

The photographs in Adiós Niño give eloquent testimony to the lives of Guatemalans, and they reflect the sensitivity and commitment of those who took them. I am lucky to have accidentally found the work of Victor J. Blue, whose terrific pictures enhance this book. I also thank Donna DeCesare,

Jonny Raxón, Nancy McGirr, Anaís García, and most of all, the gifted Andrea Aragón, whose haunting photographs of street youth grace the book's cover and interior.

Above all, I give my gratitude to my life-loving, ever-original, and insightful daughters, Jasmin and Ana. They form my supreme *caracol* of humor, good times, ideas, and hope. Words are not enough to express my love. *Adelante.*

THE RISE AND FALL OF TOMORROW

The child, the future of nations, must be tended to with all the elements necessary to the production of civilization, progress and social perfection.

　—Ramón Rosa, *Primer Congreso Pedagógico Centro Americano 1893*

The military raped them [women]. It didn't even respect the right to live of those not yet born. The Army [soldiers] grabbed pregnant women, they cut them, they opened their stomachs, they took out their babies. They also murdered the newly born, they took babies from their mothers' breasts and one-year-olds and threw them into the river and they drowned. One of the soldiers who threw a child into the river called out, "Adiós, niño."

　—Massacre at Río Pixcayá, Aldea Estancia de la Virgen, San Martín Jilotepeque,
　　March 18, 1982, Caso Ilustrativo numero 50, Memoria del Silencio

When the woman entered the small apartment [in Guatemala City's Zone 3] that she shared with her nephew [a member of the gang Mara Salvatrucha], she saw a blurred rush of movement and heard her nephew yell, "Get out of here!" She stood for an instant, shocked to realize that her nephew and several boys hovered over two girls whom they had tightly tied up. The woman turned and ran for help. A few hours later, the dead bodies of these two girls, marked by rape, were found in the street a few blocks away.

　—Personal communication, Guatemala City, November 2003

In the 1800s and most of the 1900s, first the Guatemalan Liberal Party and later reformists and revolutionaries envisioned "La Juventud" (Youth) to be in the vanguard of a modernity that would arise from within a city conceived as a beacon in a rural and savage wilderness.[1] Following the defeat of the popular and revolutionary organizations and years of neoliberal policies, by

2000 Guatemala City was among the poorest and most dangerous cities on the continent, and La Juventud had gone down the drain with it.[2] Catapulted from the category of "heroic" into that of "criminal," urban youth replaced los subversivos as the enemies of society. For two hundred years a symbol of beautiful tomorrows, La Juventud has been turned upside down to signify the radically dangerous present, chaos and death, an obstacle to the future instead of its herald.

The experiences of urban youth at the outset of the twenty-first century are haunted by the last century's catastrophic failure to win the struggle that shaped it: the fight for a different Guatemala, one with a dignified life for all, one beyond mere survival.[3] The terrifying boys and the murdered girls in the third epigraph live and die within the legacy of devastation shown in the second one. The ideological use of the child in the first represents the salvation fantasy of liberalism: the continual displacement of the inequalities of capitalism to a more just future that has never arrived and that now seems to have vanished from the horizon. Today the big question for many youth is how to cross borders to find work.

When I first arrived in Guatemala in 1978, the now-infamous gangs called Maras had no discursive or literal presence. Instead, the vitality of the popular movement permeated everywhere I went, from aldeas in Huehuetenango to Guatemala City. The year before, over 100,000 Guatemala City residents had turned out to greet 80 Maya Mam miners who had walked from the Cuchumatanes Mountains to the capital to publicize their struggle to win a union in a tungsten mine, and all along the way, down the 370 kilometers of the winding Pan-American Highway, villagers and townspeople had prepared food, fiestas, and sleeping space for them. In 1978, shantytown dwellers, bus drivers, factory and state workers, students, and almost everyone else in Guatemala City brought it to a halt to raise wages and stop an increase in bus fares. In mid-1979 the call for a democratic and revolutionary Guatemala was pervasive, and many people sat by their radios listening to the Sandinistas take Managua. In early 1980, the entire workforce of the plantations and mills of the Southern Coast struck, arming themselves with machetes and with the esprit of their slogan "Cabeza Clara, Corazón Solidario, Puño en Alto" (Clear Head, Strong Heart, Fist Raised). It did not seem unrealistic to think revolution was on the horizon. Not only did tens of thousands join the revolutionary fronts in the late 1970s and early 1980s, in some areas of Guatemala these new recruits pushed the guerrilla leadership to take stronger military initiatives.

Urban youth have a long history within this landscape of social protest. Even though they were a numerical minority in the midst of their peers, the primary, secondary, and university students who joined political movements were a dominant presence in the public school system from the 1950s (if not earlier) until the early 1980s. They were among the first to openly challenge the post-1954 military regimes, when a handful of secondary students from the Escuela Normal and the Instituto Rafael Aqueche organized the dynamic and militant Frente Unido del Estudiantado Guatemalteco Organizado (United Front of Guatemalan Students, FUEGO) in 1958 and configured a new generation of radical militants, even before the Cuban Revolution.[4] Thousands of city students became activists over the coming decades. Urban students joined rail and other workers in April–May 1962, Guatemala City's "May 1968," six years early. They enthusiastically—even euphorically—supported peasant and worker groups throughout the 1960s and 1970s. They went into the countryside to learn from the rural poor; they secretly joined the guerrilla groups; and, despite increased disappearances of students, they marched against the state in Guatemala City in the tens of thousands after the Panzós Massacre in 1978. On May 1, 1980, they marched in greater numbers, this time with their faces covered, under banners reading "For a Revolutionary and Democratic Guatemala," and "Nicaragua Today, Guatemala Tomorrow," in the last truly massive demonstration of the century.

The uproar about the Maras came on the heels of the military's breakneck defeat of that possible future of popular revolution that was achieved by the scorched-earth genocidal campaigns of the early 1980s. The Maras made their first public appearance in 1985, when they joined students from the Instituto Rafael Aqueche to protest a bus fare increase. The subsequent massive publicity generated by the media, politicians, and the National Police about the presumed dangers of these new gangs contrasted sharply with the absence of news about the army campaigns in the countryside. This new discourse concerning unruly urban youth not only furthered the silence surrounding state violence in the 1980s, it put into motion an astonishing reversal of truth, a lie that was part of the war: youngsters were the source of violence and other dangers from which the state would protect its good citizens in order to create a new social reality. A study done in these same years, however, refuted the propaganda that the Maras were a threat: it showed that the *mareros* offered clues, but not danger, to the world around them. Although anxious about life, they celebrated it, and they concerned themselves with the communities that surrounded them. Their "us" included the poor, and the *burgueses* and the "asshole wealthy" constituted their "them."[5]

But the Maras changed. By the time of the 1996 Peace Accords the gangs had become morbid, and that has only increased with time. Worlds unto themselves, the gangs have come to form a subjective "us," and everyone else, including the poor, constitutes "them." Too many gang members in Guatemala City have become the victimizers that they were once falsely accused of being (see figure intro.1). Although without a doubt still accused of far more crimes than they commit, as the Mexican scholar Rossana Reguillo Cruz points out, the Maras also "unfortunately actively participate in the propagation of their own legend."[6] Invented and real, they huddle together around violent identities and practices that make them more than "a series of photos and video clips" to turn the public toward *mano dura* (iron fist) politics.[7] Within them has settled, to quote the Guatemalan epidemiologist Dr. José García Noval, "a violence that . . . concretizes itself in actions of extreme cruelty."[8]

Cut Out of History

The youth in Maras have become increasingly involved not only in violence, a term that describes many modalities, but in violent deaths. I argue that their turn from life toward death is related to larger transformations that have taken place in a short period of time in Guatemala. I suggest that the way the gangs changed, and not just how they are in a frozen snapshot in time, needs to be understood within a historical context of several overlapping dynamics. One is the defeat of a decades-old urban subculture in working-class barrios that emanated from the popular movements of 1954–80. Another is the inextricably related means and effects of that defeat, which include a military victory through genocidal war, neoliberal policies that have diminished social services for the urban poor, unemployment in a city where employment refers to a physically exhausting job at not even survival wages, and a legal system that is currently in complete collapse. In addition, and most emphasized by journalists and many researchers, in the mid-1990s members of two gangs from Los Angeles, Mara-18 (M-18) and Mara Salvatrucha (MS-13), arrived, and they had ties to the sale of drugs. The growth of the drug trade, and of drug use in urban neighborhoods, has been rapid. By one estimate, by 2000 almost 80 percent of the cocaine shipped from South America to the United States flowed through Guatemala. The appearance of skilled entrepreneurs who use violence as a marketing strategy in a country in permanent economic crisis is an element in the history of the gangs. One thing facilitates another: a weak economy and an inoperative legal system allow global organized crime to flourish and to incorporate mareros as cheap labor within a system of networks that employs down-and-out youth everywhere in the world, and keeps them that way by making sure they have little cash.

FIGURE INTRO.1 Mareros in El Hoyón Prison, Escuintla, 2005. However real, this photograph of threatening and tattooed mareros exemplifies the clichéd image that has been used with success everywhere in Guatemala to incite fear, to garner support for politicians from the extreme Right, and to justify increased military involvement in civilian life.
Credit: Victor J. Blue.

I underline historical specificity and politics to argue that in many ways these young people's coexistence with violent death, including with their own murders, is intimately related to what can be framed as the Guatemalan state's successful use of spectacular and reverberating necropolitics.[9] Starting roughly in 1980 and into the 1990s, sovereignty rested on the absolute negation of life in order to put an end to over fifty years of unfinished history in which radical political movements had polarized Guatemala in a battle for its destiny. The cohabitation with death that has come to inform Maras is tied to the success of a violence that was, in the words of the Guatemalan writer Juan Carlos Mazariegos, "an excess of reality."[10] It is the product of what this military victory and its consequences have spawned in subjectivities and everyday life: a Guatemala wherein practices and mentalities of solidarity, trust, and mutual concern have been ripped apart to strain and erode, in the words of the late Jesuit psychologist Ignacio Martín-Baró, assassinated by the Salvadoran Army in 1989, the "collective capacity to work and love."[11]

An extreme and a minority among youth in Guatemala City, a small painful intrusion that hurts and impairs, the splinter in the eye that is the "best magnifying glass," the apolitical Maras have crystallized necropolitics into what I call necroliving.[12] In the city, the postwar mareros control life through their power to take it away. For many youth in the Maras, threatening to kill and killing have become practices about the scarce daily options for earning a living, and about maintaining order, teaching lessons, and achieving identity and respect, especially for young men for whom the values tied to other male identities—such as the gallant breadwinner—and the possibilities of achieving alternate masculinities have diminished. This does not mean that every marero kills. Rather, I am suggesting that within the mareros' social imaginary, in Charles Taylor's sense of that "common understanding which makes possible common practices," violent death controls the management of life, short as that may be.[13] The average marero is murdered by the time he or she is twenty-two. Perhaps even worse: one's own early demise is part of the marero imaginary, and the average gang member *expects* to die by that age.[14]

Hardly any members of the violent Maras of the 1990s and onward directly experienced war, although a few did or thought they did. Most were born in the 1980s or later, and they came of age in a Guatemala City largely remade and reassembled by violence. They remember the stories of cadavers and not of the struggles for social justice. In her commentary on the juvenile mareros in a reform center who danced after tearing out the heart and other internal organs of a teacher named Jorge Emilio Winter Viaurre on March 3,

2009, a Guatemalan journalist wrote that Guatemalan children live in "a society in which problems are generally resolved by death."[15] Immersed in the legacy of political sovereignty through the manufacture of horrific deaths and surrounded by violent deaths, by murdering or by imagining death in their magical religious rites, gang members struggle to control death as well as life. Necroliving deracinates death. The Guatemalan psychiatrist Rodolfo Kepfer points out that mareros' preoccupation with death is part of a prevalent thanatophobia. He thinks, "In Guatemala death is perceived as a traumatic event that depends on others, it is not seen as a natural part of life. This creates the phobia that death is everywhere, lurking in other people and 'I too' [referring to youth] can arrest it with violence."[16] Murder becomes "natural death," the normal way to die. Making the living dead starts to seem to be what humans do to one another, by their very nature. This materializes what the Chilean psychologist Elizabeth Lira calls the "devaluation of life," hatred or the dehumanization of self and others, that has its grand finale in the morgue.[17]

A Planet of Gangs

Guatemala City's Maras are not the only gangs or the only very violent ones currently in cities on our "planet of slums," and the literature devoted to them is vast.[18] A variety of approaches are evident in sociology, psychology, criminal justice, communications, and several other disciplines, with no single definition of "gang" emerging. However, some strong common core arguments are apparent. Most studies of urban gangs in Central America and the rest of the Americas see them as consequences of an array of "multiple marginalities"—a key phrase in the literature—that includes urban decay and unemployment; social abandonment and domestic abuse; school absenteeism; and the lack of mobility, community, social recognition, and identity.[19] In addition, many authors emphasize that for males gaining masculine identity can be particularly important aspect of gang life, and they underscore how lethal "performing male" can be when violence, masculinity, and gaining respect bleed into one another.[20] However, neither the pursuit of masculinity nor multiple marginalities explain change or differences, describe subjectivities, or suggest how cruel or kindly a turn masculinity can take.[21]

From those outlaw bands of Robin Hoods and the gangs that fortify urban political machinery, to the Almighty Latin King/Queen Nation (ALKQN), a gang that developed a male identity based on respect for women, different gangs have varied worldviews, principles, and social relationships, and they change over time. Within their short lifetime, Guatemala City's Maras have gone, as *Adiós Niño* discusses, from protecting neighbors to abusing them. All that is encompassed by history—whether unemployment, racism, military recruitment, or the criminalization of immigration—counts. This point is elucidated in many studies, such as those by José Miguel Cruz about Maras in El Salvador, and the works of David Brotherton and Luis Barrios on the ALKQN, of Tom Hayden on gangs in Los Angeles, and of John Hagedorn, whose book about global gangs makes arguments similar to mine about the connections between gangs, the fall of social movements, and the rise of neoliberal polices.[22] The Mexican writer Marco Lara Klahr wryly underscores that gangs evolve out of contemporary histories in his book *Hoy te toca la muerte: El imperio de las Maras visto desde dentro*, when he quotes the distinguished Honduran dramatist Tito Estrada: "Look, after all is said and done, what we should ask about the Maras is what happened to the Latin American working class."[23]

Adiós Niño focuses on the connections among transformations in the Maras, Guatemala, and Guatemala City. It is situated within an emergent literature about youth gangs in Honduras, Guatemala, El Salvador, and Nicaragua, where the misleadingly dubbed "Central American gangs" exist.[24] Generally these studies are based on respect for what gang members say, as well as on surveys and official data, and on considerations of the tattoos, language, music, graffiti, and clothes that distinguish them. No one doubts that graffiti stake a gang's urban space or that clothes mark a collective identity. Most writers approach gangs as emotional communities, and try, to quote Rossana Reguillo Cruz, to "develop a vision that doesn't lose youth as subject but instead understands their multiple 'roles' and social interactions."[25]

Adiós Niño addresses several questions that hover over this growing literature. One concerns the notion that the gangs and their violence are apolitical. I argue that this is a misleading conceptualization. While it is descriptively accurate that neither the Maras nor their violence fall within the realm of what one sociologist defines as political violence, a "politico-ideological conflict between authoritarian states and more or less well defined armed or unarmed opponents," the Maras have come out of a political crucible, and politicians have found political uses for them that range from no doubt paying them to disrupt rallies for rival candidates to using images of them to garner support for right-wing candidates.[26] The politically generated depoliticization of youth is in itself a historical watershed that has changed Guatemalan urban politics. That Maras are not "political" is politics.

A tendency to depoliticize the discussion about the gangs is inherent in

studies that downplay the importance of state violence in favor of a..
that invokes a more general barrio violence that has origins in, and is .
twined with, social exclusion.[27] This is a second knotty theme within d..
cussions about gangs in the Central American region. Using declared war as
the marker, a deductive argument gets made that because Honduras had no
such war, the wars in El Salvador, Guatemala, and Nicaragua could not have
much explanatory power in relationship to the Maras and, by extension, if
these are "LA gangs," war has no significance whatsoever because Los Angeles has not been the site of declared war since 1846. Yet Honduras has had
extraordinary state terror, as the Honduran sociologist Leticia Salomón discusses in her work. Official wars are not all that is at stake in terms of histories of political violence. Nicaragua, which had a war, has far less violent
pandillas. The war was different: the 1980s Contra War was not about Nicaraguan state terror against its own population, and the destruction of political
groups in Managua did not take place on the scale of that in Guatemala City.
No doubt many distinctions could be added. In emphasizing the influence
that the means and results of state terrorism have had on the history of the
Maras in Guatemala City, I keep company with the political scientist José
Miguel Cruz, who urges researchers to complicate their analysis of gang life
in San Salvador and go beyond focusing on the "back and forth" between
San Salvador and Los Angeles by giving greater consideration to the impact
El Salvador's long war has had.[28]

The related question in the literature is, simply put, whether or not the
gangs are "LA gangs." The relationship between Maras in Los Angeles and
those in Central America is a subject that has attracted scholars, particularly
given the interest in global and transnational studies, as well as journalists
and agencies such as Homeland Security. The dynamics of the cross-border
movements of youth and organizations between Los Angeles and San Salvador, and the effects of these on urban geography that Elana Zilberg and
Juan Carlos Narváez Gutierrez analyze, seem more intense than do those
between Los Angeles and cities in Honduras, Nicaragua, and Guatemala,
where a murder in Pico-Union at dawn does not spell a killing in Guatemala
City at dusk, to use Narváez Gutiérrez's example.[29] But even in the case of
San Salvador, what does it mean, as José Miguel Cruz asks, that most youth
in San Salvador's gangs have never been outside of El Salvador?

The topic of the consequences of peoples, institutions, and cultures mov-
ing across borders is a vast one. At least since the heyday of the Mexican
Pedro Infante movies and on through Mexican rock 'n' roll, Pink Floyd,
heavy metal, and so on, Guatemalan youth have felt the effect of "world"
youth cultures. Because of immigration and new forms of communication,

n amazing rate. There is a difference between living in Guate-
∫tening to the Beatles and living in Guatemala City and being
th kin, even with their U.S. friends, in Lynn, Massachusetts.
the manner in which youth interpret and use received cul-
rmined by that culture, and questions concerning how it is
l how it changes remain. Discussions about the global pro-
edge the fundamental importance of "local actors" and con-
ditions.[30] The young man in cholo-style pants who related to me the MS-13 "born in Ramparts" story and used codified hand gestures from LA street gangs is part of an "imaginary community" whose members may never cross borders.[31] As we talked, we stood in front of his mother's barely roofed-over two-room home in Tierra Nueva II, a shantytown partly inhabited by war refugees and their children, and one with a turbulent history of political mobilization and demobilization. He has no work, and he left school because, as he puts it, it was "a waste of my time." His gang world in Guatemala City is as much if not more about the close-ups of political, economic, cultural, and social geography as it is about the Los Angeles that he and others evoke. Although Adiós Niño looks at the Maras at three levels of analysis—the transregional, the national, and the city—it privileges the last two.

To situate the young men and women in these gangs in Guatemala City's barrios and in Guatemalan history does not mean that the Maras are not informed by events, cultures, people, and commerce beyond national borders, as I make clear. Likewise, to argue in favor of the Maras' historical specificity does not imply that the Guatemalan gangs do not share similarities with gangs elsewhere in the world where cities have high rates of unemployment, drugs, violent officials, and a population in which almost 50 percent is under twenty-five years. No doubt for youth everywhere, there exist versions of the banners on the border between Guatemala and Mexico that advertise the wages, three meals a day, and "security" offered by Zeta, the Mexican drug mafia.

Unfortunately Guatemala is not the only country in the world in which anxious elites try to handle the growing numbers of those excluded from the labor market through forms of terror, and convert those without steady work into a central piece of their politics of "citizen security."[32] In addition, it is hardly the only country where state terror has a home. The manufacture of slow and horrific deaths by sovereign power is not so uncommon, and "the state of exception" is less exceptional than suggested by much scholarship about modern political power that has concentrated heavily on political control through the smooth operations of social engineering. Guatemalan military and civilian professionals learned terrorism from their counterparts

10   Introduction

from, among other places, Algeria, Argentina, France, Israel, the United States, and South Africa because, from Europe to Africa and other parts of the world, the modern condition has included acts of genocide and political control through psychologically and physically crude and sophisticated methods of inflicting pain. Moreover, ritual mutilations and the savor with which they have been carried out belong to a few centuries' worth of modern cross-cultural, racist, and political atrocities that include the lynching of African Americans and grotesque massacres of Native Americans enjoyed by victimizers and onlookers. Whether public or private, state terror has been a part of a modern global times in every continent, and so have the consequential troubled individual and collective subjectivities.

Especially within the last few decades of the twentieth century and the first of the twenty-first, violent urban gangs have multiplied within what Robert Desjarlais and Arthur Kleinman title "violence and demoralization in the new world order." It is not inspiring to younger generations that the increase of poverty in countries that have immense wealth continues, and that the world's greatest material production is of the means to destroy life. That this is accompanied by the ever-creative market-bound manufacture of complex cultural arrangements consisting of images, sounds, and narratives that display varieties of violent deaths and make clear the adrenal thrills and existential highs of killing, and sometimes of being killed, in countless movies and other increasingly intimate forms of media hardly encourages what can be called "respect" for human beings among our world's youth or adults. Still, to talk of a "new world order" does not mean that the world has become one place.

Childhood, Adolescence, and Violence in Guatemala's Dumpy Modernity

Informed by Philippe Ariès's much criticized yet indelibly influential book *Centuries of Childhood*, the framework often used for studies of the history of childhood and youth in Europe and the United States would by implication allot the lives of many Guatemalan children and youth to the categories premodern or traditional or, most arrogantly, "underdeveloped."[33] Instead of cataloging Guatemala as a "not-yet" or a developing country, we need to recognize it as a modern country, and its modernity is just what it is. The juxtaposition of old and new, the so-called traditional with the latest now "modern," the computers in homes without running water, the *huipil-clad* Maya girl who sells used clothes from the United States (that might have been originally *hecho en Guatemala*) in front of a shelter for street children sponsored by a Catholic center located in New York City; the sickly shoeshine boy with his fashionable sunglasses; the rip-off fashion jeans; and the Che T-shirts that fill the street markets to the fascination of foreigners and nationals alike—all speak not only of poverty and creativity but also of a historically specific modern condition.

What might appear oppositional has been allied or unified into its own field of the modern. By the year 2010, this capitalist modernity could not provide Guatemala City with a safe walk or a regular—clean or dirty—water supply in its mundanely named Zones 1–8, 11, 12, 17–21, and others not in the confined wealthy areas, much less develop national wealth and distribute it to an increasingly poor population. More frustrating is the reality that gains fought for and won at some point in the twentieth century—such as the right to unionize, social security, land reform, a legal system, a living wage, the extension of public education and medical care, paved roads, and adequate bus service—have either been destroyed (unions, a living wage, land reform), stand in permanent disrepair (roads, bus service, railroads, public education), are continually falling apart (medical care, social security), or exist in name only (the legal system). As presented in James Ferguson's *Expectations of Modernity: Myths and Meanings of Urban Life on the Zambian Copperbelt*, the resourceful and modern Zambian former copper miner named George Kabamba, who is holding on to life despite being "destitute, sick, living in rags in a leaky tent in a malaria-ridden swamp," would find kindred lives in Guatemala.[34]

The Argentine philosopher Enrique Dussel wrote that in Latin America, modernity was born with the Conquest for both the conquered and the conquerors, as well as those imported from Africa as slaves. As many have argued, the brutalities of colonialism, slavery and forced labor, racism, spiritual suppression, and the robbery of common resources in the hundreds of years since 1492 have been historically inherent to, and not an aberration or disfiguration of, modern capitalist times. Exploitation and the superexploitation of the socially constituted "darker races"—whether through the postcolonial forced labor systems, child labor, sweat shops, or maquiladoras—are not some gray transition toward the modern or the developed any more than these are on the periphery of capitalism.[35] Being situated on this violent "underside" that is at once an ignored center has been the complex condition of Latin American and Caribbean modernity and capitalism, not a sign that these are not there.

The construction of La Juventud played an especially important part in this trajectory of modernity in Guatemala, where capitalist modernization has meant keeping part of the population excluded from liberal rights. In the 1860s, Enrique Palacios, a member of La Sociedad Económica de Amigos del País (Economic Society of the Friends of the Nation) who worked to develop Guatemalan export agriculture and trade relations with England, wrote clearly about the relationship between modern times and a Maya population that he did not want to disappear in the blaring light of the new: "The majority of the population will not be an active element of progress, but rather an instrument [of it]."[36] This instrumental majority was the Maya labor force of children, youth, and adults on coffee plantations, one guaranteed through forced labor laws and other legal and extralegal mechanisms of control. The sophisticated delegates to the Guatemala City 1893 Conferencia Pedagógica, who planned to implement innovative pedagogy nationally, equivocated when it came to the Maya, who composed most of the population within the national territory. They concluded that the children of los indios were to be given kindergarten education within plantations, one adapted to their special condition as agricultural workers. For this reason, it was decreed that "school hours be reduced to the minimum . . . without exceeding three hours a day, finding in each area the time most adequate with regards to the climate, the seasons, cultivation and other specific circumstances."[37] "Progress" depended on these "qualifications" within liberalism. Throughout the first part of the twentieth century and until 1944, Liberal Party dictators obstructed the development of an all-encompassing national citizenry; it was a privilege conferred on very few.

The social construction of La Juventud as non-Maya, urban middle- and upper-class students became vital to the new nation. In the course of the nineteenth century, La Juventud was projected repeatedly not only as a vanguard of modernity, but also as a solution to the so-called Indian Problem, the dilemma of how to build a "civilized nation" in a territory where the majority were uncivilized "indios." Initially drawn to John Locke's notion of a child's mind as a blank slate, intellectuals concerned with the question of building a modern nation and a citizenship saw public education as salvation. If children's minds were blank, an ideal and monocultural education could rescue children from the complexities of their family origins. At first rejecting or ignoring social Darwinist ideas as these appeared in Guatemala, they focused their attention on new pedagogies coming from Europe, and thus their attraction for the German Friedrich Froebel's kindergartens, especially (theoretically speaking) for Maya toddlers.[38] But Guatemala could not get away from keeping "indios" as noncitizens, who composed an exceptionally cheap labor force for its modernization through export agriculture. That plans for a territorial-wide public education ran afoul again and again did not stop the ideological uses of La Juventud, which grew to be an inflated and racialized symbol. Children of los "indios" and of all rural people, fell out of the category of La Juventud soon enough, leaving it non-Maya and urban.

In the late nineteenth century, Guatemalan elites and intellectuals marked off infancy, childhood, and youth as stages in "the perfection of civilization" and mankind.[39] A veritable cult of La Juventud developed around annual Festivales de Minerva of the Liberal Party dictator Manuel Estrada Cabrera, in which costumed schoolchildren and youth paraded around cardboard floats representing "La Ciencia" in celebration of "El Progreso."[40] By the 1920s, adolescence had become a keyword in national discourse. At mid-century, President Dr. Juan José Arévalo, one of Guatemala's premier states-men, an educator, and author of *La adolescencia como evasión y retorno*, saw the cultivation of adolescents as the nation's most urgent task to prevent what he described as the psychological disease of fascist and feminine submis-siveness that threatened human history. He urged creating strong mascu-line leaders through his innovative Escuelas Tipo Federación (Federation Schools) school system.[41] After the 1954 coup, it was above all the political Left that kept alive a mythology around La Juventud to the effect that it had a revolutionary essence and a responsibility toward the nation, now redefined in terms of "el pueblo."

Although infancy, childhood, and adolescence have been constructs used by Guatemalan professionals to describe so-called universal truths, these "stages" have not been widespread experiences. For the well-to-do minority, childhood and adolescence have long pointed to times and spaces of pri-vate schooling; art and sports lessons; university education; foreign travel; long engagements; clubs and parties; and, for fifteen-year-old girls, elabo-rate quinceañeras, which are not, as they are among the urban poor, followed by a life of paid or unpaid labor. For decades, having or not having this ado-lescence has been inside the consciousness of all city youth, whether they are poor or wealthy. It has become a "norm" in which the majority of youth do not participate. The notion of teenager, with its connotations of volatility, rebellion and fun, was not employed until the second half of the twentieth century, when it became an aspiration of many.[42]

In contrast to representations of urban youth as either a heroic vanguard of modernity or a decadent plague, at no point has there been a homoge-neous "Youth." Embedded in distinct kin life and history—and growing up within particular class, gender, cultural, and community constructions, experiences, and relationships—children and young people are hetero-geneous, and they have varied relationships to power. Looking at specific young lives yields the complexity of the general issue of being "young" and the limitations of framing childhood and adolescence as "modern" or "traditional" or of defining a society or culture as "child centered" or "adult centered." This is a city where, at the beginning of the twenty-first century, child labor is significant within the family wage economy, and so is the all-important modern education that families see as a solution to their economic woes. Walter, a friend of mine who is adored by his parents, attends a public secondary school and works at night in his father's tailor shop stitching imitation Levi's jeans to sell in the informal economy to style-conscious youth at *colegios* (private schools) in order to buy food in the open market for his extended family.

Whether rural or urban, Maya or Ladino, prepuberty or postpuberty, most youth in Guatemala have had little time or space for themselves, and the borders between childhood, adolescence, and adulthood have long been blurry in the eyes of the beholders. A nine-year-old who looks after his relatives, works, or both might be considered and treated as a young man, not a *niño*; a fifteen-year-old soldier is a man; and a fifteen-year-old mother from *las clases populares* is a woman. A pregnant fifteen-year-old from the upper classes who can have an abortion in Miami is just a "niñita tontita" (silly young girl). Street children are called children, no matter their age; gang members are youth criminals, not children, no matter their age; and the elite have applied the term *niños* to Mayas of all ages since the 1500s.

The institutions of public education and the law make distinctions between age groups, even if the wider community and the work world do not, and the state violates its own codes. Legal minors end up, illegally, in adult prisons. Children can legally work at age fourteen, yet children under fourteen have been and continue to be agricultural, construction, transport, domestic, and sex workers; vendors of goods and services; and laborers in high-risk jobs in the production of limestone, coffee, and fireworks, as well as in high-risk situations along the border with Mexico.[43] In the new times of the 2000s, the large Legumex factory, part of the "modern" as opposed to "traditional" sector of the economy, employs children under fourteen from 7 AM until 7 PM to cut hundreds of pounds of vegetables and fruits daily for export. They stand in cold water, receive one half the Guatemalan minimum wage, and get no benefits.[44] These children are having their childhoods; they are not short adults in an old-fashioned society. Disappointing adults, exploitation, abuse, and violent everyday upheavals have made small delights too scarce and dependency on adults too fragile. For decades there have been children and youth who have figured that they might be better off on their own.

In *Minor Omissions*, one of the few volumes concerning the history of Latin American children, Tobias Hecht suggests that the study of children is indis-

pensable to the understanding of the larger society and ought not be sub-
sumed within the history of women and families.[45] I add that it is especially the marginal minorities among the young—such as war orphans, gang
members, and youth who make homes in the streets—who reflect and address central problems and not subcultural or subsidiary ones. Sitting at the
intersection of the personal, subjective, social, and familial on the one hand,
and larger categories such as modernity and capitalism on the other, young
people are uniquely located, and through them our historical lens widens.
We can see the mareros of today that way: a warning about all the points of
that complex crossroads.

"The Law of the Conservation of Violence"

The state terror that went on before the war escalated in the 1980s was horrific enough, but opposition to it and an explanatory discourse about it
prevented it from being absolute. Children who grew up in the late 1970s
formed the Maras from within a broad social imaginary of class solidarity
that still persisted in the early 1980s. But state violence escalated rapidly, in-
tensifying in ways that were clearly traumatic.[46] In response to a first draft
of this manuscript in which I described several massacres, an anonymous
reader for Duke University Press who was astutely cautioning against sub-
stituting shocking description for analysis wrote: "[A] concern I have . . .
[is] the explicit representations of army violence. . . . I understand why it is
important, [but] I found the chapter deeply traumatizing—arbitrary details
haunted me for several days after reading it. I wonder whether it is necessary to traumatize the reader." The violence in Guatemala cannot be communicated adequately, as is suggested by the many discussions concerning
the crisis of representing the reality of the unimaginable. That is part of the
power of an "excess of reality," of something that cannot be real and is real.
Yet depictions and approximations must be made in order to avoid further-
ing the silence surrounding it, leaving it as if incomprehensible and iso-
lating those who experience it.[47] Trying to place the reader closer to these
experiences is an attempt to communicate reality. The manuscript reviewer
was right on the mark to find the material traumatizing. Trauma is *exactly*
what readers need to know.

In his book *How Societies Remember*, the sociologist Paul Connerton argues
that the body "re-enacts the past" of social history by "conveying and sus-
taining memories" through inscription and incorporation.[48] I am not suggesting that killing people is a "cultural posture" in Guatemala, although a
few cynics might. The insight that bodies reenact society's past at least sug-

gests the possibility that the extreme violence of the mareros in the post-war period is a mimetic way of having or storing the war, especially because it is neither completely remembered nor completely forgotten. Someone is "acting out," to use Dominick La Capra's formulation, what went on without a clear idea of it.[49] Pierre Bourdieu puts a similar thought in motion in other terms when he writes about the assault on the welfare state in Europe: "You cannot cheat with the *law of the conservation of violence*: all violence is paid for. . . . The structural violence exerted by the financial markets, in the form of layoffs, loss of security, etc., is matched sooner or later in the form of sui- *socologist* cides, crime and delinquency, drug addiction, alcoholism, a whole host of *an* minor and major everyday acts of violence."[50] In Guatemala, this "law of the *klue*" conservation of violence" is complicated by war, trauma, and the silences about both, which is not to say that Guatemalans are all suicidal and criminal, but the "whole host" is everywhere evident.

Despite the lack of immediate and satisfying answers, the question of the relationship between history, violence, and trauma must be kept in mind. There is too much extreme violence and trauma in the world to risk leaving aside the historical weight of these realities on the grounds that we do not fully understand them. Cathy Caruth has suggested that being traumatized by what breaches "the mind's experience of time, self and the world" is necessary for surviving the unimaginable. To be traumatized is constructive in the face of destruction.[51] This paradox, in which the displacing of what cannot be "placed" due to the inability to absorb the unimaginable—this distancing from experience even as it happens, as well as afterward, as protection—has a terrible catch to it. The experience, in one way or another, returns "uncontrolled and repetitive" to have a strong continued life "because violence inhabits, incomprehensibly, the very survival of those who have lived beyond it that it may be witnessed best in the future generations to whom this survival is passed on."[52]

Criticism

This study does not *prove* a relationship between trauma, the "law of the conservation of violence," and escalating postwar violence of the Maras in Guatemala City. However, it is a plea to pay heed to the historical agency of horror and trauma, an entreaty that adds fuel to the argument that should need none concerning the urgency of breaking public silences and ending impunity. If the law of the return is valid, and if Guatemala does not end impunity, "claim" its experience, and know its history, then it might drown in another sea of blood in the name of nothing. Ordinary Guatemalans need be the protagonists of their history and bring the entire miserable crew that has engineered this apparatus of political violence to justice, and then some. Healing is an elusive concept, and if healing means the restoration of mind,

Healing is elusive

heart, body, and soul, it may never happen. Truth telling and trials cannot change what Martín-Baró calls the "underlying problem of the traumatogenic social relations that are part of an oppressive system that led to war."[53] Over and above telling the truth and bringing the guilty to justice, the whole social, political, and economic structure needs transformations based on human solidarity and our revolutionized imaginations.

Part of the problem concerning the evolution of these gangs is that the revolutionary groups did not think much about the gangs at all. In the 1980s, representatives of revolutionary groups called mareros lumpen or—worse—spies, and turned their backs on them. This helped leave youth open to recruitment by professionals, including those in army intelligence, for whom violence is the means of business. Why turn our backs on gangs? There is nothing at all wrong with a gang as a type of social organization. Youth form groups as spaces in which to speak emotional truths, refashion identities, and cultivate their own opinions and voice. The strong points of the powerful relationships among young people who have been marginalized can be intense trust, loyalty, friendship, and love, as Aragon's beautiful cover photograph of two boys living out on the streets suggests. Perhaps the life expressed in their faces and in the gentle gesture of one boy's hand on his companion's arm can avert the death foretold in the fumes the other sniffs from the glue bottle he clutches.

The Structure and Genesis of This Book

Adiós Niño is a history of the present dedicated to not saying good-bye to children. This introductory chapter has placed my basic argument within discussions about the gangs, and in the framework of the larger history of a modernity that has its constructions of young people and its uses for them. Chapter 1, "Death and Politics," describes in broad terms the two historical periods—the 1950s to the 1980s, and the 1980s to the early 2000s—that formed the universe in which Maras evolved. It gives the background, and sometimes the foreground, for the material presented in chapters 2 and 3, in which many of the events, people, and places first presented in chapter 1 reappear as the camera focuses in, so to speak, on the Maras and specific aspects of city and national life. Chapter 2, "1980s: The Gangs to Live For," takes the reader back to the times in which the Maras first appeared, and chapter 3, "1990s and Beyond: The Gangs to Die For," follows them forward into the 2000s. Titled "Democracy and Lock-Up," chapter 4 continues by discussing the discourse around delincuencia and citizenship, and the rise of a prison system that revives violence to presumably ensure democracy and citizen security. The concluding chapter, "Open Ending," concerns the alternatives that young men and women who leave the gangs face. *Conclusion*

I am an oral historian, which in this particular case involved doing fieldwork and writing down my observations as well as conducting interviews. The research for this book took place over more than a decade in different parts of the city, including some in which I lived, and in different settings, ranging from homes to shelters for the homeless. I spoke and spent time with youth in and out of the Maras, social workers, psychologists, neighbors, parents, and others, some of whom I came to know personally. Those whom I quote are cited, and dozens more are not, even though in one way or another they are all present. Conversations varied: some went on intermediately for long periods of time, and others were short; some were structured or semi-structured interviews and others were informal. In addition to fieldwork and interviews, I have also drawn on newspaper articles by investigative journalists, essays and reports by professionals, and other published material, including surveys and data on gangs gathered by a variety of organizations that each have had their own researchers and perspectives.[54]

No one book can do everything. With luck, this study about what Saskia Sassen calls "concrete localities" can serve others in the community of people studying gangs in Guatemala and elsewhere in Central America to deepen knowledge through comparison and contrast.[55] I hope this book will also help the English-language reader to comprehend Guatemala and empathize with its people, who constantly revitalize their lives.

In the final months of my writing and cutting and more writing and more cutting of this manuscript, the still-life paintings of the Italian painter Giorgio Morandi repeatedly came to mind. Over and over again, he painted similar objects, which entranced him and whose integrity he wished to respect. This book feels "over and over again." It has been a long time in the making. I first studied the gangs before my first child, Ana, was born in 1987 in Guatemala City. After my second child, Jasmin, was born in 1990 in New York City, I returned to Guatemala to look at the general question of urban youth. After taking up residence in New York City and then in Boston, I kept coming back to Guatemala City to see my friends, do research, and finish *Hacer la juventud: Jóvenes de tres generaciones de una familia trabajadora en la Ciudad de Guatemala*, which was published in 2005. Mareros kept coming my way, especially while, accompanied by my daughters, I kept meeting street children.

The last time I talked with a young person in a Mara was in 2008; I was alone, an older woman from the United States. Have I been the adequate or appropriate person to write about youth gangs? Can we "fit" in some psychological, sociological, or historical sense with what we study? It has become customary for scholars to make arguments about why they are suited to their particular topics and themes. I cannot make any claims that I am a good match: I did not grow up in Guatemala City, much less in a gang there or anywhere; I have never spent more than a night in jail, and not in Guatemala, and so forth. It is simply that one thing led to another.

Because I wanted to understand how ordinary people make exceptional history, in the early 1980s I researched and wrote *Trade Unionists against Terror: Guatemala City, 1954–1985*, a book about urban labor activists who fought for life against all odds and who ultimately turned state murder around into an inspirational tool and thus kept their dead compañeros present, and life meaningful. Still living in Guatemala City in the mid-1980s and working with a new research institute, I and others researched mareros for a political reason: we needed to understand these new gangs because the publicity about them that was creating new fears in a wartime city was based on absolutely no information. Subsequently it became hard for me to let go of this thread, especially after it was clear that the opposite of what had protected the sanity of the labor movement was under way: murder was and is being utilized to indeed kill life. I spoke with street children who were joining MS-13 and M-18 in the late 1990s, and most of those youth are dead. One young man, Estuardo, an M-18 member murdered in 1998 by MS-13, was dedicated heart and soul to historical memory, and his most important memories were of his mother's memories. Because I knew Estuardo and other youth, it fell to me to write this book.

Morandi kept painting those bowls, bottles, and other containers over and over, a bit differently each time. Writing this book, I kept drawing and redrawing the same terrain over and over, reframing the material from the same interviews again and again. Looking at his paintings and my manuscript, I worry that the gang members are too shoved against one another, that they do not have space to breathe, and don't quite emerge, that the table or surface upon which they rest is not wide enough. Hopefully this book gives enough so that readers can pick them up and look at them again with the consideration and compassion they all deserve.

I feel terrible when I talk about all this. I don't want to upset [anyone].

> —Excerpt from the unpublished autobiography of Rodrigo Sic Ixpancoc, ex-soldier
> of the Guatemalan Army, El Periódico, November 4, 2010

"To Remember Is to Feel a Knife Tear into You"

Sitting on a chair in small apartment in Guatemala City's Zone 3, Victor recounted that in 1985, when he was fifteen, he and his friends founded Mara Plaza Vivar Capitol with companionship and competing in an up-coming break dance competition in mind. But a few months later, he explained, Army Intelligence (G-2) stopped him and a few others who were hanging out in a semi-occupied shopping center on the main strip of the shabby downtown Sexta Avenida in Zone 1, shoved them in a van, and took them to a military base, where they received a few days of training. Then, in his words, "They took us up to the mountain in a truck with some *nicas* [Nicaraguans] to some village . . . and we had on rubber boots and pretended to be *egyptos* [members of the guerrilla group Ejército Guerrillero de los Pobres (Guerrilla Army of the Poor, EGP)], the *nicas* called a meeting and people [the villagers] came and the soldiers came down all of a sudden and killed everyone . . . [it was] a massacre." He went on to say that he was soon dumped back on to Sexta Avenida, and within days he had taken off to Mexico in fear of G-2 because, he said, "the others [the *mareros* with him] were killed." In Mexico, he worked with the Mexican drug ring La Eme for many years. At age twenty-eight, a full thirteen years later, he said, he returned in 1998 to a changed Guatemala City and joined Mara Salvatrucha (MS-13), which had arrived in the 1990s.

The abrupt and murderous military intervention that changed Victor's life almost beyond recognition in 1985 is a small version of the experiences of millions from 1980 to 1996, when over 100,000 primarily unarmed people died violently in massacres that came at dawn like thunderbolts, and millions fled without destination. Marked by this history, Victor mentioned only fragments of it to me. We spoke in 2002, six years after the Peace Accords officially ended the war. Victor told me that he has no idea what the war was about. He said, "It just was."[1]

The 1996 Peace Accords that formally stopped the thirty-six-year war between the Guatemalan military and revolutionary groups over Guatemala's destiny brought tremendous relief because, at last, the war had ended. Among other important agreements, the Accords mandated constitutional amendments to redefine Guatemala as a multicultural nation, limit the army's mission, resettle displaced peoples, allow civil society groups, and reform the judicial system. However, virtually none of its provisions were or have been implemented because, basically, the war concluded with a victory for the Guatemalan military, the state, and the economic status quo, and with the demise of a long revolutionary era.[2] To begin to understand how deeply this defeat cut into and transformed Guatemala City in the last decades of the twentieth century, when the Maras evolved, it is necessary to appreciate that since the 1954 coup that overthrew a democratic government, the very existence of strong resistance to oppression and repression was as important as the oppression and repression. In the decades following the 1954 coup, many Guatemalans understood and portrayed the power of the state and of wealthy elites as temporal and historical, not absolute. Even with its ups and downs, the popular movement made exploitation and state violence in some way or another provisional because these could be assaulted by demonstrations, strikes, occupations, and citywide uprisings, as well as by a social imaginary that made challenging domination possible. The movement generated the knowledge that violence is the political tool of the state and of elites. From that perspective, Victor's 2002 understanding of the war indicates a loss of ideological mooring; the war was not something that "just was."

In other words, what ended with the Peace Accords was more than the civil war. A way of knowing the world and acting within it had been shattered. The dynamism of an urban subculture of class solidarity wherein jokes get made, songs created and heard, leaflets written, small newspapers mimeographed, banners painted and seen, and political conversations held, was no longer there. To put this into the subjective and emotional framework in which life is lived: the ability to give voice, the "euphoria of ethical activism," the existence of a sense of historical purpose on a grand scale, and the vivacity and hope that animated the popular movement had prevented people from succumbing to fear for generations; then, abruptly, all that life was lost and death emerged exultant.[3] After decades of struggle against what was widely perceived as an immoral political economy, the chance for an immediate alternative was vanquished. Grinding into dust the project of progressive social change cut down collective understandings of life as humanly malleable for humanistic aims. By the twenty-first century these visions seem to have become charred remains of plans for a future that required a revolutionary human praxis. What could have been memories of deaths that served to secure revolutionary victory now elicit despair and anger because so many died in vain. In 2010 an artist from the generation of the 1970s said with infinite sadness: "To remember is to feel a knife tear into you."[4]

Political violence in the second half of twentieth-century Guatemala was spectacular. It exceeded that of other countries in the Americas: Guatemala had the highest per capita number of "disappeared," it was one of two countries where acts of genocide took place, and it was there that the worst military massacres on the continent happened.[5] Guatemala was also distinguished in this period by the force of its popular and revolutionary movements. The depth of the state violence that did not stop them is one measure of their profundity, and so are the even greater horrors that it took to finally destroy them.

Violence takes many forms, has varied consequences, and conjures up different images.[6] The extreme forms of political violence that overtook Guatemalan history and came to have a cultural weight and political role in it, held together and overlapped with structural, symbolic, and everyday forms of violence.[7] Yet these are not all equivalent. Given that violence is varied and embedded in daily life, we need to distinguish a limited sense of this term and concept to capture the violence that "consciously or purposely breaks into the inner existential shell of a person i.e. into that room in which there is no other hiding place. A room from which there is no escape, the body of the human being."[8] To make explicit the varied worlds of power, hope, pain, and conflict in which the youth who joined gangs grew up, this chapter continues by contrasting two periods, 1954–80 and 1980–2000s, decades during which the kind of violence that converted life into a "space of death" emerged as a historical protagonist, as if on its own.[9]

Normal Guatemalan State Violence: 1954–1980

Guatemala was politically globalized on a grand scale in June 1954, when, in full anticommunist armor, the United States allied with Guatemalan elites to violently end the country's singular attempt at a democratic reformist government, one based on electoral politics, civil liberties, and national capitalism. In the years that followed the famous 1954 coup, a symbol of Cold War politics everywhere, the United States and the Guatemalan military and political and economic elite developed a system of rule consisting of electoral politics supported by a liberal constitution that guaranteed civil liberties and of constant state terrorism. These forms of sovereignty went hand in hand. The United States showcased Guatemala as a model of its foreign policy of promoting democracy, poured in investments that furthered manufacturing and large-scale capitalist agriculture, and collaborated with the Guatemalan state to build an extensive system of terror based on thousands of informants and on death squads that brought so-called subversives into secret centers and slowly tortured them to death in the tens of thousands.[10] During the apogee of electoral democracy, modernization, and economic growth under the reformist government of Julio César Méndez Montenegro (1966–70), death squads disappeared an average of forty-three persons every five days.[11] This durable arrangement lasting decades distinguishes the Guatemalan experience from those of countries such as Argentina, Brazil, and Chile, where the suspension of constitutional rule signaled comparatively shorter periods of outright military rule and terror.

This mix of terror and constitutional rule started in the wake of the 1954 coup. In the months following it, many 1944–54 government officials and supporters were charged and often shot or imprisoned for "subversion" under anticommunist legislation. But soon thereafter and especially after armed opposition emerged in 1960, activists and their friends and families rarely went to jail. For the most part, punishment meant death, and it happened without accusations, trials, bullets, electric chairs, firing squads, or gallows and trap doors. Death arrived slowly via ropes, bites, sticks, matches, knives, machetes, fingernails, rocks, and blowtorches, by means that were, to quote Michel Foucault on the ancien régime, "inexplicable phenomena that the extension of man's imagination creates out of the barbarous and the cruel."[12]

Foucault's discussion of the creation and reproduction of the body politic through mechanisms of discipline and punishment offers insight into modern Guatemala, although with a twist. The types of violence and physical torture of bodies that Foucault argued were foundational to an archetypal ancien régime underwrote capitalist modernization and constitutional rule in Guatemala. In the case of Guatemala, in Foucault's formulation of the biopolitics that manufacture the life of members of modern nations as "a power bent on generating forces, making them grow, and ordering them, rather than one dedicated to impeding them, making them submit or destroying them," the words "in addition to" need to replace "rather than."[13] Foucault recognized the rule over life through death.[14] He conceptualized sovereignty as the ultimate power over life and death, but he wrote that a shift occurred in the modern age: "One might say that the ancient right to take life or let live was replaced by a power to foster life. . . . Now [in the modern period] it is over life, through its unfolding, that power establishes its domain; death is power's limit, the moment that escapes it; death becomes the most secret aspect of existence, the most 'private.'"[15] In post-1954 Guatemala, death was not "power's limit." The death-squad tortures produced death that was not "simply the withdrawal of the right to live." These tortures rested on the "whole quantitative art of pain," calculated to "carry pain almost to infinity." The death squads' vocation was that "art of maintaining life in pain" in ways not unlike those that Foucault describes in great detail as "the spectacular of torture."[16]

One difference is that these slow tortures were not part of the sort of public spectacular to which Foucault refers. Instead, a phenomenon perhaps more insidious and even more terrifying replaced this or added a new dimension to it. Within the death-squad system, grotesque torture to create the most painful death occurred in secret, but the catch is that almost everyone in the city knew about it. It was on view within the imagination because the bodies turned up, and their gashes and mutilations told stories. Foucault wrote that in ceremonies of public execution, "the main character was the people, whose real and immediate presence was required for the performance." He thought that if execution took place in secret, it "would scarcely have any meaning."[17]

But what if "real and immediate presence" is in the imagination, a sort of modern individual private theater that everyone had? The scarred bodies provided the public performances in which the mind's eye had to do a horrible double work of staging the scene and being its impotent spectator at the same time. Where does the mind go when the newspapers report in detail about a man who turns up dead in a ravine, burned with a blowtorch on the stomach and elsewhere, his tongue cut out and his face beaten in so severely that his lips were swollen and his teeth broken, or about a woman and her baby found tortured and murdered? Her breasts had bite marks and her underclothing was bloody. Her two-year-old son had had his fingernails pulled out. What the bodies told of their deaths became the public spectacle. That bodies appeared with their proverbial "signs of torture" "reactivated" state power because the agony of an excruciating death was on full display, a spectacle of what happens and can happen to anyone, one that takes place first somewhere unknown, and a second time in the imagination.[18] This death-in-life state barbarism was already part of politics before the massacres of the 1980s, the period many call "the war."[19]

What the Italian philosopher Giorgio Agamben delineates as the "camp," in reference to concentration camps established at various points in modern history and most notoriously by the Nazi Party, in which "the most absolute condition inhumana ever to appear on Earth was realized," belonged to Guatemalan death-squad victims over and over for decades in concealed locations and to the imagination of those who were not there, except that they arrived in their mind's eye, without presence or power, again and again.[20] Tortures seemingly beyond the power of conceptualization, much less execution, went on, conceived and executed. This was national political rule, not a concentration camp, not a strategy to exterminate a group from the body politic, but a strategy to control the entire body politic. Those who were not tortured—the witnesses who had no access to the event that they had to actualize in their heads—were not called upon to coproduce this system of terror, as Germans were in their acquisition of and complicity with anti-Semitism in what the historian Claudia Koonz calls a "Nazi conscience."[21] Racism against Mayas saturated and saturates national life, but the Guatemalan state organized fear and sadism, not Ladinos (the common term for non-Maya), against an urban popular political movement that included both city Ladinos and Mayas.

In the late 1970s, Gabriel Aguilera Peralta, Jorge Romero Imery, Enrique Torres-Lezama, and Ricardo Galindo Gallardo did quantitative research on Guatemalan state violence in the post-1954 period. Their findings were published in Costa Rica in 1981 under the title Dialéctica del terror en Guatemala. Many have repeated and none have improved on the book's principal argument for the years 1963–79. Dialéctica del terror details how the counterrevolutionary state renewed its power through waves of terror.[22] When popular discontent and mass struggle advanced, so did state brutality, which in turn caused social conflict to decrease, and with that so did state violence. Made even more determined by the repression, the popular organizations then took advantage of the diminished repression to emerge with even greater force and so forth until, so the authors optimistically believed, the movement would inevitably triumph. Tragically, even before the book's publication, Romero Imery and Galindo Gallardo were kidnapped. Imery's mangled body turned up months afterward, and Galindo Gallardo was never seen again. By then the state had started to turn its "normal" terrorism into a massive terrorist onslaught that upended predictions about an ultimate backfiring of violence.

Years later, to clarify the base level of "normal" state violence before 1980, the archdiocese report on human rights violations, the *Recuperación de la Memoria Histórica* (Recovery of Historical Memory, REMHI), memorably noted: "For decades—and not including the war—the appearance of tortured corpses was part of waking up every morning, whether reading the newspaper or traveling footpaths and roadways."[23] Footpaths and newspapers: this violence was rural and urban; it has always been and remains today much worse against the Maya population in the countryside. At the same time, in this period state terror had a specific visibility in the city. The several daily newspapers covered demonstrations and assassinations and carried photos of the disappeared and of severely disfigured bodies. And because Guatemala City was at once the country's political, administrative, financial, and industrial capital, it was central to protest and repression. It concentrated spaces of power that ranged from the national public university, with its radical schools of law, engineering, journalism, and medicine; to the land government agency to which peasants brought their disputes; to the offices of the labor union headquarters and the rooms where clandestine revolutionary cadre met; and to the "Telecommunications Center" that housed state intelligence and loomed tall behind the National Palace for all to see. Terror and state violence permeated everything from jokes to literature. There was hardly a poet, essayist, or novelist of the period who did not write about it; a journalist who did not report almost daily on it; a visual artist who did not represent it; or a city resident who did not know of someone "disappeared."

The Power of Life

The Lazarus-like urban popular movements that these 1954–80 levels of state sadism failed to destroy had strong wellsprings. One was the indelible legacy of the 1944–54 years, which was sustained by the quick underground regrouping of Guatemalan communists after the coup and by the overwhelming popularity of that brief era.[24] Although the ten years of reform government were not utopian ones, they represented a new Guatemala. For government to have even contemplated, much less realized, a land reform, improved working conditions, housing, day care, and medical attention, constituted a historical miracle in a country with a centuries-long history of the vast majority's subjugation. A new Guatemala was not a dream: it had happened once, it was taken away; and it could happen again.

The 1944–54 nationalist discourse rooted in the concept of self-determination of nations became markedly anti-imperialist after the coup.

This radical nationalism was reinforced by the 1959 Cuban Revolution, an event with specific resonance in Guatemala because it validated armed revolution in contrast to the decision made by President Jacobo Árbenz in 1954 to not take up arms against U.S. military intervention. Radical nationalism resulted in a serious challenge to the Guatemalan state, when anti-imperialist military officers in Guatemala City tried to stage a coup in 1960 and, in the wake of their failure, started the country's first armed guerrilla movement, one that was soon informed by Marxism and strengthened by students who entered its ranks following a citywide insurrection in 1962.

Anti-imperialism, versions of Marxism, and radical nationalism were powerful ideologies among many, including professors, workers, lawyers, and schoolteachers—the latter being a group vital to the 1944–54 leadership and one whose influential union stayed on the Left. Intertwined with these views was the unfolding of remarkable changes in the church that reverberated throughout Guatemala. Clergy and lay religious workers who were revolutionized from being supporters of the status quo to instigators against it, made the Gospel an argument for class militancy, and configured Jesus as a militant who blessed the struggle of the poor against the rich.[25] The effects of this potent combination of perspectives included the growth of the labor movement and the disruption of many disciplinary institutions, including the urban public school system.

The Normal Schools, the teacher-training institutes that presumably "normalized" youth to "normalize" other youth, are one instance of a breakdown and an inversion of the machinery of sovereignty. Opened in the 1880s to regulate youth by ingraining the small and large features of discourses and bodily social behavior that would perpetuate the national status quo as it shifted in the late nineteenth century, the Normal Schools were basically militarized until the 1944 Revolution. In accord with its social aims, the generation of 1944 revolutionaries intentionally reshaped the Normal Schools into progressive and internally democratic institutions that defined nationalism in terms of specific programs for the popular social good, for instance, land reform and labor laws, and that trained free-thinking leaders destined for national prominence.[26] After 1954 and for decades thereafter, the students, teachers, and even administrators of Normal Schools held on to those ideals, and graduates were more likely to join radical groups or turn into leftist professionals than become stolid and conformist cogs within the disciplinary machinery (see figures 1.1 and 1.2). Hardly a school term passed without a major protest in Guatemala City's Instituto Normal Central para Varones or the Instituto para Señoritas Belén, to name the two most prestigious public teacher-training schools for boys and girls, respectively.

FIGURE 1.1 Student review parade at the Instituto de Varones, a Normal School, Guatemala City, 1914. The Liberal Party dictator Manuel Estrada Cabrera (1898–1920) mandated that military studies be added to the positivist curriculum. These students were emblematic of the educated youth who, if obedient, symbolized "Progress and Order." Photographed by José García Sánchez. Credit: José García Sánchez. *Desfile del Instituto de Varones*. Ciudad de Guatemala, 1914. Colección de José García Sánchez. Fototeca Guatemala, CIRMA.

FIGURE 1.2 Student demonstration against the militarization of government, Guatemala City, 1960. Soon after the 1954 coup against the reformist government of Jacobo Árbenz (1951–54), girls, boys, and young women and men organized FUEGO in schools such as the Normal Schools and boldly took to the streets to demand rights. Many of these students joined the armed struggle in the countryside that started in 1961. The prominent sign to the left reads "FIRE, NOT ASHES." Anonymous photographer. Credit: Anónimo. *Pancartas y carteles de la manifestación en contra del Gobierno de Ydígoras Fuentes. Ciudad de Guatemala, Julio de 1960. Archivo de fotografías de El Imparcial. Fototeca Guatemala,* CIRMA.

The shallow discourse of anticommunism and developmentalism could not fend off the associative enthusiasm that resounded in the city. The regime's political economy brought little or no hope to Guatemala City's emerging working classes during a period in which manufacturing, transport, and the service sectors grew.[27] Developmentalism permitted urban social programs to flounder and brought new industries that hired mean managers, paid miserable wages for long hours of hard work, neglected safety, and had no respect for employees or labor laws that permitted unions and guaranteed conditions. The post-1954 coup Constitution's guarantee of liberties such as the right to organize and to form electoral parties encouraged labor unions and other urban groups to try to use it in their favor, with few successes. Again and again state brutality threw off track trade union and grassroots legal struggles as well as campaigns for structural change by reformist politicians.[28] With the failures of progressive electoral parties and the chronic inability of the Ministry of Labor to address labor disputes in the background, by the second half of the 1970s many people had grown weary of legal means and were attuned to ideas about armed revolutionary change. This was especially the case after the state responded inadequately to a 1976 earthquake, as well as following an October 1978 uprising in Guatemala City that united workers of the state and private sectors, students, and neighborhood youth and other *pobladores*, who went on strike, barricaded streets, took over barrios, and fought security forces to bring the city to a complete halt. They successfully prevented a ten-centavo bus fare increase and raised the minimum wage. It took this urban rebellion to make these hardly revolutionary changes, and victory was short lived, because a flood of kidnappings by state agents and the refusal of authorities to actually grant a new wage minimum quickly followed. It is impossible to think that the youth who grew up in Guatemala City and joined Maras in the early 1980s missed this weeks-long episode of the urban population in open revolt.

Between the 1954 coup and the 1980s war, urban children and youth and the adults surrounding them lived in many milieus, and not just one of terror, that both directly contested terrorism or "simply" kept sensibilities of humanism and solidarity vibrant. The public face of what could be called a plebeian culture of people united by social class and a tumultuous history that had an unfinished air because the 1954 coup had derailed a new Guatemala was constantly visible. It was evident in so small a detail as the pleasure taken by most residents in the annual Huelga de Dolores (Strike of Sorrows), in which masked students disrupted the city with their satiric floats and placards making fun of the country's dominant institutions. It was even more apparent in the May 1 marches, which did not primarily honor a distant past of repression and worker unrest. Every year Guatemala City's International Workers' Day march and rally revitalized itself by directing attention to that year's ups and downs, and by the flow of old and young eloquent speakers who called for immediate changes and kept alive notions of alternate possibilities. All this had the effect of restraining despair and unfocused angers. During all these years and right into the 1980s, there were no especially violent youth gangs in the city. Going at least back to the 1940s, boys and young men sometimes joined minor street gangs called *pandillas* that engaged in petty crime and brawled against one another without dominating or tormenting neighborhood life or killing one another.[29]

For decades the social life of many boys and girls and young men and women in the popular urban areas had more or less centered, for better or worse, on romance, tedious low or unpaid work, family, school, sports, and even church activities. Within the context of everyday life the discussion groups and the social improvement agenda of the Young Catholic Worker movement attracted youth in the late 1950s and into the 1960s, when more radical priests and other religious figures drawn to liberation theology had influence and support in the barrios.[30] Although young people knew about state terrorism, its tactics belonged to an "other side" that had not yet overtaken the city, and not to their side of the proverbial tracks. In the 1970s young people were often students in the politicized public school system and/or workers who sometimes joined labor unions (or at the very least knew about them), neighborhood betterment associations, street protests, or, hand in hand with their families, the land invasions that followed the 1976 earthquake. They lived near older militants and others in neighborhoods that were milieus of active class solidarity. A trade unionist characterized his neighborhood in La Parroquia, Zone 6, in the late 1970s with the words "when it came to demonstrations everyone went."[31] At least they did up to a point.

The War in the 1980–1990s

The military made a qualitative leap in its methods in the 1980s that had continuities and ruptures with the state violence that preceded it. Of course it continued to be extremely cruel. Among other changes, an official suspension of the Constitution legalized state barbarism; it became massive and aboveground; uniformed soldiers and members of official Civil Patrols rather than death squads committed it; and it came very fast to quickly reach unparalleled levels of sadism, even for Guatemala. This upsurge in terror affected the city drastically, and it had far worse results in rural Maya communities, where the military committed acts of genocide premised on its racism and its historic fear of Maya rebellion. In the Maya highlands, the military had a strategy that was, to quote one army official's unknowingly perfect formulation of necropolitics, "planned down to the last detail to destroy every sign of life."[32] This intensified war's aim was, for once and for all, absolute annihilation of, rather than containment of, popular movements in both city and countryside.

Writing about the countryside, the historian Greg Grandin places the start of this escalation in March 1978 in the town of Panzós, Alta Verapaz, when army soldiers fired an unarmed crowd and killed over thirty Q'eqchi' Maya women and men who had gathered to discuss threats to their lands. In the city, where tens of thousands of urbanites protested what they immediately named "The Panzós Massacre," there was in 1978–79 a sharp increase in kidnappings in Guatemala City. It could be argued that the police firebombing that killed over thirty people who had peacefully occupied the Spanish embassy in January 1980 to protest and publicize the war in rural areas made the war "official" in the city. What followed left no doubt that the state had declared all-out war there. Uniformed police kidnapped students from the funeral march for those killed at the Spanish embassy a few days after the assault on it. Thirty-one secondary and university students and factory workers were kidnapped in one day during the May 1 protest that year. On June 21, the narcotics squad division of the National Police "disappeared" twenty-seven trade unionists in broad daylight out of a labor central's office a few blocks from the National Palace. On July 14, uniformed police shot and killed nine students and injured forty more on the University of San Carlos campus. On August 24, seventeen trade unionists were kidnapped from a presumably secret meeting. By September 1980, the open popular movement had shut down, and the revolutionary groups endeavored to stage hit-and-run propaganda actions in the city.

In the first few months of 1981, the Guatemalan Army formally stepped in. Soldiers, tanks, and helicopters launched a full-fledged urban counterinsurgency, destroyed the safehouses of the revolutionary groups, and killed or captured dozens of cadre, while others fled to the mountains.[33] Even though the city seemed a graveyard, some thought the coordinated revolutionary fronts would respond to this urban counterinsurgency with an urban offensive, as had recently happened in Nicaragua. These supporters felt part of a national guerrilla military campaign because at the time the Guatemalan Army started its scorched-earth campaigns in 1981, the population of entire parts of the largely Maya departments of El Quiché, Huehuetenango, the Verapaces, and Chimaltenango were supporting and joining revolutionary fronts.[34] Residents—especially those in the poorer areas of the city, where the distinction between city and countryside is blurred by the steady movement of people between them—heard bits and pieces about both advances of the guerrillas and the army's massacres in rural areas during the early 1980s, but it took time for city people to realize how weak the revolutionary fronts were. Left-wing discourse still remained relevant in Guatemala City despite the army's advances. When the Maras first formed in the early 1980s, the military's use of violent death was already proving to be a definitive way to control life in rural areas, but the gangs did not utilize death in that way, or at all.

One Becomes, and Is Not Born, a Killer

According to the United Nations Report of the Commission for Historical Clarification (CEH), in the first years of the 1980s, the army and other state forces committed 91 percent of the human rights crimes carried out between 1962 and the 1996 Peace Accords.[35] These crimes consisted of 626 massacres that left more than 100,000 people dead, more than 55,000 children orphaned, and well over 1.5 million internal and external refugees.[36] Of the 626 massacres between 1960 and 1996, 554 took place between 1981 and 1982. By the close of those two years, the number of dead later counted as victims of acts of genocide was complete. The Guatemalan Army was unconstrained, the guerrillas could mount no large military offensive, and the international community remained silent. Massacres that the Guatemalan anthropologist Ricardo Falla has described as "collective torture," rather than battles, constituted these campaigns, according to the thousands of testimonies collected by the UN CEH and the Guatemalan Archdiocese.[37] When the military escalated the war, it obliged a large percentage of the Guatemalan male population to participate in turning the death-squad system of sadism into public spectacles in hundreds of "red" and "pink" zones in the countryside.[38] The army involved hundreds of thousands of Guatemalans, mostly Maya, in causing "pain almost to infinity" to hundreds of thousands of Guatemalans, who were in their majority Maya, in a short period of time. As a case in point, in a twenty-four-day period the Maya municipality of Rabinal in Alta Verapaz alone experienced twenty-eight massacres in which around five thousand people were killed, representing almost 20 percent of the population in that area.[39]

Part of the manufacture of death was the production of those who killed, as in any war, but in this case that did not include relying on or constructing patriotism and an image of an ideal nation for which war must be waged, except in the most superficial sense. Manolo Vela Castañeda's research on the military shows that the regime did not build an army in order to pursue "war in the name of life," to use Foucault's description of twentieth-century war and genocide.[40] Bereft of the support of the urban majority in the early 1980s, frightened to wade into the waters of openly recruiting from among a concentrated population that had as recently as May 1, 1980, marched under banners of "democracy and socialism" in numbers of over fifty thousand, the military made little attempt at propaganda designed to win the city over to, much less explain, the war. For a few months in the early 1980s, General Efraín Ríos Montt, Pentecostal and chief of staff, gave Sunday "sermons" on television to explain the "crisis" as a moral one that could be answered only by "cleaning house."[41] In kind with other urban war propaganda, his talks aimed to frighten and not to convince. In this period, the army television channel showed the Guatemalan Army's pride, its elite force of killers called the kaibiles, "cleaning house." They grabbed hens, pulled the feathers out, and ate them live with the animal blood splattering all over their contorted faces.[42] On other channels, these scenes of kaibiles interrupted soap operas.

The principal mechanism for constituting a fighting force to massacre in the countryside took place in the countryside, where military commanders forced Maya males into the army. For the most part they were rounded up in village markets, then hauled away on trucks to military bases, where they were barbarized through three months of abuses to turn them into cruel soldiers who lacked any trace of idealism.[43] In his unpublished manuscript, Rodrigo Sic Ixpancoc, from Rabinal Baja Verapaz, describes what happened to him: A local military commissioner arrived at his home to inform him he had to "ir a comer arroz [literally, to go eat rice]" and serve in the army. During his three-month training, he was beaten repeatedly, stripped naked, not allowed to eat or sleep for long periods, screamed at—"Chicken," "Indio shit," "Guerrillero"—tortured, taught to torture, and told that "if his mother was a guerrillera, an india shit, he had to kill her." His manuscript describes details that repeatedly emerge in the UN CEH's Memoria del Silencio report of training that included the promotion of Maya self-hatred, beatings, rape, and even debt peonage among its forced recruits. This was a war devoid of love between officers and soldiers or among soldiers or of nation.

Recruits spent twenty-seven weeks receiving instruction in absolute obedience and "contempt for life and the savoring of violence."[44] The recruits repeatedly recounted the presentation of pointless murder as if it were an exhilarating event. As one reported, a training instructor "yelled to me, 'Hurry, you are missing something good.' And when I got there they only had one of the boys [referring to three either recruits or civilians brought into the base] left, and they were cutting off his head. That is what I was missing."[45] Recruits were exhorted to take the so-called step of death: killing someone as a proof of competence. Instructors encouraged recruits to compete with one another in designing ways to torture the communist guerrillas. One recounted: "The instructors gave lessons and awoke the creativity and the imagination so that each one would think of a torture even more refined than the last. One said he would take off the guerrillas' shoes, make a wound and put salt and lime in it. The next invented something else. He would poke out eyes with needles and on it went."[46] At the end of 1981, military commissioners organized the Patrullas de Autodefensa Civil (Civil Self-Defense Patrols, PACs). The PACs incorporated all male villagers between fifteen and sixty, armed them with sticks and machetes, and ordered them to rape, steal, murder, and massacre in their neighboring and sometimes their own communities, or be killed (see figure 1.3).[47] At the height of the war, the PACs included almost one million Guatemalans in a country of eight million; over 40 percent of the entire male population was forced or socialized into fratricide. A former PAC member stated that these groups were not created to protect villagers, as the military had claimed; instead it was, he said, to "kill our own brothers. . . . We are all are sick with what they made us do."[48] The PACs carried out almost one-half of the massacres in some areas under the orders of military commanders.[49]

The murder of children is perhaps the strongest example of the design to inflict "infinite pain." In massacre after massacre, soldiers drew and quartered or decapitated children with dull machetes, raped them, and ripped the unborn out of pregnant women in front of relatives and other community members.[50] In one massacre, an entire village had to listen to the gang rape of one small girl for hours before she and the others were killed. In a variation of this, soldiers raped mothers in front of their children.[51] People remember the massacre at Cuarto Pueblo in 1982, and they told how soldiers put "wires, red, red hot from the fire into them [the villagers], stuck them into their mouths, and all the way down to their stomachs . . . not caring if the person was a little child."[52] In the case of the community of Río Negro, on March 13, 1982, soldiers and Civil Patrollers entered the village, pulled people out of their homes, ate breakfast, played marimba music, made women and girls dance with them, and raped the youngest ones. A survivor testified that the soldiers then killed 70 women and 107 children; in the words of one witness, "they hung some from the trees, they killed others with machetes and they fired at others. They took the little children and threw them against the stones."[53] In another massacre, soldiers went into a

FIGURE 1.3 The uses of youth: this photograph of Civil Patrollers in the countryside, July 1985, suggests the ages at which almost one million males, for the most part Mayas, were obliged to join the Civil Self-Defense Patrols. Behind them, children watch. Credit: Anónimo. *"Patrulla de Autodefensa Civil" organizada durante el conflicto armado interno.* Guatemala, 28 de Julio de 1985. Archivo de fotografías de El Gráfico. Fototeca Guatemala, CIRMA.

hamlet and seized twelve men and boys and twelve women and girls. After directing the women and girls to get twelve hens and pots, they ordered the sons to kill their fathers. A witness stated, "If the son was the one not complying, then the father had to stain his hands by killing his son." After that the clay pots with the twelve hens inside were put on fire, and the women began to cook. A survivor testified: "The army screamed at them to make sure the food was well-prepared. . . . While the food cooked, the men died and the soldiers burnt them. . . . When they were all burned up, they [the soldiers] applauded and started eating."[54]

The above descriptions come from survivors in answer to set questions asked by human rights researchers in the late 1990s. Despite the problems involved in taking testimonies, witnesses of massacres detailed how in community after community, large numbers of soldiers arrived before dawn and quickly set up what can only be called death spaces in which they "destroyed every sign of life." The military did not miss much in its calculations. Soldiers burned the houses and fields, ate the animals, arrived on religious days, made sure the children and the unborn died first and in the most horrible ways, poisoned wells with dead bodies, and killed the esteemed elderly with old work tools.[55]

Perhaps the words beyond words of a survivor of the massacre of 350 of his fellow villagers at the Finca San Francisco in 1982, words that he used to describe his state of mind when he arrived in a Mexican town after fleeing across the border, break though the numbing literal descriptive style of the accounts given to human rights workers, and open onto the sheer incomprehensibility of existence and knowledge in the aftermath of an episode that obliterates the known world: "Is it 11 in the morning? I arrive in Santa Maria. Like a drunk I cannot see if it is daylight. I come without sadness. I think nothing. Without food, without food, without a jacket. Without clothes. I am nobody. Without a hat. Completely nobody."[56] Another villager who had fled that massacre testified that a soldier had taken out a child's heart and put it to his mouth.[57]

After the 1980–83 massacres, the army expanded its control over territory and local structures and placed survivors in resettlement camps that provided food, work, and Pentecostal services, and thus it could be said that it started cranking up the machinery of life, such as it was. By the early 1990s, the majority within the military high command felt secure enough to start a years-long period of negotiating to reach a final accord. As victor, the military could began to advertise the new discursive reality of "peace" and "democracy." The guerrilla fronts still existed, and they engaged the army in skirmishes, but the fronts had lost popular support definitively by the late 1980s, and the 1996 Peace Accords ended an armed struggle that was already over.[58]

How could this war, terrible in the city and much worse in the countryside, not have an effect on the evolution of urban gangs? However formulated or expressed—whether in ways very fragmented, hardly unrecognizable, or more colored in—all this history and all those who lived through it, got around. Millions of people suddenly left one place and went to another, and sometimes on to others. Thousands fled into the mountains, where *(refug)* some joined hidden settlements called Comunidades de Pueblos en Resistencia (Communities of People in Resistance) to live off the land, and thousands crossed the border into Mexico, where many went into refugee camps. Others became undocumented immigrants who either stayed in Mexico or traveled to the United States, where they disappeared in large cities, especially in the Los Angeles area in the 1980s and 1990s. It is estimated that between 50,000 and 200,000 left the country, yet 1.3 million fled the four hardest-hit highland departments.[59] Uncounted numbers of displaced moved about within Guatemala.

At least fifty-five thousand war refugees came into Guatemala City and quietly moved into the poorest areas of the city, where, if they were Maya, they often shed their clothes and languages for fear of being pursued. The mother of Estuardo, an MS-13 member killed by Mara-18 (M-18) in 1998, escaped into an area of Guatemala City called Tierra Nueva I after a massacre killed the other members of her family in the early 1980s. In 1984, at fourteen, Edgar Guarchaj came from the Department of El Quiché to live in the streets of Guatemala City to make money to send back home so that his father could pay another man to serve his shift in the PAC in order to have the time he needed to work his land to keep the family alive.[60] Edgar remained tied to his family and stayed with relatives in the city, but thousands of orphaned children turned up on Guatemala City streets. Soldiers even brought orphans to a group home for children. In the words of a social worker there: "The same army [that massacred] would bring these children and say that so and so 'was the only survivor of a battle'; to us this meant of a destroyed hamlet. This was very hard. . . . These children did not talk, at first we social workers thought that they were deaf mute, but little by little we discovered it was from the trauma of being present at the assassination of their parents and of their community. . . . We did not dare keep records for fear of reprisals, and we became human archives."[61]

Escaping war and seeking opportunities, tens of thousands of Guatemalans and Salvadorans went to California in the 1980s and 1990s, where they were pulled toward the long-standing Spanish-speaking neighborhoods of Los Angeles. Norma Stoltz Chinchilla and Nora Hamilton discuss how large numbers of these immigrants settled in Pico-Union, a part of Westlake, located within the Ramparts division of the Los Angeles Police Department in the southern central part of Los Angeles, an area relatively cut off from others by freeways and other obstacles. They brought a new presence to this small dense world, one of the poorest areas of the city and 80 percent Hispanic by the 1980s. Life there was as difficult as in the worst of urban areas in the United States: the average income was $15,000; it had an 85 percent high school dropout rate; and it was plagued by crowded schools, overcrowded housing, inadequate services, and a dearth of recreational facilities, conditions that would deteriorate with the recession of the early 1990s.[62] This was a period of urban deindustrialization and the deregulation of government programs such as drug and alcohol rehabilitation centers and English as a Second Language classes. As in other cities in the United States facing similar problems in these especially hard times, gangs and drugs dealers increased in Pico-Union and neighboring areas.[63]

Los Angeles, including Pico-Union, has a long history of gangs, written about by James Diego Vigil and others.[64] Gangs and youth clubs probably date from the White Fence in 1929, which was started to protect Mexicans and Mexican Americans from racism. The story of gangs in Los Angeles history includes the heyday of zoot suit cultures of African Americans, Mexican Americans, and Mexicans in the 1940s, and the more recent Crips and Bloods. According to Vigil, none of this was characterized by excessive brutality toward others or themselves. What Vigil calls "escalating violence" in the 1950s and 1960s was "self-contained" and involved "set battles." He writes, "The modern notion of the ultraviolent street gang or predator did not prevail." Major transformations came with crack and guns in the 1970s and 1980s, and sharpened in the 1990s, with the incorporation of gang members into the Mexican drug ring La Eme, and the arrival of Central American youth marked by war.[65]

Numerous writers have emphasized that MS-13 and M-18 in Guatemala City are Los Angeles gangs because they started there; nonetheless, they also started as specifically Guatemalan and Salvadoran gangs in Los Angeles.[66] Boys and young men who came from Guatemala and from El Salvador, where twelve years of civil war ended in 1992, brought memories of war-related experiences that had to be recontextualized in the midst of new difficulties of racism, rejection, and unemployment in an unfamiliar city.[67] Especially given the push within academia to go beyond the boundaries of nation, it has been tempting to treat these gangs as a "global" phenomenon because of this Los Angeles nexus, as well as the Mexican one. Then again, even though these youth move across borders and experience the transcultured worlds of Los Angeles and of Mexican towns and cities, and they pick up meaningful slogans, names, institutional frameworks, and tactics— for example, the Southern United Raza (the nonaggression pact between gangs)—they are still what cultural historian Peter Fritzsche calls "bounded subjects" whose subjectivities had been shaped by the "national experience" and whose bodies are sometimes literally scarred by the nation-state.[68] In their studies, James Diego Vigil and Tom Hayden both connect the violence of the Central Americans gangs in Pico-Union to state barbarism in Central America.[69]

From my perspective MS-13 and M-18 could well be placed inside an as yet unwritten history of ex-soldiers from Central America that someone should research. An ex-soldier from either the Salvador Army or the rebel army nicknamed Flaco Stoner founded Wonder-13 in the 1980s to defend his compatriots from Mexican Americans gangs. It soon became known as Mara Salvatrucha, to honor its Salvadoran members, although it welcomed Guatemalans and Hondurans excluded from other Latino gangs.[70] In addition, with the numbers of Central Americans coming into the area, youth from El Salvador, Guatemala, and Honduras took over an older, once Mexican American, 1950s gang known as 18th Street and later called M-18, Mara-18, or Barrio-18.[71] The impact of both military training and the more general war experience was evident to them and to others. The Los Angeles Police Department heard that MS-13 gang members were "outstanding" in their cruelty because they had been trained by no less a talent than that of the U.S. Special Forces in El Salvador.[72] Neighbor youth noted that these gangs of Guatemalan, Salvadoran, and Honduran youth brought a new level of violence to the area, which soon provoked escalations of violence in other gangs. One young man in Pico-Union described the change in M-18 after Salvadorans took over: "[Before] they [M-18 members] were junior high school guys . . . like punks in the way they dressed, T-shirts with skulls and long hair. . . . The truth is later [M-18] became so large and so different from the *cholo* gangs, this stuff of just looking for violence and no more than that . . . they [the Salvadorans] just kill [because] some *bato* [dude] gives them an ugly look. . . . They always shot to kill."[73]

Ernesto Miranda, another founding MS-13 member and ex–Salvadoran military solider explained the intensity of MS-13 brutality: "[In Salvador] we were taught to kill our own people, no matter if they were from your own blood. If your father was the enemy, you had to kill him, so the training during the war in our country served to make us one of the most violent gangs of the United States."[74] In the following description, a perceptive and astute young man in MS-13 captures this connection between the heightened cruelty of Salvadoran and Guatemalan gang members in Los Angeles, and the state terror in their home countries:

> The difference between the Mexicans and Salvadorans or Central Americans in general is this: Mexicans usually come from states like Michoacán. They live in a small town and are mainly agricultural. They do have violence from feuds, drug war, or now LA barrio violence. Generally speaking, they are not initially violent when they come to the US. El Salvador and Guatemala are another story. It was common to walk out of a *tienda* and see a street splattered with brain particles and blood. People in Guatemala were getting kidnapped and tortured to the point of insanity. In the main university in Guatemala City, students were forced to give classes due to the fact that all the professors had gotten smoked, one by one. . . . If you reach the age of 15 in Guatemala without having to identify [the body of] a relative you were blessed. These people [Guatemalans] saw carnage that even the Faces of Death [snuff videos] chose not to use.[75]

In his view, the pornography of snuff films, with their raw footage of—among much else—real life in real-time rapes, massacres, train crashes, murders, and bodies flying out of exploded buildings, cannot hold a candle to the experience of violence inside the social wreckage of a collapsed moral universe in which you leave your everyday corner store to find brain particles all over the street outside.

With the many sweeps that the Los Angeles police made in the Ramparts District, members of M-18 and MS-13, including Flaco Stoner, ended up in the California prison system, where (accounts claim) they made tight connections with La Eme. When and why a deadly rivalry between MS-13 and M-18 started is not clear, but it predates the U.S. Immigration and Naturalization Service (INS) massive deportation of Central Americans back to their countries of origin. What started as a trickle of INS deportations in the early 1990s turned into a flood that included incarcerated gang members by 1996. Taken from prisons and flown home in shackles, these deportees brought with them MS-13 and M-18, as well as whatever slogans, clothing styles, hand signals, and vocabulary had not already traveled to Central

America through the media and immigration. MS-13 and M-18 absorbed and reorganized local Maras in Guatemala City into clikas with names such as "Los Locos," which then formed the base of the MS-13 or M-18 pyramids. Each clika was under the supervision of a veterano; veteranos designated palabras (words) who communicated between the clikas. Members of M-18 and MS-13 with whom I spoke in Guatemala City in the late 1990s told me that the youth of each clika had their identities affirmed by going through initiation rituals—for instance, receiving the MS-13 baptism of thirteen blows to the body and the cult knowledge of the changing meanings of the gang symbols that came from Los Angeles.

"Shadows of War" in Guatemala City

The war and its aftermath combined with changing demographics and an economic crisis to alter Guatemala City. Neoliberal restructuring programs affected Guatemala City, as they did Los Angeles and other cities around the world. Perhaps no more social services, for instance public clinics, got eliminated in Guatemala City than in Pico-Union, but residents had even fewer resources at the outset. The substantial industrial development that took place in the 1950s and 1960s under the Central American Common Market had already started to unravel by the late 1970s as a consequence of the 1973 oil crisis. The cutbacks in production in workplaces such as the large unionized CAVISA glass and ACRICASA thread companies turned into shutdowns in the last two decades of the twentieth century, making worse already drastic problems of gainful employment in a city that was booming demographically. Low-wage maquiladoras, the sole growth industry in the 1980s and 1990s, did not offer enough jobs to compensate for those lost in the 1980s, much less create new ones in a city with one of the world's highest growth rates. The population had gone from less than a million in 1975 to almost three million by 1996, with those under twenty-five constituting over one-half the urban population.[76] The áreas marginales, exceptionally poor areas (see figures 1.4 and 1.5), grew as they never had before: of 161 identified in 1998, a full 111 formed after 1991. A 1996 survey of áreas marginales found that 34 percent of the households earned less than a "survival" income.[77] Most analysts argue that war refugees, whom the sociologists Santiago Bastos and Manuela Camus evocatively name "shadows of war" in a study of urban settlements, account for their rapid growth.

Even though the displaced in the city rarely spoke directly about the massacres in fear of the consequences, which included reprisals, new designations and much else signaled the war.[78] Where once rural-to-urban migrants

FIGURE 1.4 Two boys standing around on a stretch of the Avenida Bolívar in Zone 8, Guatemala City, a city with little to offer youth, 2000. Credit: Andrea Aragón.

FIGURE 1.5 A mother, Guatemala City, 2002. The city streets hold out even less for young people with children. From the series *Inhalando muerte*. Credit: Andrea Aragón.

had identities that reflected their work and place of origin—the tailor from Todos Santos or the saleswoman from Totonicapán—now there were refugees, victims, ex-soldiers, ex-PACs, survivors, widows, and orphans. Like those who went across borders, war refugees in the city carried terrible memories into a situation where they were often alone, with few to console or understand them. Despite their silence about the war, in one way or another they communicated their feelings as well as some version of their experiences to their children and others. Because human rights workers generally did not gather testimonies in the áreas marginales, the memories of these refugees in the city were not reconstituted and affirmed as part of a "collective war memory," however complex that notion, its production, and its uses may be.[79] Without some community in which to develop a collective understanding of how mistrust, uncertainties, anger, hopelessness, and fear are grounded in specific events and people, all these sensations became unspecific and even more overwhelming because they seem to have no roots outside of a blur called "the situation" that was out of their control.[80]

The growing number of poor areas and the presence of a war-related migrant population constituted one shift in urban life. Another was that the more established city neighborhoods changed radically in the late 1980s and 1990s because they all but lost their politics to the state terror.[81] Neighborhood involvement became tied to the infrastructure of global nongovernmental organizations (NGOs) by the early 1990s. In many areas, vertically structured civic life replaced the horizontal political life of the earlier period. The number of NGOs increased dramatically, and institutions representing city and state departments, such as the medical clinics and pharmacies run by the municipality with funds from the Ministry of Health, diminished. In contrast to the 1970s, grassroots groups became few in number and only local in perspective. This meant that grassroots agency and everything that went with that—from starting from scratch in someone's front room and getting up the nerve to go door to door, to developing analysis, strategy, and tactics in relation to the Guatemalan state and its agencies—had all but died off. By the 1990s, community improvement committees generally sought financing and advice from hierarchical agencies with international ties. Outspoken residents became entangled in trying to win changes "from above" rather than in mobilizing "from below." With many NGOs working in barrios, competition about funding from these agencies often divided community leaders. Communities tended to become further depoliticized because the NGOs encouraged residents to resolve their problems through the medium of the NGOs, instead of bringing them to the attention of the broader public and the state, as had grassroots organizations in the 1970s, when neighborhood residents boldly inserted themselves into national politics (see figure 1.6).[82] To confound this new absence of horizontal solidarities, the barrios had lost to state violence the left-wing religious workers who had envisioned creating "God's kingdom on Earth." Tierra Nueva, later called Tierra Nueva I, started by a liberation theology priest in 1976 and where the Mara Las Cobras was born in the early 1980s, is an example of a community built with a new world in mind.

The history of its offspring, Tierra Nueva II, illustrates the deep political change in barrios. In 1985, the teenage son of a religious left-wing organizer of the original Tierra Nueva I launched Tierra Nueva II with his friends. A Mara called Mara Nene were born with the invasion; it was part of its "heat," as one described the marero support for the new community.[83] But within a few years, the combination of well-funded NGOs and selective state violence undermined the power of the original organizers and of their visions for a community-run Tierra Nueva II. Death threats forced one organizer into exile and others out of activism. What was once a rivalry about break dance contests between the Maras Nene in Tierra Nueva II and Las Cobras in Tierra Nueva I became a violent one over *territorio* that included neighborhood streets, stores, and women's bodies. Las Cobras destroyed Mara Nene at the end of the decade and went on to become violent within the gang and neighborhood.

Much had changed in these milieus. By the late 1980s and increasingly as time passed, dozens of Pentecostal sects dominated Tierra Nueva I and II and other areas. Trucks mounted with sound systems blasted taped messages of sin and salvation incessantly to summon residents to services that went on during the day and evening for hours. Unlike liberation theology adherents, most pastors believed, in the words of one, that "the poor will always be with us. The poor choose to be poor."[84] Pentecostal pastors emphasized that nothing could be done about the fact that life was hell, and this portrayal of earthly impotence and hopelessness resonated in the wake of the defeat of projects for social change.[85] The Pentecostal message emphasized the constancy of crisis and the absence of human control outside of individual willpower about the individual self. Nothing could have seemed truer. These churches grew like wildfire. For young people, this city life in the 1990s bore few traces of the experiences and ideas of the popular and revolutionary movements of the 1970s. The majority in Guatemala City was under eighteen, and what were startling transformations for older generations made up normal life for young people. This was a city that was losing its cultural texture, one in which people continually experienced the instability of the nation's relationship to its past.

FIGURE 1.6 The neighborhood of Esperanza in Mezquital, Guatemala City, 2005. Fifteen hundred families led a land invasion in 1984 to establish the urban settlement of Mezquital in Zone 12. War refugees were among the tens of thousands who came to live here. Over the years, Mezquital has been the scene of the twists and turns of grass-roots organizations, nongovernmental organizations, state repression, Pentecostal churches, Maras, community initiatives against Maras, and "social cleansing" campaigns. Credit: Victor J. Blue.

The growth of violence following the war is notorious, and it happened in this urban crucible stripped of its political and ethical past. Today, Guatemala City is one of the most dangerous places in the world, with an average of a murder by gunfire "for every hour of the day," as one newspaper journalist phrased it.[86] The Guatemalan human rights ombudsman Sergio Morales stated that in 2008 there was more violence each day than there had been daily during the war.[87] Most deaths are by gunfire. Most of those who die are youth. By one count, 80 percent of gun-related deaths are of youth between fifteen and seventeen.[88] This violence is generally not related to the political views of those killed, but that too continues. Women and men who have opposed mining companies and hydroelectric projects, occupied unused lands to prevent starvation, and sought to protect the environment have been killed, and so have workers trying to unionize.

There is complete impunity. In the wake of the war, the state has shown itself either unwilling or incapable of preventing crime. The new National Civil Police, the presumably reformed police mandated by the Peace Accords, simply does not pursue criminal investigations. A 2002 study revealed that for every hundred cases reported to the judicial system, only ten received any response at all, and in 2005, only 1 percent of those accused of "crimes against life" were ever brought to a hearing.[89] Mental health professionals— who seem the chroniclers of the period—report that this impunity causes despair, fear, paranoia, physical illness, and rage ignited over and over by helplessness. Impunity has led to the formation of barrio vigilante groups that beat up and even kill real or supposed young criminals. Impunity means that there exists absolutely no buffer between the community and crime except community action, which can take many forms. Impunity functions as a model whereby transgression of the law is seen as the normal way and the only way.[90]

Violence has taken a long journey. In the 1950s, 1960s and 1970s, notions of violence were qualified and analytical. Violence was not perceived, understood, discussed, measured, or judged outside of a particular context. Although in countries such as Colombia, the term "La violencia" was a familiar one, it was uncommon in Guatemala. Whether in social science and humanities publications, banners, or the bulletins of campesino leagues, Maya cultural organizations, urban trade unions, and university and secondary student groups, violence was represented as state terrorism, structural and everyday oppression, and armed self-defense. Not only the revolutionary movement but also the popular movement and many religious figures defended armed violence as necessary and just. It was not until the 1990s that the defense of revolutionary violence and people's war became increasingly subdued in the face of military successes. The military has never muted its defense of its actions, which it defines as "restoring order," the opposite of the chaos of violence. It justified its own behavior, which it never called violent, in terms of "social cleansing," or it used the language of the Cold War National Security Doctrine to argue that the cancer of subversion needed to be cut out, a medical rather than a military phrasing.

Now ubiquitous, the unqualified term "La violencia" started to be used after the decisive massacres of the early 1980s, and it has held different meanings depending on who uses it, where, and when. It became a code for state violence for survivors who lived under military rule. For some, "La violencia" was and has remained a euphemism for state violence, a way for survivors to speak about the past in seemingly apolitical, and thus protected, language. It also became a way for the army, Pentecostals, and others to describe "El conflicto." For many, especially younger generations, "La violencia" (and not the history of popular movements, guerrillas, state power and military strategy, struggles for land and higher wages, ideas, and ideals) tells the story of Guatemala's past. Within this vision, a faceless "La violencia" consumed the past, and the present must be protected from it. The historically focused *Memoria del silencio* report, which analyzes causes and assigns blame, has been poorly circulated in Guatemala. For those who attend school, most curricula deal superficially with "El conflicto" and "La violencia" as the past from which Guatemala has evolved into a "post-conflict" democratic society.[91] This new public sphere rhetoric of "conflict" and "post-conflict" suggests that conflict—surely a necessary condition of a healthy society—is negative. Whether the issue is land invasions or protests against mining, anything that questions the status quo is viewed as negative because it reintroduces conflict and drags to the foreground the muck of "La violencia." Progressive groups have had a hard time reclaiming a language of resistance. Everyone must be nonviolent; otherwise they are part of "it."[92] In everyday talk now in Guatemala City, "La violencia comes," "La violencia arrives," "La violencia prevents us," "La violencia surrounds us," "La violencia forces us," "La violencia frightens us," and so on. And "it" does all these things.

Of 170 children under the age of eleven, questioned in 2010 in what the National Civil Police call a "red" (high-crime) neighborhood in Guatemala City, 135 said that they had witnessed murders, and they could often describe in detail where the bullets went and the way the blood squirted out to quickly turn clothing red. Given an average of eighteen violent deaths daily in the first months of 2010, no doubt most of these children actually did see murders, and not on television (see figure 1.7).

FIGURE 1.7 Neighborhood residents watch the scene of a murder in Zone 5, Guatemala City, 2005. Credit: Victor J. Blue.

Marco Garavito, head of La Liga de Higiene Mental, a mental health collective, describes how the police typically put up a yellow cordon around the crime scene, but they place it right next to the body. "Why not at thirty meters?" he asks with the enormous frustration because so simple a change would help keep these deaths at least at a spatial distance. Children slip under the ropes to look closely at the bodies, which are often of youth from the neighborhood. If not literally known, the dead are familiar types, the people the children might be a few years later. A reporter asks Garavito, "What will happen to these children? What psychological damage will they suffer, what will happen to them in the future?" Garavito replies, "It takes no investigation to see that violence affects them . . . to the degree they become accustomed[,] they reproduce it. They see it as normal, natural."[93]

To challenge this, La Liga runs a program that takes as its point of departure and arrival the notion that violence is a "decision, not an obligation." If young people have internalized violence as the natural means of living, they assume life demands it, or in the words of the Liga, "obliges" it. To invert this and say, "violence is a decision" denaturalizes it, makes it someone's responsibility, and brings youth back inside the "old" social imaginary of cause and effect and human agency and away from the passivity of Victor's "it just was" discourse.

To return to Victor, introduced at the start of this chapter: In what massacre did Victor take part? Was he trying to impress or frighten with a tall story? He gave slight information, but what he said could certainly be true. The "high-intensity" massacres were over by the time the army picked him up, but "low-intensity" ones continued. If he did make it up, he did not invent the material. Clearly he knew things about these massacres, and this knowledge was part of his archive. His description was flat, without remorse or horror. If the military did not seize and train him, and then take him to the highlands to play a part in a massacre, perhaps he told this personal narrative in order to belong somewhere in the larger Guatemalan story of war, about which he had no shame or pride because he was part of what "just was."

1980s: THE GANGS TO LIVE FOR

I joined because there was emptiness inside me, a little loneliness, a bit of sadness. Maybe we are all alike in this. I joined through a bunch of girlfriends with whom I was very heavy. We've shared sorrows and joys. I think the Mara is a group of people who need affection. Some of us want to escape the mess in our homes. Sometimes we think we can create a new world.

—Researchers' interview with Maritza, Mara de la 4, March 1987

When he was nine years old, Aníbal López told his parents that he had had a vision of an earthquake. A few days later, in the early morning of February 1976, a 7.5-magnitude earthquake with an epicenter close to Guatemala City struck. More than twenty-three thousand persons, most of whom lived in conditions of poverty, died as a result of this tremor and a strong aftershock, and tens of thousands more were injured and left homeless. The López family's rented apartment in Barrio La Florida, Zone 19, was badly damaged, as were most of the over ninety thousand *casas precarias* (precarious homes) in the city.[1] In late March, the López family was one of many who joined a well-organized land invasion led by a revolutionary Catholic priest onto a defunct coffee plantation on the outskirts of Zone 7, not far from La Florida. This response to disaster was the result of theological reflections into the meaning of the earthquake between the priest and a small group of residents in the old barrio El Gallito in Zone 3, a neighborhood so poor that families lived in one room that served as all rooms. The group decided, in the words of one member, "the earthquake had been a warning from el Señor to leave El Gallito shantytowns" and develop "a communitarian identity." They christened their settlement Tierra Nueva.[2]

For a few years, a neighborhood committee that was inspired by liberation theology's emphasis on building a here-and-now Reign of God on Earth ran Tierra Nueva with "the notion of a little socialism in terms of solidarity" and "without bars or houses of prostitution."[3] The settlement grew, and over time residents mobilized to obtain water, electricity, paved streets, garbage collection, and a sewage system. They provided themselves with a medical clinic and started discussion groups as well as a daycare center in part financed by workers from the radical Coca-Cola Workers' Union. Years later state violence, corruption, and the imperatives and finances of the state and NGOs undermined Tierra Nueva's politics, but for a period of time, this attempt at an alternate everyday modernity emerged in both the imagination and practice.[4] Problems such as alcoholism or unemployment were framed in social terms and widely discussed in community circles. This was a loose form of a "creative imaginary," wherein individuals and collectives attempt to define themselves, in contrast to the ontology of "being determined."[5]

The radical politics of Tierra Nueva belonged to the milieu of solidarity and social justice that prevailed in neighborhoods, factories, and schools. With fewer than one million residents in the 1970s, Guatemala City was the country's commercial and political center, and it had recently become the site of Guatemala's singular industrial development. Stretched out over a high plateau cut through with deep ravines and edged by mountains, the city was divided into twenty-one zones. The zones were packed with people and housing, but green areas still dotted neighborhoods, many of which were the consequence of unplanned urban spread. Except in the wealthy sections of the city, social life took place in empty lots, green areas, and designated soccer fields; at church and home and in streets, bars, houses of prostitution, the city's central plaza, and its downtown in Zone 1. At midcentury, the urban population consisted of skilled artisans; a small middle class; an elite class; and a lower-class majority that labored in service, transport, construction and other sectors, was poor and primarily Ladino or mestizo, with a far smaller number of Mayas. In the 1970s, these social classes remained; the city, however, was also becoming a proletarian one and rural migrants were adding to its numbers and ethnic texture. Factories gave many zones a new profile, and some of these factories even seemed a centerpiece for their size and bustle. The hard work, general mistreatment, low wages, and managerial violence against women and men in these new factories were challenged by workers.[6] Unions were big news: factory sit-ins and strikes were on the radio and in the press, with workers taking their grievances to the public. A major event in the city, International Workers' Day on May 1, drew tens of thousands to the city's central plaza with prounion and antigovernment banners. As was discussed in the last chapter, city residents mobilized again and again. Aníbal's generation was perhaps too young to enter the ranks of revolutionary organizations or the other groups that students and young workers joined, but it came of age within the ethos or the *habitus*, in Pierre Bourdieu's sense, of the decades-long fight between the state and the popular movement.[7]

Because Aníbal had predicted one of the worst earthquakes in Central American history, as he grew up in Tierra Nueva, his extended family brought their worries to him, placed a lit candle in front of him, and asked him questions such as "where is so and so?" or "is so and so hurt?" His successes—for example, correctly envisioning an uncle delayed on the highway but not injured, dead, or missing—won him a reputation as a seer, and he was treated with special respect. Encouraged by his older brother, in the early 1980s he joined a new Tierra Nueva gang called Brek Las Cobras—*brek* as in break dancing—and later named Mara Las Cobras, which consisted of neighborhood boys and girls in their teens. His art career began in those years.[8]

For Aníbal, being in Las Cobras enhanced his sense of himself among peers who appreciated his talents.[9] He designed the graphics on Las Cobras' signature black T-shirts. He loved the group favorites, Jethro Tull and Led Zeppelin, enjoyed dancing, and was proud to win the title "Rey del Brek" in an annual dance contest in which gang members competed in 1985. That same year, another new gang, Mara Nene, took part in a land invasion led by the seventeen-year-old left-wing son of a founder of Tierra Nueva and established the settlement of Tierra Nueva II right above what then became renamed as Tierra Nueva I, discussed in chapter 1.

The mid-1980s was the period when, without ending the war, the Guatemalan military returned the country to constitutional rule after evaluating the success of its counterinsurgency scorched-earth campaigns in rural areas. Even if what became known as a "transition to democracy" was a tactic designed by the military to garner respectability while it continued the war, it provided at least enough space in the city for small mobilizations that remained informed by progressive ideals. In 1984, over four hundred Coca-Cola workers occupied the Coca-Cola facilities for an entire year to protect their union. An attempt was made to start a radical labor confederation to replace the one destroyed in 1980, and a new organization, Grupo de Apoyo Mutuo (Group of Mutual Support, GAM), which united relatives of the disappeared to demand their loved ones safe and sound, held its first public march in 1984.[10] Urban land invasions, such as the one that created Tierra Nueva II, grew, and in September 1985, just before president-elect Vinicio Cerezo of the centrist Partido Demócrata Cristiano (Christian Democratic Party, PDC) took office with his promise of a "government for and by the people," secondary students from the Rafael Aqueche Institute in downtown

Guatemala City took to the streets to stop an increase in bus fares, with the support of the bus drivers and the participation of youth from the neighborhood breks. In retrospect, these urban demonstrations in the mid-1980s were the last in the twentieth-century city with those kinds of 1970s left-wing politics. The point here is that gang members were part of this brief reappearance of protest.

The mid-1980s also saw the first massive advertising campaigns aimed at the urban youth market. Brightly colored ads portraying happy youth wearing Levi's jeans, Reebok or Nike footwear, and expensive accessories appeared on television, which was becoming ubiquitous in barrios for the first time, and on billboards. This relentless multinational crusade to get youth from all social classes and ethnic backgrounds to desire goods that formed part of a fantasy "world youth culture" had effects. It was impossible to live in the city and miss this loud second coming of capitalism, in which messages about the benefits of consuming what were virtually lavish goods replaced the discredited promises of the post-1954 economic development. This consumerism intensified life for working-class youth, who already faced many demands and dilemmas. Desires to have a youth style that required its own expensive international accoutrements had the potential to push to calamity already-untenable emotional, cultural, and economic situations wherein youth from poor homes were expected to work, to study, and to be a stable part of the time-honored family wage economy. It is in this context of a fading Left presence, a return to civilian government, and a marked growth of advertising that the Maras emerged.

Real Maras Become Imaginary Ones

By 1987, boys and girls from age six to late teens had created over sixty gangs, which were sometimes dubbed breks but more often Maras. They gave them names that suggested mischief, rebellion, fun, trouble, a place, gringo-isms, masculinity, or some combination of these traits. Maras named Los Guerreros, Las Pirañas, El Ruso, Los Pulpos, Los Garañones, Tigresa, Ángeles Infernales, Las Brujas, Los Angelitos, Nais, Relax, Vacas, Botudos, Sexta Calle, Los Motines Paraíso, ADI, Los Títeres, Guevudos, Zope, Callejeros, Mara 33, Apache, Miau Miau, 3 de Julio, Las Llantas, Motley Crew, El Ceviche, La Isla, and Mara FIVE came to include as many as one thousand children and teenagers who joined together to socialize; listen to the music of Led Zeppelin, Jethro Tull, the Grateful Dead, Queen, and other groups from the United States and Great Britain; and live with group and individual style, attitude, and personality. They earned reputations for their own striking character. Their lower-class "strutting" drew fire from better-off students at private *colegios*, who even started gangs called Bourgeois and Anti-Brek, which declared "war" on the Maras for being "vulgar" and "uppity." Decrying the appropriation of break dancing, a member of Bourgeois and Anti-Brek explained: "I fight with the breks because they are servants, vulgar types, because they rob, because of the way they dress. When brek dancing was in style, the bourgeois started to dance brek until it went out of style, but the poor kept dancing."[11] Victor, a founder of Mara Plaza Vivar Capitol, and Carlos Rafael Soto, head of Public Relations of the National Police, told me the same story about the origin of the widespread use of the term *Mara* for these gangs. They both separately said that the National Police spread the use of the term *Mara* in September 1985 during the protest against the bus fare. Soto remembered, "The September protesters used no organizational form or name so we called them 'Maras' from that Brazilian movie." Victor recalled, "The guys from the press and the cops said 'here comes the *Marabunta!*' and that's how it came to us and we started to be the Mara Plaza Vivar Capitol."[12]

A year later, these Maras were front-page news. Under the headline "Grenade Exploded in Discothèque," the daily El Gráfico reported that a youth in a "yellow bus with a black strip" threw a hand grenade at a crowd of teenagers in front of a discothèque named La Montaña Púrpura. One of the wounded, a ten-year-old on his way to Zone 1 to get a pair of sneakers, recounted to the journalist from El Gráfico that Mara youths in a school bus descended upon him and his friends, snatched gold chains, and fled.[13] Within a day, the National Police spokesperson Soto explained to the media that the grenade had exploded in front of this discothèque at which loitered drugged youth who belonged to Mara 33, a criminal band from Zone 6 that had its origins in television programs from the United States and in misguided parenting. In his words, "This evil affecting our youth is the fault of irresponsible parents who have permitted their children to live in complete freedom."[14] Common images of delinquent life—such as the abuse of school property, weapons, gold chains, free-wheeling minors, Zone 1, and discos—materialized in the story, and Soto used many of the loaded words—drugs, foreign, bad parents, drugs, freedom—of the ensuing anti-Mara narrative.

Without evidence, the National Police, press, and politicians quickly linked these Maras to urban problems such as street crime, prostitution, and the sale and use of drugs. The magistrate for minors, who directed the frail juvenile court system, pointed to the "disintegration of the family."[15] Social workers, even female ones with children, cited "women working outside the home" as the "fundamental cause" of juvenile delinquency.[16] Catchphrases about "imitating foreigners," "foreign movies," "lack of nationalism," and "imitating Negros" occurred again and again. The head of the juvenile delinquency bureau of the National Police told me: "Rock music incites youth to fight. We copy a lot . . . we don't appreciate our own culture. Guatemalan citizens who work abroad bring records, this infiltrates our culture, there is also the effect of the Negroes in the U.S., the Maras are like Negro gangs, or like Stallone's Cobras." Speaking without irony, in the midst of civil war, he added, "Or look at that movie *Warriors*, now that had impact!"[17]

Members of the Pentecostal movement were emerging in the mid-1980s as the city's new professionals in the wake of the military's destruction of the intellectual community in fields such as psychology and sociology, and they incorporated this mix of nationalist, racist, and pro-family rhetoric into a religious discourse of Satanism that surpassed that of criminalization. Pentecostal fanaticism had echoes of what the historian Virginia Garrard-Burnett suggests was Guatemala's religious language of war, one best exemplified by nationally televised speeches of the early 1980s that proselytized about the urgency of the covenant between God and man to cleanse society of evil, and were given by Pentecostal general Efraín Ríos Montt, who directed acts of genocide.[18]

With unchallenged authority, Pentecostals became in the 1980s the most organized and outspoken experts on gangs in the city, and they drew on the international fame of born-again Christianity successes with gangs such as New York City's famous Mau Maus. Pentecostal members, as chapter 4 elaborates, became important officials in government agencies who did not hesitate to be outspoken about their conservative religious vision of the roots of social problems. A Pentecostal counselor working in the Welfare Secretariat insisted to me that "the term Mara is Hindu for 'death to the soul.' . . . They are Satanic, they use the anti-Christ number 767 and their music encourages incest and necrophilia."[19] A widely circulated Pentecostal pamphlet titled *La música roc y sus peligros* warns that the Maras played rock music incessantly to promote "Satanic themes, pornography, materialism and chaos. . . . The popular singer Michael Jackson casts spells of terror in his music and video 'Thriller.' AC-DC has songs like 'Injected Poison' and the Evil Way on their album 'Highway to Hell.' The group 'Queen' has been popular. . . . Many think that 'Queen' means "queen" but aside from that, 'queen' is an expression used in the street for homosexual transvestite. Theirs is a Satanic philosophy of homosexuality and the number one danger to which we must be alert."[20] A respected Pentecostal psychologist, Roberto Morales del Pinar, who directed a home for runaway girls and young women and wrote a regular newspaper column, described in horror to me how, in one U.S. rock video, teenagers throw their father out the window. According to him, "In the Mara Satan appears to them [mareros], blood flows, wounds open, hate grows. . . . Satan conducts their death cults." Morales del Pinar thought it took fire to fight such fire, as it had, he pointed out to me, against the communists.[21]

The newly elected ruling PDC did not use this particular language. It made the "crisis of youth" a central issue and set up an underfinanced agency called National Plan for Youth to provide alternatives to gang life. It sponsored conferences, and even gave a few Mara youth office space in the National Youth Institute, an older establishment that trained future leaders. The PDC directed the new Ministries of Culture, Education, Labor, and Health—not the National Police or religious group—to confront the challenge of the Maras. However, the PDC did not confront the Pentecostal view, though party officials knew that the gangs represented no danger because the PDC had commissioned a study that showed the Maras to be composed of fairly average urban youth who at the worst broke minor laws. That these findings were not publicized and circulated facilitated confusion and fear, allowing the PDC to maintain favorable ties with the burgeoning and well-financed Pentecostal movement.

Research about Mareros

Young social scientists within the National Plan for Youth, who were genuinely concerned that their work would contribute to making party policy, directed the PDC's study. They conducted two straightforward surveys that consisted of asking young women and men in the gangs multiple-choice questions. Forty filled out a questionnaire in 1987, and a year later, five Mara leaders who worked with the National Plan asked 290 gang members the same questions. The two surveys coincided on all but matters of age and gender. In the smaller study, 20 percent were female, and in the second, larger study in 1988, 44 percent were female. In the first survey, 80 percent of the youth were ages fifteen to nineteen, and in the second, 73 percent were ages twelve to fifteen. The sheer percentages of females and children who belonged to the Maras undercut the images that the media, the police, and the Pentecostal descriptions evoked, as did all the results.

According to both surveys, of the religious majority in the Maras, 24 percent belonged to Pentecostal churches and the rest were Catholic; 27 percent checked "no religion." Eighty percent lived at the birth family's home. Ninety percent were born and bred in cities; 86 percent were single. Most spent their free time "hanging out" with Mara friends with whom they had "very tight" relationships, and few regularly watched television. All were literate, 61 percent attended elementary or secondary school, and the rest had dropped out of school. Eighty-three percent did not work either because they studied or because they could find no work; 21 percent occasionally stole items. Most who worked in the formal economy earned little. When the questionnaire asked about aspirations for the future, 55 percent stated they wanted to study, 19 percent wanted to work, 2 percent wanted to form a family, 1 percent wanted to immigrate to the United States, 19 percent had "no aspirations," and the rest had no reply.

Queried about what might improve their future prospects, 64 percent replied "nothing," 24 percent "study," 9 percent "work," and 3 percent "rob." Over half had taken illegal drugs, usually marijuana. Over 80 percent felt "happy" in their Maras, and 85 percent were "in agreement with the rules guiding the Maras because they were not imposed norms, but arrived at through consensus." Almost 100 percent had a positive view of their Mara as "angry, but with internal solidarity and respect" and declared that they had entered because of the "necessity of youth to unite." Only 8 of the 290 youths in the second survey said that they wished to leave the Maras in order to become "good citizens."

Whatever their shortcomings, the surveys at least revealed that Maras were composed of young people who seemed to be more or less "normal," except that they were better educated than most city youth, they stole goods, and they moved within milieus of their own creation. Probably a citywide survey of adults would have found comparable replies about religion and wages but not about literacy, immigration, stealing, drugs, and, most important, belonging to a space perceived as one of solidarity, respect, happiness, and democracy. The PDC researchers, themselves products of the 1960–70s, realized that the Maras had a relationship with that immediate political legacy. They concluded their report by defining the Maras as "a phenomenon of organized protest," which was not a negative description in their eyes.[22]

That same year, wishing to analyze the abrupt, shrill emphasis on juvenile crime in a nation racked by extraordinary state violence and shaken by the loss of dynamic popular politics, the social worker Nora Marina Figueroa, the psychologist Marta Yolanda Maldonado Castillo, and I did a qualitative study of the Maras under the auspices of the independent research institution the Asociación para el Avance de las Ciencias Sociales en Guatemala (Association for the Advancement of Social Sciences in Guatemala, AVANCSO). I wrote up the results in a monograph titled *Por sí mismos: Un estudio preliminar de las "Maras" en la Ciudad de Guatemala*, published by AVANCSO in 1988.[23] We had decided to study these gangs of children and youth because publicity about them had become alarmingly predominant at a time of complete silence surrounding the murders of the tens of thousands of children and youth in the highlands. The dangers these gangs posed might well be fantasy, we thought, and meant to distract attention from military massacres, yet the anxieties being created were real. Giving answers to simple questions concerning who these youth were, what they were doing, and what they thought they were doing aimed to clarify the public discussion. We interviewed dozens of members about family, work, school, violence, their gangs, their social lives, and their general views of life. And, after we spent several months passing time and talking with mareros from ten different Maras, we made the general observation that most of them were calm, well spoken, and thoughtful, not mindlessly imitative, obsessive, or hostile. Concerned about love and acceptance, they did not want to be misunderstood by us or the media, and they were usually eager to talk (see figure 2.1).

The young people and children with whom we spoke came from poor, working-class, and lower middle-class families. Their parents labored in the informal and formal economies, most commonly as vendors, artisans, construction workers, day laborers, and domestic servants. They often described home life to be tense because of financial and emotional strains. Silvio, an eighteen-year-old member of Mara FIVE, depicted his family: "My whole life has been a Calvary because my father is an alcoholic. There is no way to stop him! But my mother is the best in the world, everyone says so. I have a sister and the two of us suffer. . . . He doesn't have any money, not even so we can eat. Today he came home drunk at 5 PM. But I have a grandmother who lives in the USA . . . she loves us, she helps us, thanks to her I study."[24] As this predicament of alcoholism in Silvio's "whole" family illustrates, troubles were not confined to the single-parent households. Speaking of her emotional ties to her hard-working nuclear family, Lupe explained in a disheartened tone and without cynicism, "I have almost no relationship with them. . . . I don't know what to talk to them about."[25]

The gang members' views about the family, which they clearly perceived as the basic social unit of life, revealed deep feelings about what constituted a problem and what a solution. In all but ten of the descriptions of family life that we heard, fathers and other men such as stepfathers and boyfriends were irresponsible, alcoholic, and violent. Yolanda, age fourteen and a member of Mara Belén, explained that her mother, whom Yolanda adored, was a prostitute in a nightclub in Zone 1. Yolanda was furious at her mother: "I'm mad at her because she wants to marry some guy and I don't want him to live in the house. I haven't talked to her for two months. My little brother

FIGURE 2.1 Snapshot of Miguel, a member of Mara FIVE, taken in Guatemala City in 1987 by the author. Despite the publicity about the Maras' Satanic criminality, in the 1980s no professional photographers were taking pictures of Mara members, who were hardly menacing in appearance. Credit: Deborah T. Levenson.

doesn't like him either. This guy is rotten. He beats my mother."[26] Rafael, a seventeen-year-old from Mara 33, said of his family, "The truth is that I don't even know my father. I live with my stepfather, but he fights with me and I have to confront him all the time. My mother sells food, she makes stuffed chilies, tostados, atoles. . . . One day I'll invite you. My stepfather is a drunk who likes to fight, he's always loaded and my old lady and my brothers and sisters and I have to put up with this because there is no other way."[27] A sixteen-year-old Mara 33 member, Hernán, lived with his mother and father, but his relationship with his father was "terrible, a mess, because he is hot-headed."[28] Sixteen-year-old Marvin from Mara Garañones did not know what happened to his father: "I lived with my grandmother until I was fifteen, when she died, and so I had to go live with my mother and stepfather. I don't get along with him. Every so often he beats me and kicks me out."[29] Even worse than this general violence that many recounted to us were accounts of sexual abuse. Girls and young women told us of fathers, uncles, or stepfathers who had raped them in their households, in familial beds or patios, on floors or tables. Angeles, a fourteen-year-old former member of a Mara, recounted that she and other young girls wrote a play that represented the girls' tribulations for a project named Chicas de Hoy (The Girls of Today), run by a private organization. The plot was one of adult male against young female, and it told the tragic "every young woman's" story of a girl first deserted by her father and then raped repeatedly by her stepfather.

These descriptions were about men, and not all family members. Out of all the mareros with whom we spoke, just one thought that his household was an unconditionally good place and a "real home." Berlin, an eighteen-year-old from Mara 33, an orphan who lived alone with his grandmother, commented that he and his grandmother got along "super bien, we have good vibrations."[30] Even through the praise Berlin gave his family of two was unique, grandmothers always, and mothers sometimes, emerged in the family stories as good people and as saviors, in contrast to adult males. Silvio's brief portrait of his family was common: his father wasted family income on alcohol, and, as he put it, his mother was the "best," and "everyone says so." The working maternal grandmother in the United States who paid for the children's expenses out of her wages was a common figure in these families. Lucia, a thirteen-year-old from Mara de la 4, lived with younger siblings, a father who drank and, in her words, "yells at everyone in the house," and a disabled mother who depended on her mother's monthly Western Union money wires from New York City. Lucia pointedly credited her grandmother for paying her mother's medical expenses, which included an expensive wheelchair.[31]

Social workers used the vague concept of the "disintegrated family" in order to explain youth delinquency and as a synonym for "familial crisis," yet conversations with these professionals made it clear that they knew that male alcoholism and domestic violence created crises in many two-parent households, and that they saw wife beating and machismo as widespread problems that "everyone knows about."[32] That awareness of "what everyone knows" did not become operable knowledge. The aim of the social work with youth was to unite children with their families and reinforce child–parent relationships, and not to honor and support youth, especially females, who had the sense to detest the men in their households. In addition and no doubt related to the wish to repair "broken" families, social workers looked at us in despair when we suggested that legal steps be taken against these men.

In contrast to the social workers, these youths did not seem to want to mend their birth families, nor to hold as dear a vague ideal of the nuclear family. Their knowledge of what the general concept of "familial crisis" meant came from their emotional experiences, and they had their own solution: a redefined family, the Mara. They consistently used the term *family* to refer to their Maras. Without deserting their birth kin, the young women and men with whom we spoke wanted better families, not the status quo "traditional" ones. These young people slept at their birth family's home most of the time, and at the same time they created new families inside their Maras. They often ate together, a traditional family activity, in fast-food restaurants, and they kept track of one another's whereabouts. Yolanda, who lived with her mother, said, "Like the others say, for me the Mara is my family, the best one in the world. There you have someone who loves you and tells you so." Sitting next to Yolanda in a Wendy's restaurant, where our conversation took place, sixteen-year-old Tono added that their Mara was "like family, but nicer, because no one bawls you out. Instead each person is like who they are, and that's all there is to it."[33] Here was the new family, simply enough, warm and accepting. Hernán evaluated family in relation to his views on freedom and acceptance: "I think that family puts a lot of pressure on you, and because of that you seek your own group, a new family, so you can be free to be what you want to be and not how others want you to be." For Calixto, at twenty-four the oldest Mara member we met and the only one who had immigrated to Mexico and the United States to work, Mara ADI was his Guatemalan anchor. He said, "The Mara is all I have . . . it's my only family. There are friends, girls, and a lot of things that I cannot explain. When I am far away, there's someone here for me, someone to write to, someone you want to see."[34] Silvio said that he "joined the Mara through friends. You talk, and go along getting to know each other, until it's like a really good family." Maritza, whose Mara de la 4 was at one point an all-girl gang, explained: "I joined because there was emptiness inside me, a little loneliness, a bit of sadness. Maybe we are all alike in this. I joined through a bunch of girlfriends with whom I was very heavy. We've shared sorrows and joys. I think the Mara is a group of people who need affection. Some of us want to escape the mess in our homes. Sometimes we think we can create a new world."[35] Being encircled by affectionate and empathetic peers made up Maritza's new world, and that interrupted, and thankfully so, a life spent being constantly at pains with a "mess."

Articulate in the conversations that we initiated, the youths had never sought out a priest or a nun, a friendly schoolteacher, or any other adult for guidance or solace. Their space belonged to them, and in their space they did what they enjoyed, at a distance from adults. Sexuality was central to this distance because the new family of the Mara did not disapprove of sex for young people. It did not necessarily introduce sex, but the gang members admitted to it. Inside the Maras, sex flourished as exploration and as an item of conversation. What was a silent truth elsewhere—that many girls willfully had sex with boys before marriage—was not hidden, which is not to say that there existed sexual equality or that abuse did not go on during this early phrase of the Maras, as it would constantly in the 1990s. Notwithstanding serious problems, in the mid-1980s arguably the only space where youth heterosexuality and homosexuality were undisguised and unashamed realities was within some of the Maras. Hernán cheerfully described his Mara in the working-class neighborhood where he had lived all his life, as consisting of "twenty eight guys and two dykes." His own lover was male. He explained, "The heavy thing is that in the Mara you learn to be freer in every sense. So, if a guy has sexual relations with a guy, no big deal. Same thing with the girls." Maritza, who had had an amorous relationship with another girl, said that her greatest wish was to "find a girl or boy who in all honesty loves me and loves that I love her or him."

However, in drawing a closed circle around their Maras, the gang members did not leave their birth kin emotionally. They were loyal and proud members of the family wage economy as well; they never complained about this fact or rebelled against it. Everyone in their households worked, and—this was the only departure from the CDP report in our findings—so did the mareros. Lupe, the fifteen-year-old member of Mara Pirañas, hawked clothes in the large El Guarda market, her mother sold fruits juices in a smaller one, and her father worked in construction. Another fifteen-year-old, Joel, from Mara Belén, had a part-time job in a shoe factory. He explained to us, "My father leaves at six in the morning and comes home at eight at night. . . . My mother works in a store. My brothers and sister each work on their own, and I'm almost never at home."[36] Rocío, a twelve-year-old girl, who had just joined Mara 33, worked alongside her mother sewing fashionable clothes that her older sister then sold to shops in Zone 1.[37] Maritza picked coffee alongside her mother when she was small, then washed clothes, and more recently worked in sales earning Q150 a month. Earning Q160 a month, América worked sixty hours weekly in an upscale bakery in Zone 1, and gave part of her earnings to her mother.[38] Isabel, a seventeen-year-old in the Mara Plaza Vivar Capitol, made thirty quetzals a week baby-sitting to help pay her younger brother's school expenses, such as a uniform, a notebook, and a pencil.[39] Rafael explained, "I have worked in everything, like the rest of us [in the family]! Can you believe that when I was a little kid, I collected plastic bags in the garbage dump? After that I gathered old newspapers and sold them in the market. After that I worked as a mechanic, which is very tiring work, and after that in a supermarket. There are eight of us plus my mother—it is a lot [to support]." Hernán worked in the informal economy, selling nail clippers, scissors, sunglasses, key chains, and change purses out of his school knapsack; he averaged Q150 a month. He said, "With that I can help my mother and buy my own things, because my father does not even have money to buy his own cigarettes." Marvin earned one hundred quetzals a month as a carpenter's helper and gave most of it to his mother. He hated her husband, who hit him and sometimes threw him out, but by giving her money, Marvin remained an indispensable son inside the circle of kin. Having money was obviously a form of power. The mareros' ability to get money, and not necessarily their ability to hold down a job, gave them a positive sense of themselves and allowed them to help kin.

Within the context of the Mara as a means to empowerment and self-esteem, robbery noticeably widened the horizons of many mareros. As workers, these youths were poorly paid for what was generally unskilled labor. As thieves, they made more money, a point many learned while working, and they also had the opportunity to develop interesting skills. When the Pepsi-Cola Company employed Alejandro, a sixteen-year-old Mara FIVE member, at fifteen quetzals a week as an auxiliary on a delivery truck, he discovered he and others could make fifteen quetzals a day stealing and selling crates. In 1987, as a full-time thief who stole from tourists traveling to the colonial town of Antigua, Alejandro was king: he earned eight hundred quetzals during Holy Week that year. He was proud of his abilities, and he explained at length his exploits riding back and forth on a bus between Antigua and Guatemala City, happy to allow *gringas* to "practice their Spanish on me," while he cut their backpacks and slipped out whatever his fingers could

Money

manage to mine. That was his specialty. He said that mareros usually had one, whether it was opening car locks, stripping cars, cutting glass, slitting pocketbooks and pockets, or fencing goods. Like others, Alejandro stressed that this sort of activity meant "nothing really serious" to those robbed, and that he took "nothing of importance," such as a passport.

By working or more productively by stealing, the mareros could award their new selves new necessities, provide old necessities for their families, and maintain their accustomed selves. Hernán explained, "I have money for my father's cigarettes, and I get what I want to," as he waved a handsome gold wristband around. Lupe pickpocketed to provide cash for "my mother and sunglasses for me." Robbery could yield the new material culture of youth without hurting one's family. Berlin, for example, looking great in a brand-name wool sweater, fashion jeans, and new clean white Nikes, explained to us how he had acquired his stylish apparel: "I stole the sneakers from a burgués [a bourgeois], these pants from another, and that's how I get along, getting what I need to live."

As Berlin said, he and other youth in the Maras stole from burgueses, snobs, and those who had money, or had the nerve to appear as if they did. They positioned their victims as the class enemy, and their crimes class justified. Calixto, who helped support his mother and siblings, explained, "I've robbed everything from a piece of bread to a car, and with that I am saying everything! I am a professional thief, which is a bit more elegant then 'delinquent,' but I've always robbed from people who have money, robbing from the poor is evil." Silvio said, "Look, the only people I steal from are people with money, because robbing from an equal would not be right. I grabbed chains from the chicks at Monte María, Belga, and other private schools." Rafael, the seventeen-year-old from Mara 33, said, "I've taken what I need, and I have robbed from the rich. Taking from the burgueses is like taking a strand of hair from a cat, and you have to survive one way or another." Lupe explained, "I slit the pocket books of two burgueses. . . . I took stuff from some others as well. . . . Last year I bought my mother a pair of shoes for Christmas so she doesn't have to use sandals anymore. You want to know what else? I bought a Christmas tree. It was the first time we had a Christmas tree. We in the Mara, we have to steal from the burgueses because they have things we don't have, and it doesn't affect them." Even if they sometimes stole from the lower middle class, even if they categorized potential victims as bourgeois in a purely visual and unreliable way, mareros were self-conscious about presenting their actions as belonging to the class world of the deserving poor. If robbing helped their own, it was morally correct. Their language and recognition of their social location reflected a class and moral awareness that came from the recent urban movements. They never robbed within their own neighborhoods, and this represented a significant and a, sadly, short-lived consciousness, a choosing of sides that came from a critical awareness, a framing of their situation, and not from a "primitive" or subconscious "speaking" that the oppressed "have" by virtue of oppression.

A few of them had been at the margins of activism. Maritza was involved in a movement to fire a reactionary school principal. Silvio had been in a secretive political association in public school. His social commentary on his school days was meant to educate us, the researchers. He explained that he was expelled because of his membership in the student group, but he was more interested in pointing out the following: "I want a different education, something that is really helpful and not a lot of crap that what the hell do you want to waste your time with it anyway? It would be great if the teachers taught in an interesting way and not just by dictation after dictation. You get tired and then you lose interest in your studies because you are treated as an object that should not talk, move or think, basically [someone] who should not really exist." Silvio called Mara FIVE a weapon of social justice. He said he initially joined it "because I have a strong desire to fight for my rights, which society has denied me."

In addition, their cultural taste exemplified their proximity to the popular movement and their alertness to the dilemmas of youth, war, and unhappy families. La historia oficial (The Official Story), an intensely emotional Argentine film that condemns dictatorship and advocates in no uncertain terms for victims of the Dirty War, was one favorite. The other was Pink Floyd's The Wall, a music-driven movie depicting the construction and the possible demotion of a young man's separation (the wall) of self from self and from the world; this young man came from a family damaged by war. It would be hard to think of two movies from that era that spoke, and spoke in generationally distinct artistic styles, so deeply to the Guatemalan realities of parents and youth struggling inconclusively to get loose from webs made tight by violence.

Their other opinions reflected their political and social sensibilities. They unanimously described Ronald Reagan and President Vinicio Cerezo, a member of the PDC, in negative terms—Cerezo as "a greedy asshole"—and they painted Archbishop Próspero Penados del Barrio, a campaigner for social justice, in positive terms. They dismissed Madonna as empty headed and Michael Jackson as a "sell-out" because they thought he rejected his own roots. They overwhelmingly selected Rigoberta Menchú, whose autobiographical narrative was published in Spanish in 1983, and Che Guevara as the "people I most admire." One young man had an artistically arranged

Che Guevara
a great
admired...

scrapbook, which he regularly updated, of clippings about the Nicaraguan Sandinistas that went back to 1979. In reply to the question "What would you do if you were president?" came answers such as "Fight so that all can live equally," and "I'd bring down the rich and give it all to the poor." Most identified the worst problem in the city as the cost of living.

In 1987, a handful of trade unionists in the city, including some from the Coca-Cola union, decided to hold a May 1 demonstration, the first public one since 1980. With the media image of the mareros in mind, and in order to forestall any problems, the labor activists approached Mara Plaza Vivar Capitol about the march because this Mara was close to its route and final rallying point. Mara Plaza Vivar Capitol told them that "we mareros are from the working class and we would never harm the working class."[40] And after a right-wing attempted coup against the civilian government on May 11, 1988, Mara FIVE (Silvio's Mara) ran a classified ad in the newspaper *Prensa Libre* that read, "This business of wanting to put an end to government is no good. Youth wants peace, not violence. When will we be heard? Mara FIVE."

These young people defended themselves against class wounds, including the modern urban one of being excluded from style. In the 1980s, when advertising introduced Reebok, Adidas, and Nike, the power footwear priced at the equivalent of a worker's monthly wage and that only upper-class youth could afford, it turned into a class problem. Berlin's narrative of the origins of Mara 33—with over one hundred members, it was one of the largest gangs in the city at that time—illustrates how close the gangs stood to class organizing, and how, instead, they took the road of class stealing. For decades and through the 1970s, boys played sports in nationally produced INCATECU sneakers. He said,

> It all started when we played soccer on the Barrio San Antonio team [in 1985]. We qualified for the juvenile championship, and we were supposed to play in the final, but some burgueses had up to a couple of pair [of Nikes] each. We watched them, and then we jumped them, and we took their shoes and some other stuff. . . . You begin to realize that even soccer is only for the burgueses. We started going to parties. We got to know other guys, and we started to get together to talk about the problems each one had. Then we realized the desire to stick together. When one of the guys was really down, we helped out, but all of a sudden, we realized that we could have everything that was in style by ripping it off, or as they say, "borrowing."

Berlin brought together many elements of lower-class life in the city in the 1980s. It was virtually impossible to carry out the daily activities of life (e.g., the simple leisure activity of soccer) without struggle. With no movements for higher wages, stealing became one of the few avenues through which working-class youth could obtain material improvement. In the case of soccer, they thought that if they had Nike footwear they might win the game, and all the esteem that accompanied victory. In any case, why should Berlin and his friends not have those same high-quality goods? At points in his description, Berlin could have been talking about the formation of a trade union or grassroots neighborhood group. After all, his Mara was a local organization devoted to getting the needs of working-class met, except that some of these needs were defined by a global generational code; they were outside of the accustomed social essentials, and the means to their satisfaction was robbery.

One of the most pensive teenagers with whom we spoke, Maritza, explained her crime in terms of power relations and injustice, and expressed ambivalence about the consumerism that flooded the city:

> Yes, I have robbed. You, what do you know? Maybe it never hurt you not to have what others had. I don't know the explanation, the why of social classes, why some have and others don't. Lady, this pain I carry inside me drowns me, and I don't know how to stop it. The first time I stole was from a teacher who asked me to help her carry some oranges to her house. I waited. It was very hot. I thought she would give me one. But she didn't. I took one and also an ornament. I was scared. I thought she would find out but she didn't. . . .
>
> You want to hear something? I love perfume. But it would be a sin to ask my mother for it, because she has nothing. So once I was on a bus and I took some [a perfume flask] from a snobby-type girl. I was frightened and I felt guilty but there was no other way. . . . Here in school they ask you to buy materials—they told us to buy special paper once and I didn't have a penny, so I stole some from a companion. I wish someone, maybe you, would explain to me why one has to have objects and things one cannot buy. A while back, I stole a Parker pen from a girl. The saddest part was that when I had it, I didn't feel what I thought I would feel.

Maritza wove a world of class injury and class defense into her account of robbery. Hurt by elitism and abuse of a child's obedience to a teacher, she expressed anger and humiliation. Wanting to have the perfume yet sensitive to her mother's poverty, she protected her mother and her own desire by robbing someone she imagined would not be adversely affected. Needing items required by her school (an important arena for Maritza), she stole from companions. But she recognized that she was talking about robbing peers, not the wealthy. She stopped her narrative at precisely that moment to interrogate her petty thievery. Maritza was a thoughtful young woman, and she questioned her pursuit. What was so good about these commodities if obtaining them in this way risked friendship and brought nothing but anxiety? It was impossible not to be on her side.

Several youth in the Maras, including Maritza, cautioned us about the Maras. She told us that in some Maras, boys gang-raped girls. Rafael made the haunting comment that his Mara was "very tight—it follows you everywhere because it is inside of you. Sometimes you feel good with the group but sometimes there's a prison inside you that you can't escape." As much as these young people were not mindless imitators of television, dulled by bad habits, or cowed by the dominant ideas in Guatemalan society, and as much as the Maras could provide a better family and at least some space to act and think creatively, the danger of authoritarianism existed. Rafael went on to say, "The only thing I don't like inside the Mara is that one is apparently free, but inside one's head one is afraid to do things for fear of being rejected." Maritza commented: "You can say the Mara doesn't influence you, but the moment comes when you realize that to have their support, you have to be and do what others want. And that's where you get confused. I try to be myself, but I have trouble, so the result is that sometimes I end up being what others want me to be. . . . Well, here's another angle which is a consolation: it [the Mara] is not so great, but it would be worse without it."

As appealing as the young people we spoke with were, we concluded our study without too much optimism. Despite the powerful critiques and commentaries of society that these young women and men made, they were not trying to alter the already rapidly changing world of Guatemala City. They spent time together smoking marijuana and hanging out, not organizing. The moral affirmation of stealing from the "burgueses" and giving to themselves and other poor people was an important part of the mareros' identity, but we knew that they knew they were not always stealing from the rich to give to the poor and when they talked about having stolen particular car parts from a particular model car, they had no idea whom they defrauded.

Some of the robbery went beyond gold chains, sneakers, and perfumes. The market dictated much of their robbery, and the more money they wanted, the more the market controlled them. Consequently, they ended up "expropriating" from the not-so-well-off. In 1987, the high demand on car parts for Toyota sedans and pickups made these makes prime targets. These were two models often used by lower middle-class and working-class people who had saved long and hard to purchase vehicles in order to start a small business, such as one hauling sand to construction sites. Moreover, the more a particular Mara became involved in theft as a primary activity, the more hierarchical and secretive the gang became. In one Mara gang, all the goods went "up" to a leader who fenced them, and then some money came "down, to be divided equally." According to two irritated members of that Mara, the price the goods brought remained a mystery. In that particular gang, a gendered division of labor meant that pickpocketing belonged to females because of their small quick fingers—the same reason used for employing women in textiles—while boys stole and sold "heavy goods." As a consequence, girls earned less.

An original and daring sexual frankness and openness to love characterized some Maras. However, the gendered life within them was sometimes no worse or better than that in Guatemalan society in general, and there also existed an exaggerated masculinity, a hypermasculinity. Mara youth, male and female, tended to appear to be very tough, a trait commonly gendered as male. A macho style among homosexuals and heterosexuals was apparent in the Maras, even though it did not dominate all the members. There seemed to be little prejudice against male homosexuality and "masculine" lesbians, the "dykes" that Hernán mentioned, but "feminine" girls did not stand out, and few wanted to converse with us. Timid, they would become the target of abuse, as the next chapter discusses.

We concluded our 1987 study thinking that the Maras and their members were diverse and complex, and that these youth and their gangs were challenged and framed by the deep and fast-paced changes going around them in the city. Life in the gangs offered friendship, love, music, dance, sex, money, and excitement. Above all, Maras gave a sense of a life-affirming identity and community in the face of social decomposition and the transformation of old communities, yet without disconnecting them from their families and their old communities and without destroying their identities as sons and daughters, friends, and neighbors. These gangs etched a new geography: they had constructed a place called mibarrio in which a new family of generational peers could flourish, and at the same time this space for discovery did not replace or irrevocably divide them from el barrio. Some violence went on, but it was neither an imperative nor as dangerous and hateful as the violence in their households, their city, or their nation. Mareros spoke about what they construed as critical matters, such as love, sexuality, money, family, identity, and leisure, without violent tropes and metaphors. Juan Carlos Núñez, a Jesuit anthropologist doing fieldwork in Barrio

San Antonio in Zone 6 in the 1980s, described the local Mara as being vital and having solidarity: "To live in the Mara is to live in a network. It is about creating a soccer or basketball team, it's about creating community organization."[41]

These Maras came out of the generative environment of the revolutionary and popular urban movement, a milieu that included an anticapitalist discourse that emphasized the morality of class solidarity and social equality, precisely when those political groups were being destroyed. Because the Maras were gangs of young thieves disarticulated from radical political organizing, they combined two legacies, one of *pandillas* and the other of left-wing student and worker movements, into something new: affectionate groups that had a measure of critical consciousness about relationships and a sense of solidarity with the poor that did not become involved in politics.

Based on friendships that often preceded their existence, the Maras of the 1980s seemed to have faded, at least from public view, by the end of the 1980s. By their late teens or twenties, most Mara members we had met had left the gangs to enter the ordinary, everyday life of the urban poor in the 1990s, which often entailed work at low pay in the formal sector, and sometimes immigration. Although an unusual story in many respects, the trajectory of Aníbal López, the artist who was once a Las Cobras member, is suggestive of the creativity of the mareros and of the power of the subjective world in which they grew up. Like many other youth in and out of gangs, he emigrated in the late 1980s. He went through Mexico without documents. He made his way by drawing pictures of Christ in exchange for food and lodging in small towns along the route to the U.S. border, which he crossed to continue on to visit his brother, a Mormon in Utah, before making the return trip, again without papers. Back in Guatemala, he became a well-known artist. His art is marked by the sharp awareness of social realities that we found in our interviews with mareros in the 1980s. In one early piece, he printed typical surnames of Maya, working-class mestizo, and wealthy and well-known families on separate cardboard boxes that the viewer could then move around, to reorder the ethnic and class structure of Guatemala, with perhaps the Maya on top (see figure 2.2). He made images that addressed historical puzzles of national identity: in pen and ink he drew a Guatemalan male without skin and labeled him "Ladino" (the term used for mestizo that has the implication of non-Maya), under which he placed "50% + 50% = 100%" plus a stamp that read "SALE" (in English). To further capture the ethnic ambiguity and working-class quality of Ladinos, he penned common-use and imaginative definitions of Ladino on the reverse

FIGURE 2.2 Untitled, by Aníbal López (A-1 53167), Guatemala City, 1998. These cardboard boxes represent a partial reorganization of Guatemalan hierarchy with Maya surnames spread around, including near the top, slightly lower than "1492," a date that marks the birth of the "Ladino." On the bottom sits Bauer, a family name connected to the ownership of the Palo Gordo sugar plantation, one known for its repressive labor practices. The viewer can rearrange the boxes. Credit: Deborah T. Levenson.

side of the picture. Engaging the historical construction of a Guatemalan, he dates his work using the Conquest of the Americas as the baseline, and he initials his pieces with his resident card number.

As are others who joined these gangs in the mid-1980s, Aníbal is part of a generation almost suspended in historical time between what now seems the shutter-shot moment of an urban popular movement's peak and its quick bloody demise. Because the mareros carried within them memories of a breathtaking historical period in city life, and at the same time because their gangs originated on this cusp of a sharp change that would demolish the world in which they grew up, their Maras—FIVE, de la 4, 33, and Las Cobras, to name a few—were rich in life, ambiguities, creativities, and contradictions and they had the possibility of developing in different directions, for better or worse.

$$13\ 14$$
$$\cancel{144}$$
$$-\ 76$$
$$\overline{68}$$

1990s AND BEYOND: THE GANGS TO DIE FOR

3

If you talk, you are dead.

— Author interview with Short, a member of M S-13, Guatemala City, 2005

[The worst effect of war is] the undermining of our social relations because our social relations are the scaffolding we rely on to construct ourselves historically, both as individuals and as a human community. Whether or not it manifests itself in individual disorders, the deterioration of social interaction is itself a serious social disturbance. . . . . A society that becomes accustomed to using violence to solve its problems big and small is a society in which the roots of human relations are diseased.

— Ignacio Martín-Baró, SJ, *Writings for a Liberation Psychology*, 115

The mareros' thinking is military thinking that is always reproducing war, they live in war with the logic of war, thinking of the enemy's attack. [They live within] a militarized culture of obedience, discipline and the fulfillment of orders and missions.

— Interview with Rodolfo Kepfer, psychiatrist, El Centro Correccional de
Menores Etapa 2, San José Pinula, Guatemala

~ Origins

A founding member of Mara Plaza Vivar Capitol back in 1985, Victor returned to Guatemala in 1998. He was twenty-eight years old, and the war had only recently ended. He sought out his old gang because, he explained, the only family he wanted now in the city was his Mara. It was "all over" with his mother: "She does not like me." After thirteen years of living in Mexico and working with gangs there, he found that the mareros in Guatemala City had become "more sophisticated," "Mara FIVE is with 18 [Mara-18, or M-18], and mibarrio Plaza Vivar Capitol is with MS [Mara Salvatrucha, or

MS-13]." Identifying himself as a *veterano*, a name he said referred to someone who had killed, he joined MS-13 to assume a "leadership role" and dedicate himself to gang rivalry. Speaking in military terms, he told me that "everyone sees themselves as soldiers serving mibarrio [my gang / my place] in a war without any Geneva Code." His response to my query about his reference to the Geneva Code was "war without rules." When I asked him to explain what that gang war was about, he gave the same explanation as he did for the civil war: "Who knows, it's the way it is."[1]

Guatemala City had changed dramatically since Victor's teen years. Consumption of hard drugs, especially crack, had become pandemic. Video shops now dotted neighborhood blocks. Small weapons were everywhere, and private security was one of the few growing urban enterprises. Military and ex-military men had created an expanding industry of over two hundred companies that employed thirty-five thousand people by 2002, more than twice the nation's fifteen thousand policemen. Private security companies hired out men and women to protect individuals, hotels, restaurants, malls, small stores, private homes, and gated communities, the last of which were increasing in number in response to the rising common violence against people and property.[2] It was difficult to not spot guns bulging out of shirts, pants, and jackets on any routine walk through the center of the city.

It was no longer possible, as it had been in 1987, to walk down Sexta Avenida in Zona 1, change dollars on the black market in the empty lot behind Plaza Vivar Capitol, and strike up a friendly conversation with young people who called themselves breks and mareros and who sported brand-name clothes. By 2000, youth in and around Maras had become secretive. At the same time, photographs of them as muscular tattooed young men stripped to the waist or behind prison fences had become ubiquitous in the media. Tall tales proliferated. By the early 2000s, mythological numbers had appeared: the Federal Bureau of Investigation (FBI) claimed that 200,000 mareros, an army, "operated" in Guatemala. The National Civil Police, reorganized from the ill-reputed National Police, gave wildly divergent numbers without explanation: a 2002 figure of 50,000 was reduced to 10,833 in 2003.[3] Another source, the Association for the Prevention of Crime, stated in 2006 that 165,000 youth belonged to Maras nationally.[4] These fluctuating numbers, tattoos that were said to be Satanic symbols, and the constant evocation of the Maras' "international links," one that for some had echoes of the old "international communist plots," spread panic. Without proof or hesitation, the influential U.S. Army War College scholar Max G. Manwaring cited the Maras as the major reason for the dramatically increasing crime rates in Guatemala and elsewhere in the region.[5] In the brilliant noir police novel of the late Mexican novelist Rafael Ramírez Heredia, La Mara, set in the diseased and rotting no-exit southern border town Ciudad Hidalgo, the Mara represent barbarism in all its diabolical colors.[6]

Studies by many NGOs and the United States Agency for International Development (USAID) have not dispelled or confirmed the criminal image, which in effect adds to the sense of mystery. Their findings offer little or nothing in relation to literal transgressions and offenses. These reports concur on major points: gangs are hierarchical, and most members have little status or power. The youth in Maras are primarily male, 75 percent by one count. With some exceptions, they come from poor and lower middle-class backgrounds. Most have basic schooling. The age span is broad, ranging from six to the late twenties. A report done by the Demoscopía research group under the auspices of a Swedish International Development Agency (Asdi) found that a number of youth in Maras are parents, and that the majority of mareros work at odd jobs in the formal, informal, and illicit economies.[7] With its focus on combating criminal rings, USAID investigated the Maras' organizational structure. Its report presents the Maras' tight organization pyramid with "organized crime" on top, followed by, and in descending order, "transnational gang leadership," "gang cell [clika] members," "neighborhood gang members," and finally "children at risk." Having said this, the USAID report concludes with the statement "no one Mara fits all," one that leaves much up in the air.[8]

Researching in the postwar city, I found that some youth made comments such as "I am a marero," because they smoked marijuana or crack with members of one or another clika of MS-13 or M-18, were involved in fights, attended the burials, or some combination of these activities. Alberto presents an example of how different the various senses of belonging can be. He said he was "with MS-13." Since childhood, he had known an MS-13 leader nicknamed Maté who had been a barrio character infamous for habitual bullying. Maté was the offspring of a middle-class family well known because it ran the local pharmacy, and his murder caused consternation in the area, even though most people there did not like him. Mourning death, including that of Maté, was a neighborhood question. "We showed up [at the burial]. We are with MS-13," Alberto told me. He also said that he had never been "baptized" (inducted). I asked if his mother had gone as well to the burial, and he said yes, "of course the whole family, we all went . . . they [Maté's family] are neighbors." It is hard to put Alberto in the same category with youth who are violently baptized into groups, obey codes, and take actions that divorce themselves from neighborhood loyalties and the "we" of family.[9]

Perspectives and Perceptions of City Residents

Urban residents have sometimes referred to a whole range of youth when they have spoken of mareros. However, their larger, more general discussions about "Las Maras" refer to those feared by residents. Poll after poll in this postwar period has established that Guatemalans see the Maras as one of the nation's greatest threats. This belief persists even though sections of the city without Maras are plagued by crime, and no proof actually demonstrates that major crimes such as femicide are linked to them. That being stated, there can be absolutely no question about the gangs' extremely negative impact on the city's neighborhoods.[10] In contrast to El Salvador and Nicaragua, polls have showed that city communities never feel protected by the presence of Maras, who form their own rivaling "pockets" of territorio that break the larger community.[11] According to residents in barrios and colonias, social workers, and street educators, gang violence shot up in the 1990s, and it has become increasingly ugly and constant as the years pass.[12] In a 1998 study on a colonia in Zone 6, residents described acute changes in daily life that made mistrust, fear, and the acquisition of weapons realistic reactions to the gangs. There, gangs broke up community events such as dances or meetings, their presence divided people along the lines of their offspring's affiliation in rival Maras, and their constant warring with one another made walking around nerve racking and sleeping difficult. One woman said, "Ten years ago you could come in [to the area] at nine at night." By 1997 that was impossible, and in addition, between 8 PM and 4 AM, "gunfire and screaming [went] on."[13] In 2003, residents in that same area reported that gang members beat children to force them to join and sometimes killed them if they refused.[14]

Within many neighborhoods, mareros have used public spaces without reserve, whether school grounds, plazas, soccer fields, or even churches, and these have become dangerous spaces that parents caution children to avoid (see figures 3.1 and 3.2).[15] Afraid of what can happen once children leave the home, parents sometimes stop sending them to school, and even more dramatically, afraid that their children will be forced to join the Maras to gain "protection" from the consequences of not joining, they sometimes send them out of the country. In U.S. immigration courts, undocumented Guatemalans increasingly cite threats from mareros, as well as accounts of persecution, including rape and murder by mareros, to argue against their deportations.[16] Fears of persecution by mareros show up in explanations about immigration among Guatemala City residents living on Mexico's southern border.[17]

FIGURE 3.1 Life in Ciudad de Sol, a populous working-class neighborhood in the metropolitan area, 2005. Mara Salvatrucha (MS-13) dominates Ciudad de Sol. The dramatic wall mural on the left shows a cemetery with a gravestone marked RIP, the English-language initials of rest in peace. Graffiti art has become an important part of the Maras' aesthetic, élan, and territorial mapping. No renter, property owner, or storekeeper requests these murals, which represent danger to residents. Credit: Victor J. Blue.

FIGURE 3.2 A girl walks by a towering M S-13 graffiti in Ciudad de Sol, 2005. Credit: Victor J. Blue.

The effect of the Maras over parts of Guatemala City has been made worse by the fact that no dust seems to settle between the rival gangs. Residents say that the spaces mareros occupy are always contested ones, and the fights between gangs are constant. Gun fights between clikas of MS-13 and M-18 have led to fires, especially in the poorer settlements that firemen refuse to enter because police do not have substations in them. This seemingly uncontrollable violence and the subsequent rapid decline of property values have forced many residents to flee middle-class, working-class, and completely poverty-stricken areas.[18] The rivalry has been apparently even worse in several towns that border the city, such as Villa Nueva and Mixco, as well as Palín and Amatitlán to the south, where MS-13 and M-18 have had a competing presence for years.

This combination of (1) Mara violence, as well as adult crime unrelated to Maras, and (2) the lack of any meaningful official crime prevention or arrests has left barrio residents in an impossible situation. The National Civil Police has at times come into neighborhoods to "clean out" gangs, but this has led to more confusion and insecurity. Police pick up youth who are never seen again (see figures 3.3 and 3.4). In addition, street workers and others have implicated police in extortion rackets and murder. A bus driver who refused to pay "war" taxes fled the country with his family after his daughter was shot and killed by a bullet fired from an apartment belonging to a policeman.[19] One gang minister told me that the police threaten to kill the mareros unless they bring in a certain amount of money and that the police raise the sum at will, which keeps the gang members in a state of panic.[20] In this ongoing madness, nothing buffers community residents from criminal violence; even the street lights do not function. Violent civilian action in the countryside against presumed mareros has been widely reported. However, there have also been cases in the city, as the anthropologist Manuela Camus points out, of shopkeepers and barrio residents beating up or killing suspected criminals.[21] It is the logic of violence. A woman in the Colonia Primero de Julio told Camus that she would not "have someone locked up [in prison]. What for? So that in three days when that person is free they come looking for payback?"[22]

Two examples illustrate how impunity and changes in the Maras have shifted life and subjectivities on the broad citywide scale. The first involves workers at the Coca-Cola Bottling Plant in Guatemala City. This workers' union is historically famous for its heroic persistence in the face of multiple assassinations of its leaders and members by state agents, for its radical political stances, and for withstanding an attempted plant shutdown when four hundred workers occupied the premises for one year (1984–85). Two

FIGURE 3.3 A member of MS-13 watches out of a door as police patrol Ciudad de Sol, 2005. Credit: Victor J. Blue.

FIGURE 3.4 In an abandoned church in Mezquital, Guatemala City, a father speaks about his missing son to the photographer Victor J. Blue. On July 18, 2005, policemen picked up his son off a street in broad daylight. His family has looked everywhere without finding any trace of him. The ruined church was his son's M-18 hangout. The wall graffiti reads "Only for Locos." Locos is the name of his son's clika. Whether or not mareros choose to discuss their birth families in their self-presentations, their worried families are part of their lives. Credit: Victor J. Blue.

years later the union, one of the few that survived heightened repression, sponsored the first public May 1 demonstration since 1980. As the last chapter describes, Coca-Cola union leaders were among those who approached Mara Plaza Vivar Capitol, Victor's old Mara, whose members hung out along the march's planned route, and were relieved—given the negative press the Maras got—to receive the gang's enthusiastic support. At that time, Coca-Cola workers carried weapons to defend against themselves against political assassination.

In contrast, by the early 2000s the union had pragmatically backed away from radical politics. Coca-Cola deliverymen had taken to paying war taxes to those mareros who controlled the territorios through which the Coke trucks passed to supply retailers, and the union had petitioned the company for compensation for war taxes and for armed protection.[23] In 2008, a Coca-Cola deliveryman recounted his experiences. His route covered a neighborhood in Zone 7, where he regularly paid taxes to the clika of a Mara. Over time, he sensed growing tensions and to offset more troubles, he befriended a gang leader he then hired to further protect the truck for the hours that he spent in the area; thus he paid a "tax" and a "wage." Even with all that "protection," his regular assistant who hauled the crates was almost "gunned down without any motive by a kid in a gang." Reflecting on the militant history of the union, he commented, "It is one thing to die for something," and another to be killed for nothing by "some sick crazy kid."[24]

A far worse situation has developed for transportation workers. Bus drivers unionized under radical leadership in the 1944–54 period, and their union was one of the first to regroup following the 1954 coup. By the 1970s, the bus workers' union had succeeded in organizing drivers across the dozens of small and large companies that ran Guatemala City's poorly organized transportation system. In October 1978, the union allied with urban residents, students, and workers in what turned into an urban insurrection sparked by an increase in bus fares. The union struck in support of city residents, and it maintained a high profile in subsequent political demonstrations against state terror and for popular revolution. Unlike the Coca-Cola workers' union, the bus drivers' union did not survive the early 1980s waves of state assassinations. But even without a union, the drivers went out on strike in September 1985 in solidarity with young people, including gang members, who took to the streets to protest an increase in fares.

After the 1996 Peace Accords, a new and apolitical union started up, one that lacked historic ties with the old bus drivers' unions. Few drivers joined it until robberies of riders and drivers became dramatic, and the union developed its profile by petitioning for police protection, a request that was not granted. Robbing bus passengers and drivers became routine, but after the Maras initiated *impuestos de circulación* (circulation taxes), and demanded a Christmas holiday bonus, the drivers went on strike demanding police protection in 2002, and again in 2003, when the circulation tax increased from twenty to forty dollars a week.[25] Following these unsuccessful strikes, the murders of drivers and their helpers started and spiraled upward. Between 2006 and 2008, 512 city bus drivers and sixty of their assistants were assassinated. In 2008, almost two hundred were killed. They were usually shot while they drove, and presumably by the gangs who collected these taxes, although no one has been ever been brought to trial for these killings or for subsequent ones. In the month of February 2008 a dozen drivers were shot dead in two days. During one day in March 2009, two drivers were murdered in three hours; in 2009, 146 drivers and their assistants were murdered, and so it has continued.[26] One driver, companion of several drivers who had been shot dead on the job, explained to a journalist that he took home $150 a week after paying out $90 in circulation taxes, and he added that he could not afford to quit. He said, "It [the money] is not enough to live, and I might die, but I can't find another job."[27] With support from the municipal government, the bus companies have established a fund for widows and orphans of drivers who, like widows of the war, have organized.

A new crime-induced "dividing practice" seems to ally the majority of city residents, who are poor people, on the same side of the barricades with the state and the right-wing politicians against whom residents have historically fought. Yet however much anger at, and fear of, youth gangs exists, Coca-Cola workers, bus drivers, and many city people are not so naive as to think that these robberies and murders start and stop with young people or that old enemies are suddenly friends. Mareros from MS-13 and M-18 extort from delivery truck drivers and stores, and from bus drivers and neighborhood merchants, but everyone wonders what adult syndicate collects the money. Speaking generally of both the plausibility and purposes of skilled and professional manipulation of the mareros, Rodolfo Kepfer, a Guatemala City psychiatrist who worked for many years at a youth detention center, said in an interview: "The Mara is not autonomous. There are powers behind it. There is a system here, a logic, and a well-established hierarchy. There are periods when only members of a certain gang and not another get sent to jail, or periods when they are only involved in one specific sort of crime and not another. . . . All of which makes one think there are master plans that are not elaborated by these children who form the Maras. Who gives them arms? Who teaches them military tactics?"[28] Given the impunity and the obvious political and economic clout of the drug trade kings, it has been impossible to delve into this far-reaching question of the uses of mareros as cheap labor for well-structured maneuvers that land youth in jail, instead of those who pull the strings.

What can seem to be contradictory views in the neighborhoods reflect other types of awareness of the Maras' complexities as victims. Those residents who tell of terrible assaults by gang members, call for *mano dura*, and do not necessarily oppose lynching suspected delinquents on the spot do not necessarily see the Maras as monolithic or evil. Their efforts to protect their own lives do not mean they have lost sight of the larger picture. They will often bracket their horror stories with remarks such as "they are not all like that" or "that bunch just gets high and listens to music. They don't do anything."[29] They point out that mareros belong to a shared and difficult world of the barrios and that they sometimes suffer domestic abuse. It was with grief, despair, and worry for both victim and victimizer that a schoolteacher told a reporter how she saw a young gang member shoot his girlfriend in the face at close range.[30] In a lunchtime discussion among a group of professionals in a youth shelter in 1997 regarding the deterioration of city life and the problem of gangs, a social worker offered what sounded like a line from a Bertolt Brecht play: "If only we got mad at the system again."[31]

Mental health experts and religious figures situate the mareros at that same threshold between life and death at which the gang members place themselves and their victims. The most well-known figure in the world of gang ministry is the Jesuit priest Padre Manolo Maquieira, who died in 2006 at age sixty of a heart attack. In 1996, Padre Manolo started pastoral work with gang members in three poor Zone 6 colonias in which MS-13 was powerful. By 2001, he had created a youth club that provided children and teenagers with art classes, sports groups, and discussion circles, only to later realize that the rival gang M-18 was using the club as a recruiting ground to develop its capacity to wage war against MS-13 for control of the area. Disillusioned, eight years after he arrived in Zone 6, he judged the gang members to be beyond repair and shifted his attention, as did others, to "children at risk," a term for those who were in danger of joining the gangs or being killed by them, as several he knew had been.[32] He thought the gang members were self-hating and in no way rebels against society. He wrote that they were "rebels against life and against themselves," their violence was a "form of suicide, of self-punishment."[33] Working with former gang members in a reform center just outside the city, the social worker Herbert Sánchez told me that, like alcoholics who every day must choose not to drink, the youth with whom he works must "choose life over death every day."[34] Interviewed after self-described mareros cut out the heart of a forty-five-year-old schoolteacher, Jorge Emilio Winter Vidaurre, with the proclamation "he lived long enough," the psychologist and youth worker Marco Garavito stated that "a sense of life no longer exists among mareros."[35]

The Mareros' Sense: "Why Should I Talk?"

When I resumed research in the late 1990s, the first time I met mareros was when two members of MS-13 entered a leaky makeshift black plastic encampment full of street children in Zone 6, where I sat with a street educator who was doing medical checkups. Straight out of a photograph, with dark-colored tattoos on their arms and dressed in black, the two looked muscular and healthy, even jaunty, and they contrasted with the malnourished, drugged, and sick street children who huddled on filthy mattresses and looked up attentively at these two larger-than-life figures. After directing the street educator to look over a wound one had, the mareros retreated. The street educator said that they would return to shake down the children after we had departed.

To my surprise, a week later I saw one of the two MS-13 youth I had seen in Zone 6 sitting by himself in a common space inside an NGO crisis shelter for street children. We recognized one another and introduced ourselves. He said that his name was Luis Arturo, he was seventeen years old, and he was leaving MS-13. Because the penalty for that would be, he explained, death without trial, he had entered the shelter, where he bided time to "consider the options." He described himself as a "professional" drug salesman because he did not take drugs and insisted on immediate cash payment and not goods. The Mara seemed a business association, and not his friendship cohort. A muscular body builder who regularly worked out in a gym in Zone 1 in Guatemala City, Luis Arturo spoke about "mibarrio" as a sales region, one he had to fight over with other clikas. He normally lived alone in a "so-so" pension, but he now stayed in the shelter. The "involvement of the National Police in the trade" had become a "permanent threat" to his life in MS-13, so it was best to leave it all. Having listened to him, I asked him if we could take the time to talk more about his life, and he replied, "Why should I talk about my life?"[36] He shrugged, and we both drifted off. It was impossible for me to conceptualize how to "interview" anyone who did not want to talk.[37] Possibly I was the problem, for many reasons. Nonetheless, as I proceeded with my work of finding and talking to youth, the difficulties of having conversations started to become its own topic. When I later asked Short, a young man in the Maras I did befriend, about this, he shot off the statement "To talk is to die." To make the point, he refused to respond to my further queries about what that meant.[38] Perhaps if I were male, and better yet if I had lived for an extended period of time in a particular barrio full of gang members, things might have been different. Nonetheless, a sharp contrast existed between the youth in gangs I had met in the 1980s and those I was encountering in the late 1990s and 2000s.

The young women and men in gangs in the mid-1980s enjoyed conversing and turning over ideas. No one asked us, "Why should I talk about my life?" Eager to talk about almost anything in open-ended discussions, they often took the conversational initiative and hoped to present themselves as "good" within the framework of a class struggle between rich and poor. To have the myths surrounding them exploded seemed just, and to be just was part of their narrative of themselves. Why not talk? The assumption of communication was in place. But with the striking exception of those who left the Mara and a very few others, the youth with whom I spoke in the late 1990s and 2000s did not look to talk, much less interpret. It would be an understatement to say that the language of class had disappeared among the postwar mareros. Talk of "the poor" and "the rich," much less the poor *against* the rich, had diminished.

As time went on, I discovered that I was not alone with this predicament of finding it difficult to have lengthy conversations with mareros. Foreign journalists and sociologists have sometimes paid mareros in cash, goods, or favors for interviews. In the early 2000s, the Guatemalan sociologist Anneliza Tobar Estrada, who did none of that, developed a project in a high-security prison that concerned the mareros' "perception and criticism of Guatemalan society and their proposals about what should be done," research that would involve the mareros and that explicitly honored them. After conferring with their clika higher-ups via cell phone from the jail, the mareros refused to participate. "Why should we?" they said, and she shifted her research toward a few ex-mareros and the professionals who worked with gangs.[39]

Not talking, as in "to talk is to die," could be read as a pact that creates a potent sense of belonging. It is no doubt related to MS-13's and M-18's multifarious relationships with adult criminal rings that manipulate youth inside a dangerous world in which fortunes are made and talk is dangerous. But it also reflects a larger political and social landscape that does not encourage young people from the popular barrios to speak, much less to analyze. Little was brought forth by my mention of subjects that mareros "ran with" on their own in the 1980s, such as work, family matters, school life, presidents, and movies. But the deeper issue concerns what they did choose to focus on in conversations.

What mareros most wanted to pencil in was their inclusion in a tightly knitted group that aimed to fight to the death. Many youth said that friendship was what initially attracted them to the clikas of MS-13 and M-18, but in what did friendship consist? The internal life of the Maras had shifted away from dancing or the possession of expensive consumer goods to a focus on drugs, painful rites of loyalty, and annihilating the other gang. A seventeen-year-old MS-13 member named Carrito explained, "We dedicate ourselves to killing gang members who aren't from mibarrio and that's it—day after day, someone dies every day—every day our life is the same except it's a different person who dies . . . one day one of theirs, one day one of ours."[40] Thirteen-year-old M-18 member CC described to me how one day he would die in a gang fight because his life consisted of "matando a ellos, matado por ellos" (killing them and being killed by them). A boy named Gato told me, "We die one day to the next." Phrases appeared and reappeared in conversations such as "we only think about killing," "nothing matters to us."[41] Fifteen-year-old Junior said, "In the group we learn to be bad. We like to kill. We only think about killing, about revenge, about violence. Other people's lives don't matter to us." Using the beautiful name Orquídia, one youth, who was covered with what he counted to be fifty-five tattoos, insisted that to enter his clika of MS-13, one had to kill members of rival clikas. He said, "Definitely the more people you smoke, the more respect, the faster you move up in the gang," and added, "We only kill other gang members . . . my turn [to be killed by the enemy gang] will come."[42]

An amiable fifteen-year-old named Abel, a member of MS-13, explained to me that after he had been kicked out of his home, he went directly to the National Airport because he thought he could sneak on an airplane. Instead he met a kindly cleaning woman who paid him to help her and took him home. She tried but could not maintain him, so she brought him to a crisis shelter that, because Abel was stable and did not take drugs, placed him in a group home for teenage boys. It was there that he discovered drugs and MS-13. He explained: "They [MS-13] offered me a barrio. I wanted one, and they had asked me, so I joined. To join I had a baptism. They took turns hitting me, hard, thirteen times, thirteen seconds each blow. . . . You need the Mara to defend you . . . you need friends for fights. As they say, 'If someone touches you, they are touching everyone.' There isn't a night without a fight. The firemen don't come. Nobody comes. I fight. I am prepared. I don't have any obligations. If I die, so what?"[43] Later killed in a gang fight, a street child recounted his experiences in MS-13: "A bunch of us little kids entered the MS-13 together. One of us was five years old. The majority of us are dead now. They [M-18 leaders] killed them. . . . Five people died at my hands. The last time I killed was last year. I gave a *tiro de gracias* [coup de grâce] in the forehead, right here."[44]

Tattoos gave great poignancy to this constant rehearsal of killing, killed, shooting, shot, dying, dead. Although many of the youth I met did not have the facial tattoos that have attracted photographers, and many had desisted from using tattoos because these made them a target, the corporal aesthetic of tattooing had replaced the designer clothes of the 1980s. Large and small tattoos announced and named like no fashion sunglasses or brand-name jeans could. At first glance, the specifics of any one person seemed to vanish into a meta-identity signaled by tattoos of Satan, the sad and the happy clown, Christ, "forgive me mama for this crazy life," unicorns, tigers, the Mexican Virgin of Guadalupe, numbers, gang names in block letters, crowns of thorns, and wrist tattoos of thorns and chains. But what was being announced was personal identity. Tattoos were autobiographies. Carrito said that tattoos "cuenta la historia" (tell the story). Lounging on an old car seat outside of his mother's small place, two rooms of a long row of rooms in El Gallito, Zone 3, Short read out his tattoos to me: "2" represented the number of his children, "3" referred to his zone, "rest in Peace, Julio" was a reference to a friend who died, "March 3" was the day of Julio's death, "Shirley" referred to an ex-lover, "Chiki" was the name of his girlfriend, and "Los Locos" was his clika. Sitting next to Short and with Short's encouragement, Jonny read his tattoos aloud to me: "16" was the number of the months he spent in the Centro Preventivo in Zone 18, one tear drop represented the number of people he had killed, a heart represented "what I left behind, "la Chaka" was an ex-lover, and a sad clown face was a "picture of me."[45]

Short and Jonny lived in the same poor neighborhood where they had grown up, as did most of the youth I met. None of the youth with whom I spoke had been to Los Angeles, and a few had never been to areas of Guatemala City that might count as urban highlights, such as the fancy Avenida de la Reforma or the city zoo. All these youth read and wrote, but did so only minimally, except for one young man who claimed that he kept all the account books for MS-13 in Zone 18. None found school interesting. Several had common Maya surnames and were stereotypically indigenous in appearance, but no one replied to any query about ethnicity or to specific questions about the world outside of the hyperpresent gang life. They each had a nickname, and they called themselves mareros, and not indigenas, Mayas, Ladinos, mestizos, or chumos (a term for poor Ladinos or mestizos).[46] They knew that they amounted to being big, bad kids with tattoos (even if they do not have tattoos), the type who kill (even if they did not). They knew that they would all burn in hell, and they all loved their mothers, but they were loyal to their gang above all else, and for that they killed and were killed. They presented a repetitive script. They may have been making stories up or exaggerating, but violence and death were at the tips of their tongues. Sometimes tattooed and other times clean of tattoos, they spoke about the "rules," about being beaten and beating others. Killing and being killed construct life and destiny, which consists of their death. This story of and belief in the "fight to the death" for mibarrio seems to answer the puzzle of life for these youth in a world that is, to borrow a phrase, "ontologically insecure and existentially uncertain" (see figure 3.5).[47]

The question I repeatedly asked about why M-18 and MS-13 clikas fight to the death got similar responses: "Así es" (It just is like that) or "saber" (who knows). "Being malo [bad] is the only way to live, because life is bad," said one youth. The one specific explanation for the intergang killings concerned revenge. After Short's close friend Julio was killed, he told me, "After my tears dried, I did what I had to." He and other gang members caught someone in the rival gang and got even. He concluded: "It was 'an eye for an eye.'" Carrito, who describes himself as a "professional car thief," said that "life demands malo . . . it's part of life" and that is "how it is," "la violencia" is life. "It" (death/violence) happens, and the mareros have found a way around it because they are inside of "it," and not waiting for "it" to arrive. This suicidal fatalism is described by the Guatemalan psychologist Mariano Gonzáles as the mental condition of "accepting hopelessness" in which there is no "human project."[48] In a horrid reverse of modernity's theme of making one's way in life, these youth control their destiny of death by "making" their own deaths in the fight against an "enemy" who is themselves in the mirror of the rival gang.

That young men and boys from similar backgrounds and with similar troubles compose one another's enemies is paralleled by negative feelings about self. Writing about mareros he had known for years, Padre Manolo noted, "They have low self-esteem, continually they repeat . . . 'we are bad.'"[49] I heard the same over and over: "Soy malo" (I am bad/evil); "Somos malos" (We are bad/evil). When these youth say "malo," they refer to evil, bad, and badly behaved, and not "bad" as in a positive reversal. One youth told me that he wished he could change, and his family wished he could as well, but "that's life—it's evil, so it's necessary to be evil."[50] Simultaneously, mareros defend themselves against society's relentless negativity toward them. One said, "Society hates us. They hate us, and they look at us, they see a tattoo, and they judge us. We aren't perfect, you know. But all they

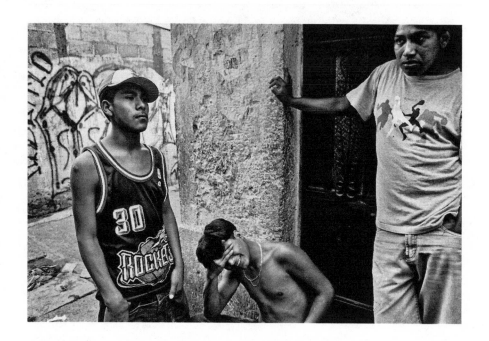

FIGURE 3.5 Members of MS-13, 2005. Not all mareros have tattoos, although in images of them they almost invariably do. This photograph is an exception. Credit: Victor J. Blue.

think is that we are bad people. They are just assholes."[51] Former marero William told the researcher Anneliza Tobar, "Society isn't ours, it belongs to others," and "when we join the gang, we look with indifference at the rest of the world."[52] Society is an enemy, the rival gang is an enemy, and each gang is entrenched in its mibarrio, a remarkable movable space given materiality by the presence of mareros who can show up in places from prisons and buses to el barrio.

Tragically, the el barrio of neighborhoods, streets, and markets where these youth have grown up and usually live appears to be configured in their geographical imagining as prey. Padre Manolo observed this to be true especially if they lived in their old neighborhoods: "Their aspiration is not to be a youth from Barrio X. It is to be a youth from outside Barrio X who owns Barrio X."[53] The "outside" from which they descend might be the Los Angeles of their desires where they may have never been, and they return to beat up on the actual location of their own history of families, schools, and the dramas of their own lives. The youth I spoke with had relatives who most likely worried night and day about them, but what the mareros wanted to highlight was that they had broken with their families, even if they still slept at home. Victor articulated this in stark terms: when I asked him where he was born, he replied, "I was born with the Mara, without it I am nothing."[54] The common tattoo "forgive me mother for my crazy life" both retains the sanctity of mother love and distances oneself from it. The tattooed youth is not leaving his *vida loca*; he is requesting forgiveness for not leaving it. When I asked Short about his kin, he replied that his mother thought that he was "malo," and he added that she was not part of "mi vida." Yet, we were sitting outside of her house, where he lived. These youth may well support families, but that was not part of their self-presentation, as it was in the 1980s. Surrounded by a seemingly endless parade of lives of poverty and failure, in their minds the mareros have severed themselves from "esa vida" — "that life." They break with it, and even literally break it.

Rosa ended up murdering an elderly woman. Here is her account to a social worker:

> We all lived in the same house. It's a really big house, and everyone went there every day. There was a kind of temple. I was supposed to cut my veins and let drops of my blood fall into a big well. Everyone in the Mara had put their blood into that well. . . . During some rituals, some people fall down, others see eyes in the flames, some see someone being killed, or the things they do to you if you leave the gang. After joining the Mara, I killed an old woman because they told me I had to kill somebody, and

to sacrifice their blood. . . . I pushed her, and when I touched her afterward, she wasn't breathing any more. She was an [old] woman who lived with her grandchildren. They were from a rival gang. I had killed their grandma. I felt so bad, like I had killed my own grandma. . . . I don't remember exactly what happened. The Mara has also tried to kill me—once with a gun, once with a knife, and another time with a car.[55]

It is hard to imagine a more radical rupture from "esa vida," or a more forced hell-fire bonding than these theatrics of death and Rosa's real-life execution of an elderly woman. Rosa said that though she thought of killing herself, she fled instead, as the final chapter discusses, and went into hiding for months.

For males, admissions of shame or fear would ruin their mystique of male power through physical talent and the ability to endure to the end without emotions. Violence was gendered as male. Padre Manolo pointed out, and I observed, that some young women in the Maras identify themselves with masculinity. Eighteen-year-old Carmen told me said that she joined a clika because she wanted to be "like a man, to be ready, to fight, to jump someone . . . to go to blows." In Carolina's opinion, "women can't get things done and machos can and that's what I need to be." I asked Carolina to what things she referred when she said "get things done," and I added that in her barrio in Zone 6, women held households together emotionally and economically. She knew that, "but you know," she replied, "when it's necessary to . . . handle a bad situation . . . all the things the clika needs to take care of, to protect, to be protected." Her reply to the question "From what?" was "la violencia."[56] According to her, females are ranked. Those who are tough enough to endure beatings as an initiation ritual rather than rape—the "acceptance" of rape signals weakness—have a higher status in the Mara and a chance at being a clika leader.

Folding violence, masculinity, and Mara into one another has left girls and young women who identify as feminine without a Mara identity, and, in conversations, they positioned themselves on the sidelines. Many said that they had joined the Maras because their boyfriends were mareros. Sixteen-year-old Chata's comments were similar to those of the other girls. Chata declared her membership in MS-13, but she spoke of "doing things for them," or "with them." She had no identity as one of "them." "They" were "los muchachos," the boys with whom one gets, in her words, "used to having sex. . . . At first you don't want to and feel terrible." Feminine females provide sexual "favors" and run gang errands—especially in the back and forth between prisons—clean, cook, and look after children and often associate themselves with their boyfriends' otherwise neglected birth families. Their status reflects that of females in the larger society, yet worse.

Foot Soldiers

The marero has turned into a gendered killer/killed persona, a male warrior, the winner of the contest to decide Guatemalan history who is also a loser, the dead warrior. Gang members routinely call themselves "soldiers" who "fight and die for mibarrio." The many meanings that masculinity has had have narrowed to one, and all others have atrophied. Masculinity has come to hinge on the capacity to give violence and take it, without limits, including the cap of mortality. This warriors' work is what the really powerful men, whether generals or members of the economic elite, have had in their back pockets for generations, and they can pull it out and put it back in as need be. In the marero's life there is only this violent masculinity, without the degrees, titles, money, prestige, social networks, mobility, and other resources that the Guatemalan elites and military men have had in plentitude and that allow for many masculine identities, whether of *padre*, *patrón*, or *patria*.

For mareros necroliving has presumably kept their lives under their control by giving them space, identity, unconditional friendship, and a way to earn a living. They can use it to wreak havoc with a world that has failed them by messing up public transportation, redesigning neighborhood life, driving down real estate values, causing decreases in school attendance, and even provoking flight across borders. Finally, it can protect them, through death, from their own futures. Boys turn into young men and then into adults in their twenties without leaving the gangs until they die from life in the gang. Padre Manolo thought the presence of adults in their early twenties in the Maras indicated a fear of entering an adulthood that would be similar to that of their fathers, uncles, and other men in their neighborhoods, many of whom have not succeeded in life. He placed both extended memberships in the Mara and the early deaths of mareros in that context: they had lived and died as "youths and thus did not fail as men."[57] Over one-half of the mareros that Padre Manolo had known over a ten-year period died in fights. They beat adulthood to the punch and did not become, as the song "Hombres Fracasados" (Failed men) puts it, "failed men who could not be what they could have been."

Often surprisingly humble, sometimes domestically abused, and increasingly disconnected and alienated, urban young men and women and boys and girls for whom Ladinismo, Maya ethnicity, and Guatemalan citizenship continually depreciate into a cultural nothingness are drawn or forced into the imaginary of necroliving. In the gangs' understanding of the world, the once clearly drawn lines between victim and victimizer, between ruler and ruled, have been blurred. It appears that only violent death can sort out who is which in a contest that is never settled for long and in which positions constantly flip as today's victor is tomorrow's victim. The lifeblood of the mareros' efficacy flows from their promise to kill and to be killed. In the late 1990s, one simple tattoo signaled Mara membership in Guatemala City. It consisted of three small dots between the thumb and the index finger that stood for hospital, prison, and morgue.

The feisty 1980s mareros are one unusual reminder of an era of social struggle. Those of the postwar period are part of the heritage of war, and they portend the permanency of the war in everyday life. Neither rebels nor conformists, they are orphans of the world, not only of Guatemala. They have been criminalized by adults and even criminalized by the U.S. Department of Homeland Security for all manner of evils. These young people bring to mind those Hannah Arendt once called in another context "the most symptomatic group," those "forced to live outside the common world,"[58] in this case, mareros who reproduce the traumas that cast them outside that "common world," to end these traumas in death.

The Maras' Smallest Veins

Mareros are part of the fraught and narrow universe of destitute children and teenagers living in the city's streets (see figures 3.6–3.7).[59] Generally ignored or brutalized and despised by adults, these youth are often addicted to glue and without the means of making a living. Their ages vary (although they are called street children), their numbers grew in the last decades of the twentieth century as a direct or indirect result of the war, and by the early 2000s their offspring formed a second generation. In a complex relationship involving protection and exploitation, these street children inhabit the margins of the gangs, and they sometimes drift into them to run errands or become more full-fledged participants. The Maras are the only social grouping that they can actually join and still be street children. Unlike humanitarian workers, the Maras do not try to tug these children away from the street living to which they are habituated, with which they identify and where their close friends are found.[60] The gangs can even hold out a pathway. Guillermo, a twelve-year-old Honduran who ended up in the streets in Zone 1 by hitching rides to Guatemala City after Hurricane Mitch destroyed his home in 1998, told me that his friends in MS-13 would help him go to

FIGURE 3.6 Young people living out on the street, Séptima Avenida, Zone 1, Guatemala City, 2002. Credit: Andrea Aragón.

FIGURE 3.7 Neighborhood kids in their hangout, Guatemala City, 1999.
Credit: Jonny Raxón/Fotokids, 1999.

Houston, where he had relatives who worked in car wash. Here were real possibilities: connections with risk takers, undocumented immigration, a job in a car wash in the United States.[61]

For some, the mareros are heroes who have mastered what it takes. I met children in a shelter in the late 1990s who proudly showed off their magic marker tattoos "MS" or "18." One boy, Carlos, looked forward to being in a Mara clika when he was "stronger." The clika seemed to be that inevitable violent defense against a painful world. A teenager named Rubén filled out the following questionnaire during one of his brief stays in a shelter:

What is your family like?
My family is my parents and my brothers and sisters. My older sister is named Ana. She is studying to be a schoolteacher. My little sister, Claudia, doesn't go to school yet. My brother is named Oscar and everyone calls him "coco." He has a bicycle and my family is lucky. We live very happily. My mother is very scared, and my father likes to fight.

What are you like?
I am cheerful. My character is rebellious and people provoke me a lot. I am respectful and responsible.

Write what you would like your family to be like:
I wish that they were very cheerful and that all my brothers and sisters were tough like me. I wish Rony and the others would study a lot and enjoy life. I wish my older brother were head of Mara-18 so that my mother would be happier, less sad.[62]

Anxious about a family that he conjured up as happy, Rubén imagined that the power of the Maras—if only his brother were "head"—might make his family truly happy. A social worker told me that Rubén joined a Mara, or at least hung out with one and "got into trouble." His file shows that he died in 1998 for "reasons unknown."

Estuardo Edwin Mendoza is another youth from the streets who joined a Mara. I met him in a shelter in 1997 when he was fourteen years old, tall for his age, pale, and sad. The first time we talked, we sat together watching the rain pour into the patio. He said that he had been sick for a "lifetime" because he had caught *susto* during the war, and it "just never went away."[63] He told me about the massacre in his family's hamlet and the dead bodies he had seen, "many many dead, some hung, some burnt." "The army killed people because the people hid the guerrillas, the army killed babies. The people did not say where the guerrillas had gone. I touched dead bodies after the soldiers had cut them up with machetes. I went running into the night.

The soldiers were painted with charcoal and they had knives. . . . The army killed four of my brothers even before I was born. I saw the soldiers throw fuel over the houses and burn them." His mother, he went on to say, escaped from the hamlet after a massacre, which probably took place between 1981 and 1982, and found her way down the mountains and into Guatemala City. Estuardo thought this was the second time war had destroyed her family and left her displaced. She told him she had left El Salvador "after her parents were killed by soldiers" and she had "walked on a highway with bombs falling all around her." He remembered that she always said, "Why did I leave one war for another?"

According to a social worker report, Estuardo had never been outside of the capital. He was born in a public hospital in Guatemala City in 1983 and lived with his mother for years in the settlement of Tierra Nueva II, one that absorbed war refugees in the 1980s and 1990s.[64] According to Estuardo, he left home at age ten because "my mother said she could not support me. My mother doesn't like me. . . . This is sad, I love my mother so much. When my mother hit me, she said it was because the blood of Salvadorans made her cruel." After making a home visit, the social worker added to her report that Estuardo had three siblings, and his mother earned Q350 monthly and paid Q350 to rent a "small, dark room without much furniture." The equation of rent and salary could have been an error. However, it is not surprising that she earned only enough to pay the rent. Even if she earned a bit more, how much could have been left for food or clothes, much less school fees or bus fares? Not atypically, the social worker faulted the mother for not being the mother she could not possibly have been. She wrote in her report, "The mother has been irresponsible with her children. There is no communication between them, she is dedicated only to her work [outside the house]."[65]

Estuardo stayed in Guatemala City's streets for the rest of his life, and sometimes he stopped by his mother's place. Beaten by policemen in two incidents, he survived for a while. Out of exhaustion, he occasionally entered this shelter near the busy downtown area in Zone 1. Here he and other boys could sleep, eat, get medical attention, and attend classes on topics such as "what must be done to improve oneself," "how to take advantage of life's opportunities," "AIDS and its consequences," and "the family and the child's role in the family," provided that they did not use drugs. He would stay in this large converted mansion with its showers and friendly staff, food, and bunk beds until he was kicked out for breaking that cardinal rule, just to return a few months later and repeat this pattern. His thin file dates back to his first arrival there 1995. It gives his vital statistics, notes that he came from a family of "refugees from the countryside," and describes his behavior during his stays—"difficult," "incommunicative," and "complains of stomach pains." A volunteer music teacher had penciled into the margins, "Estuardo loves to play guitar and drums . . . although at first he didn't like the guitar, he has the possibility to express himself musically. He is helpful and cooperative, and sometimes he has his difficult moments."[66] Small wonder, in every sense.

Not yet born at the time of the massacre in his family's hamlet, he nevertheless described it as if he had been there, even actively: "I touched dead bodies. . . . I went running into the woods." Recovering a sense of himself and his mother from these images, his experiences of other people's memories at least kept him allied with a part of his family he had never directly known yet so affected him, and these memories gave him a history that explained the situation of his difficult existence, including his mother's anger at him.[67] Feeling ill could represent a "cultural document" that kept him close to his own truths and to the larger emotional and historic "we" within his trajectory.[68]

He explained to me that he joined M-18 because he wanted to "estar en algo" (be in something); here was the jagged edge of some "we." Yet, at the bottom rung of the intense M-18 hierarchy, he referred to the gang members as "them" and admired "them because they are loyal, they know how to handle stuff, they are malo, and that is what you need because life is malo." In the gang, he felt "protected."[69] This indicates the extremity of his situation; a year later he was dead because of his membership. In revenge for a presumably M-18 killing of an MS-13 member, someone in MS-13 shot him with an M16 assault rifle in early 1998. His murder was impersonal. He could have been anyone in the gang.

The war and its aftermath run through all of this. Violent death marked both ends of his life, which spanned the Guatemalan state's production of violent death as a means of political power, to Estuardo's demise within a world of youth who can produce death as a means of getting by for a while. The war formed what Pierre Bourdieu called a system of dispositions, "a past which survives in the present and tends to perpetuate itself into the future by making itself present in practices structured according to its principles."[70] The war put his life in place, organized it, and made violent death his most familiar terrain and his destiny.

Estuardo's insistent preservation of the memory of the massacre rang heroic and moral in light of the silence surrounding the war in 1997. He talked. Even though many children were in the streets because of the war, social workers rarely alluded to it in reports and conversations in order to protect their work and the children, and there existed no public discussion of it. The transparency of Estuardo's absorption in and memory of a massacre that he knew through others was uncommon among the street children I met in the late 1990s, even though many were war orphans.[71] Recalling conversations with Estuardo, I am struck by his recollection of the massacre, especially because his memories defied the "amnesia of genesis" that overtook Guatemala in reference to military violence. It is difficult to reconcile the chronology he presents—he was not born until after his mother left the massacred village—except to say that the way he put it all together underscores his subjective sense of war's presence and power.

What chances did Estuardo have, living within the effective power of violent death because it was the greatest historical force within his life, a life spent growing up in the streets and in a "small dark" space with a hardworking and underpaid woman in an urban neighborhood pockmarked at a distance by the war? Outside of the Mara—and the crisis shelter, which never worked out for him, because he could not meet the difficult requirement of kicking his addiction—there were no open doors in his life and no way to understand more deeply his most foundational and entrenched memories. To quote Cathy Caruth in her discussion of the relationship between history and trauma, his history is precisely the way in which he was "implicated in other peoples' traumas."[72] And we (myself and other adults who passed through his life) are implicated in the tragedy of not having been able to protect this child from becoming a victim of a system of dispositions that reproduced war without the war, and a target of the many in which he took part, and from which he died.[73]

ch. 3 ↑
summary

$$\frac{\begin{array}{r} 144 \\ -104 \end{array}}{40}$$

DEMOCRACY AND LOCK-UP 4

I too have known Satan, I can bring them [mareros] to Christ.

> —Panamá, Pentecostal street worker, interviewed by the author, Guatemala City,
> March 1987

The devil is my *jefe*.

> —Words said to have been mumbled by M-18 member Áxel Danilo Ramírez
> Espinoza (alias Smiley), "public enemy number one," El Periódico, April 17, 2009

Who are we? We are the majority, worker, business executive, housewife, athlete, chewing gum vendor, we are those who drive in the latest model Mercedes Benz and those who take the bus or walk in the street. We are the people who do something constructive and positive for our country and our families and who every day confront the chaos and violence caused by "mareros," those juvenile gangs. We are humble people, normal people who work to reach what is difficult but not impossible to achieve: PEACE.

> —National Civil Police of Guatemala, teléfono 110, "Unidos Contra Las Maras,"
> public relations advertisement

The National Civil Police's "United against the Maras" poster advertises an alignment of Guatemalans who run the gamut, absurdly and obscenely, from a chewing gum vendor to the owner of a new Mercedes-Benz. No matter who they are, the argument goes, all share a normality that is threatened by the noncitizen others: the "mareros." Nothing could more invert the 1954–80 progressive social imaginary, or more confuse our understandings than the portrayal by the National Civil Police. Policemen sometimes dip into and even control the earnings from the "war taxes" mareros collect; it is likely that the gum vendor has been harassed by a policeman at some point in her or his life; the owner of that new Mercedes-Benz might well have bought it with drug money; and the business executive is not part of a "humble" majority that includes workers and housewives.

However preposterous, the poster is hardly surprising. From the moment the Maras appeared on the streets of Guatemala City in 1985, mareros have been represented as threats to democracy, peace, toil, and the everyday life. Over decades of ever-increasing clamor about youth delinquency, neither political parties nor state agencies—be these mano dura or reformist—have seriously studied the gangs in a sustained manner, or developed noteworthy programs to face up to the problems that gangs pose or that youth encounter. Attention has focused on the imaginary marero, and the real ones face a world of police, media people, and others who insist on that diabolical image and push the marero to fit what sometimes starts to stick.

This chapter deals with the complexities and the consequences of varied responses to the mareros. It first discusses how expert demonologists in the Pentecostal movement staked out the terrain of handling the Maras during the war. It then recounts what has happened to the whole configuration of Mara power and powerlessness, discussed in the previous chapter, after the postwar state laid claim to a role as engineer of a new Guatemala based on law, and moved gang members into the institutional setting of the penitentiary system. Finally, it addresses the reality that going to jail has become a new—by now routine—stage in the lives of mareros, and that controlling jails in the name of National Citizen Security has enhanced the power of military and ex-military men. Prisons today reproduce the Maras, and they fuel the success of conservative political movements led by men who present themselves as necessary specialists in the management of violence.

Neoliberalism and Pentecostals in the 1980s

Structural adjustment programs imposed in the 1980s resulted in substantial cutbacks in funds to the state's Welfare Secretariat, which since 1961 has had jurisdiction over needy and troubled youth. By its own account it could only look after 4.69 percent of its potential clientele by 1987.[1] By that year, the Tratamiento y Orientación de Menores (Treatment and Orientation for Minors, TOM), the branch of the secretariat charged with rehabilitating or protecting juveniles, housed and serviced a mere 250 children and teenagers in its five centers, and even these group homes were barely supplied.[2] In addition, the leadership of TOM had no vision of its work. Social workers—who had to scurry about after working hours to solicit money for notebooks and pencils as well as supplies such as bandages, soap, toilet paper, soft drinks, and plastic utensils from companies such as Johnson & Johnson and Coca-Cola—drew up a long list of criticisms of TOM that included "programs that do not represent the needs of the majority, inappropriate solutions, lack of rational and scientific planning, lack of evaluation and supervision."[3] Psychologists at TOM appraised it in these words: "The achievements have been minimal, especially regarding reeducation, the raison d'être of the institution."[4] One professional evaluator summed up his 1987 report by saying that the leadership of TOM was "in another world."[5]

As a consequence of incompetence, financial crisis, and the ruling Christian Democratic Party's inability to rise to the occasion, the care of needy and troubled youth was turned over to Pentecostals. Given their widespread influence, Pentecostals confronted no opposition when they assumed a role as social engineer, and their religiosity blurred the designation of privatization. As chapter 2 discussed, the Pentecostals in Guatemala had been involved in governance since the war escalated in 1980. For a period they ran a leadership training program for state functionaries and figures such as the born-again Christian General Efraín Ríos Montt, an architect of massacres who justified his actions in the language of fire and brimstone.[6] In this conjunction of a presumably reformist civilian government without funds, and the growing ubiquity of well-funded Pentecostalism, there seemed nothing unusual about TOM inviting Pentecostals into its centers. Members from the largest of these churches in Guatemala City, the Iglesia de Cristo Elim (Church of Christ, ELIM), regularly went to TOM centers to sing, talk, and give counsel. With the approval of TOM officials, they brought with them easy-to-read pamphlets on important topics such as drugs and alcohol. With the aim of orienting youth to better guide other youth away from the world of Maras, Pentecostals opened a ministry named Juventud para Cristo (Youth for Christ), which regularly sent volunteers into public schools such as the important teacher training school Instituto Normal de Señoritas Belén, and the large vocational high schools. Such was the situation of Pentecostal ascendancy that in 1987 the Judicial Magistrate for Youth joined with the UNICEF program to create an alliance, the Comisión Nacional Acción por los Niños (National Commission of Action for Children, CO-NANI), in which Pentecostals had an important part.[7] Its vice-president was a Pentecostal street worker, and the Pentecostal ex-director of the Treasury Police, who was later dismissed because of his relationship to death squads, ran the CONANI-supported groups such as one named Hombrecito. With CONANI's support, numerous Pentecostal reform centers came into being.

In the 1980s the most vocal and authoritative Pentecostals advocated mental discipline and physical punishments for wayward youth. The Pentecostal psychologist Roberto Morales del Pinar, who directed a home for female ex–gang members and homeless girls in Zone 11, spoke in a professional capacity when he said he believed in corporal punishment and in the importance of his close authoritarian relationships with the girls, who had to call him "Papi." His associate, a Nicaraguan nicknamed Panamá, went into the streets "where Satan works," to save young people. Panamá had been in the Contra forces in Nicaragua, where he developed a drug habit, but he had a revelation in which Christ walked toward him, and he gave up his addiction. He was a strong and politically shrewd young adult and a self-confessed killer. After he and I had conversed and toured Pentecostal centers together over a period of months, it occurred to me that Panamá could easily have had ties with the Guatemalan military, and with pride.

One place Panamá took me to was a group home in Zone 1 named Casa Mi Hogar, a one-story 1930s building. Inside Casa Mi Hogar was a small, dirty, foul-smelling patio, off of which were four dormitories, an office, and a kitchen. It housed more youngsters than the state-run reform center Gaviotas did at that time. The patio was the central space, and every time I visited, the more than 138 young men and boys and some 20 girls who resided there were standing up in this cramped, sun-filled or rain-soaked space, and they invariably looked distressed. According to the Casa Mi Hogar's director, the youth stood for hours "to achieve discipline and formation." What sort of "home" was this? It was one to which the National Police directly brought kids, straight from the street, and to which judges sent young people for rehabilitation. The state remunerated Casa Mi Hogar for services. In his early sixties, the director described himself to me as a former drug addict who had once been part of Centuriones, a 1960s shock brigade of a right-wing political party, and later met Jesus Christ and converted to Pentecostalism inside the ELIM church. He explained to me that he was a sinner who had been saved in order to save others. Without any prompting on my part, he further explicated that his work inside the strategic hamlets into which the military had herded villagers after massacres illustrated his dedication to the salvation of souls. Punishment such as war cleansed sinners, and once cleansed they could "love themselves and develop themselves."[8]

Pentecostalism as a neoliberal solution to youth reform became institutionalized in 1992 when the born-again Christian conservative president Jorge Serrano Elías took office, while the civil war continued. He brought the Pentecostal organization Rehabilitación de los Marginados (Rehabilitation of the Marginalized, REMAR) from Spain, and his government paid it to officially manage Gaviotas. In charge of the daily schedule and discipline,

REMAR staff regularly beat the interned boys with baseball bats, brooms, and firewood in special isolation rooms; held mandatory Bible classes; and ripped crosses off the boys' necks. REMAR expanded its services to other state institutions and established its own private centers, where adults hurt and humiliated young people, and to which courts dispatched them.[9] Despite international attention to these abuses, REMAR continued to work in the prisons after Pentecostals temporarily left important administrative and advisory positions at the time of the 1996 Peace Accords. The born-again Ríos Montt entered the political arena after 1996, but his religious language met a provisional riposte in politicians such as Ramiro de León Carpio and Álvaro Arzú who, however religious, claimed modern expertise based on education and political experience, and not on a relationship with God.

The Postwar Crossover

Whether of a new generation or survivors of older generations struggling for identity and place, urban middle-class professionals and others came to believe that any hope for creating a democratic and constitutional Guatemala rested on laws and their implementation, and not on revolution. In this context, there appeared a veritable renaissance of interest in legal means of social reform and control, and criminal justice was central to this.[10] The Supreme Court judge and prison reform advocate José Francisco de Mata Vela hailed a new 1990s Penal Code that included the replacement of the inquisitorial model with the accusatory system, "the most important moment in Guatemalan legal history." He located this event within a new dawn of "political and economical facts that have changed the sequence of human history, as have disappearance of the Berlin Wall, the end of the Cold War, the democratization of all countries . . . [and in Guatemala] the construction of a democratic country, in the constitutional state of law."[11] Now liberal democracy could flourish unencumbered by the exigencies of the Cold War and the communist threats that had so twisted it out of shape.

With optimism about the promise of an era during which nonmilitary laws and civilian structures would secure democracy, prestigious institutions in the country such as the Office of the Human Rights of the Archbishop of Guatemala, the University of Rafael Landívar, and the new Institute of Comparative Penal Science Studies of Guatemala sponsored a landmark 2000 conference titled "Prisiones: El Desafío del Nuevo Milenio" (Prisons: Challenge of the new millennium). This meeting brought specialists from Latin American and European countries to Guatemala, and it placed Guatemalan professionals inside the ongoing global discussion about the world-

wide prison crisis, one that has given new life to ideals of reform and rehabilitation programs and the protection of prisoners' rights. In this postwar
period, papers, conferences, university theses, and organizations concerned
with prison reform have proliferated in Guatemala, and they all urge sweep-
ing legislation on prisons and their administration.[12] Even if all this has resulted in little change, the penitentiary system entered into the play of national history for the first time in Guatemala after the Peace Accords.

Some context is necessary. It would be hard to argue that the claim made
for many Latin American countries concerning the centrality of the penitentiary system to "strategies of control and discipline and the construction of
hegemonic visions of society," or to "the construction of a national state,"
has been the case in Guatemalan history.[13] According to the first large-scale
study of the system, done in 2000, "there has never existed the minimum
criteria for prison administration" in Guatemalan history.[14] The novel ideas
about the penal system that developed in Europe in the 1800s circulated in
Guatemala, made a small mark, and never went further than the construction of architectural performance pieces that simulated modernity.[15] The
Liberal Party built the first national prisons at the end of the nineteenth century. Established in 1877 and based on the European model of reeducation
through moral uplift and workshops for "the women's arts," the women's
prison Santa Teresa rapidly deteriorated into no more than a filthy lock-up.
The larger Central Penitentiary for Men was carefully laid out according to
the "plans of the best European penitentiaries." Furnished with a library, a
school with twelve classrooms, and a small soccer field, it opened in 1881
to house 500 prisoners, and soon thereafter held 1,500 men in chaotic conditions of "vice, misery, horror and death."[16] This was the central national
prison for men until the end of the 1960s.[17] The Central's population remained at a steady 1,500 until the 1954 coup, when it jumped to 2,500 due
to the jailing of political prisoners under anticommunist laws, then dropped
back to 1,500, probably because death squads took over punishment.[18]

In the early 1960s, the physical structure of the Central Penitentiary collapsed. To replace it, three new national farm prisons were built, the most
important one being El Pavón, located in Fraijanes, a town near the capital.
Again, modern ideas dominated planning, and the prison grounds were land-
scaped to include agricultural and manufacturing centers to rehabilitate and
train the incarcerated through useful labor and reeducation, but, as in the
past, few programs got implemented. Soon after El Pavón opened, prisoners
massively revolted in direct response to the terrible conditions that prevailed
from the outset and to the fatal beating of two inmates by guards in 1968,
during a national state of siege directed at the urban popular movement in

Guatemala City and the guerrilla movement in the east of the country. As prisoners started to tear El Pavón apart, the army sent tanks and soldiers into the sprawling complex, and gunmen sprayed machine gun rounds of bullets on the prisoners from a hovering helicopter. An unknown number were killed, and order was restored.[19] As this chapter suggests, nothing of this nature has since taken place, though conditions have, if anything, worsened within Guatemala's growing number of adult jails and juvenile reformatories.

The adult penitentiary system now includes thirty-five prisons administered by either the Dirección General del Sistema Penitenciario (General Administration of the Penitentiary System, DGSP) or regional authorities. Among these are El Pavón, El Pavoncito, and Fraijanes 2 in Fraijanes in the department of Guatemala; El Centro Preventivo in Zone 18 at the edge of Guatemala City; El Boquerón in Cuilapa, Santa Rosa; and El Hoyón in Escuintla. The Welfare Secretariat currently manages several reformatories for minors that are in and around Guatemala City and house 430 boys and a smaller number of girls. These include Gaviotas for boys and Gorriones for girls, both of which are located in Guatemala City, and El Centro Preventivo Etapa 2 for boys, which is located in San José Pinula, a small town forty-five minutes by car from the capital.

Whether for minors or adults, these centers and jails have been incoherently organized and managed for decades. In juvenile reformatories, youths are not separated by "crime," an imprecise term in this context. According to a study done in the 1990s, over 80 percent of the girls in Gorriones were there because they were at "social risk."[20] In all these detention centers those judged to have committed deeds of "little social impact" are mixed with youth accused of homicide and kidnapping.[21] Moreover, those convicted of these acts and sentenced for longer periods are often not transferred to adult prisons when they reach eighteen. All these youth, and especially those in centers that still have staff from REMAR, face beatings, have no recourse or legal counsel, and are often there "until rehabilitated," a status that remains undefined. Few teachers, social workers, psychologists, or medical professionals are available to these young people. One study describes the youth detention center Etapa 2 as "in chaos" and the Welfare Secretariat "incapable of providing security of inmates, as recent mutinies have shown, in which adolescents have been killed and wounded."[22]

For many years, the adult prisons throughout Guatemala have housed a steady population of approximately 8,500 inmates. Of these, over 90 percent are male, the majority are from lower-class backgrounds, 40 percent are between eighteen and twenty-two years of age, and well over three-quarters are awaiting trial. Those who are convicted are incarcerated together no matter whether they have been found guilty of petty theft or multiple homicides. Prison conditions are notoriously terrible for most inmates. They live in over-crowded cells without light, air, mattresses, or sanitary facilities. Worse, water is scarce. As one example, a single faucet from which water trickles for at most three hours a day serves 330 inmates in El Hoyón, located in the hottest part of the country. Because prisoners need cash to survive and few prisons have work programs, inmates sell drugs and their bodies, and they wash clothes or clean for the wealthy inmate minority that lives in special quarters.[23] To add to this, corruption and violent humiliation of prisoners have been the operational principles of guards. An observer noted that in one center, guards "force inmates to clean toilets with their hands, floors on their bare knees, sleep standing up and other degradations."[24] Guards have accepted money for everything from renting out mattresses to facilitating escapes and opening doors to allow in extralegal executioners.[25]

It was at the end of the twentieth century that this corrupt and decrepit prison system slowly started to replace barrios and factories to become the new publicized site of urban struggles—or rather of disputes about the man-agement of power—that would become increasingly central in the popular imagination. The stage for this was set by groups of inmates who took over the internal functioning of some prisons in the 1990s in response to the disastrous state of affairs inside them. They organized Comités de Orden y Disciplina (Committees of Order and Discipline, CODs) that made prisons safer for visitors and inmates, implemented strict disciplinary codes, and de-manded fees from prisoners to provide for cleaning equipment, prison secu-rity against internal theft, and the salaries of COD staff. The most famous COD was at El Pavón, one that inmates started to stop the constant robbery and rape of visitors. Over the years, it created what journalists described as "a country within a country," or "a small town run by inmates."[26] The COD operated all the criminal rackets inside El Pavón smoothly, and it con-trolled internal strife in favor of the COD's board members. The COD sup-plied goods, liquor, drugs, and prostitutes; collected fees from the inmates who ran the prison's lively commercial center, which included a pizzeria, a pool hall, a call center, a butcher shop, a tortillería, various repair stalls, and a hardware store; charged rent for structures, land, and land use; and helped arrange the sale of homes built by departing inmates. The COD brought a sort of peace to El Pavón, which boasted of having the best housing for the wealthy minority in the nation's prison system. Although the majority of in-mates were poor and lived inside old cells with or without mattresses, the rich had well-built homes with gardens (and gardeners), refrigerators, and gym equipment.[27] For years, reformers, human rights advocates, and mano

society in prison

dura politicians all argued emphatically that the central problem in the penitentiary system was, in the words of one, that "the state has given control to the prisoners."[28] In reality, this "prisoner power" consolidated the control of a small minority of inmates that threw crumbs to lower-class ones, had ties with external elites, and tried to use the growing inmate population of mareros as foils within their behind-the-walls maneuvers.

A Place in This World

A group of researchers who minister to incarcerated gang members has suggested that by 2002, by which time the gang presence had become concentrated within the system, prison life represented a new stage of Mara history.[29] The significance of jails is one result of the policy adopted by authorities of grouping gang members together in the same prisons, and even in the same cell-blocks. With some fifteen hundred inmates, the largest penal complex in the country, El Pavón holds some three dozen mareros. This contrasts sharply with the smaller El Hoyón, which has approximately 300 mareros out of almost the same total of inmates; the Centro Preventivo in Zone 18, which has had over 250 members of Mara-18 (M-18) jammed into one small section known as the "11"; and the high-security jail El Boquerón, where some 100 mareros represent over half of those incarcerated there.[30] The same pattern of keeping large numbers of gang members together has existed in the juvenile reformatories (see figure 4.1).

Increased incarcerations and the tight grouping of mareros have had many consequences. One of these is simply that the penitentiary system has become the single most important place for mareros in Guatemalan society. It is their center of sociability par excellence, one where they continue to reference and elaborate on gang identity, maintain contact with gang members and leaders through their cell phones, and meet each other's wives and children and other relatives on visiting days, and one where one marero's visiting sister might become another marero's lover. Locked in together, they are locked into each other: already intense gang loyalties become even more high pitched; in prisons, mareros are only that, and in those closed shared spaces they can recuperate their fantasies. They use gang language and signals, get new tattoos and shave their hair off over and over; their main sights are each other's bodies, and they are together day and night, eating, sleeping, cleaning, and sitting around. Vital to their need to be physically strong, they do strenuous exercise routines as a group. According to one report, "There exists no specified area for exercise [in the jail], they [gang members] play soccer in the patios, they do exercises endlessly—sit-ups, push-ups—

FIGURE 4.1 Members of M-18 sitting together in El Hoyón Prison, Escuintla, 2005. Credit: Victor J. Blue.

wherever they can to stay in shape."[31] The many photographs of mareros behind prison fences attest to the fact that these youth maintain their bodies and their style. Categorized as mareros, they also call upon themselves to act as mareros, and they continue the war between Mara Salvatrucha (MS-13) and M-18 behind bars.[32] The mareros have marked out territories, and they fight for them.

When the mareros have opposed prison authorities, it has been to retain and expand their space within the penal system, rather than oppose their incarceration in it. The several uprisings of gang members in prisons and youth centers have involved taking guards hostage as leverage to win demands that will improve prison life for them as mareros. They have consistently sought increased visitation privileges and the right to carry cell phones at all times. However, the sharpest disputes have concerned transfers, which are matters of mibarrio solidarity, protection, and survival. The policy of putting mareros together in jails does not mean that mareros from the same gangs are necessarily together in the same centers. Mareros have rioted repeatedly to stop the reassignment of members of their mibarrio to jails that are rival strongholds, and to bring members of the same gang into the same prison. Examples of this are the taking of hostages around those paired demands at El Boquerón and the Centro Preventivo in Zone 18 in 2005; the Centro Preventivo and El Pavoncito in 2006; El Hoyón, Etapa 2 in San José de Pinula and El Pavoncito in 2007; and Etapa 2 in 2009. These disputes have usually left prisoners and hostages wounded or dead.

Taking Fire

Despite their concentrated numbers and gang adherence, mareros' power in prisons is limited. Outside of El Hoyón in Escuintla and juvenile centers such as Etapa 2, mareros have not become the authoritative group of inmates within the system because they have faced stiff competition from incarcerated state agents and members of the Colombian and Guatemalan mafias, as well as from important outside groups. Vulnerable as lower-class youth without lawyers or wealthy relatives, mareros have been targets for powerful prisoners and, above all, for politicians and military men who entrap gang members and use them, as well as the all-important uproar around them, in dangerous dramas that go beyond jails.

The first publicized case of this nature took place in the Centro Preventivo, Zone 18, where the ex-colonel Bryan Lima Oliva and a former member of the presidential guard, José Obdulia Villanueva (both incarcerated for the murder of the human rights advocate Bishop Juan Gerardi), joined together with other ex-military men who awaited trial there. Under Lima Oliva's leadership, this cohort of inmates took control of the prison through the COD and, according to testimony later taken from prisoners by human rights organizations, "demanded monthly payments from inmates in return for security, cable television, food, water, light, cigarettes and maintenance."[33] At the lower end of the prison hierarchy, mareros complained of physical abuse at the hands of Lima Oliva and his friends, and this exploded on February 12, 2003, into a fight that left over fifteen mareros dead. It also left Obdulia Villanueva beheaded. In a show of power, Lima Oliva announced from prison over national radio that his bodyguards had immediately killed Villanueva's killers in their cells. Lima Oliva explained that mareros had decapitated Villanueva because "they respond to their instincts and are hostile to military men" and that he and his "thousands [milles] of fellow inmates would begin daily executions of gang members if these were not removed." Prison administrators complied and transferred two hundred inmates, including mareros.[34] Years later, the discovery of Lima Oliva's prison account books revealed thousands of dollars in loans that were paid back in gems, cars, and furniture; the cell phone numbers of Mexican Zeta leaders and ex-kaibiles; and notes on what homes to rent for purposes of drug distribution and how to stock them — "washer, drier, television, 5 laptops, 200 hand grenades" — as well as on rental fees for chairs and tables within the prison for inmates' visitors.[35] The mareros had lost out to a trans-regional military-run capitalist company that operated on every profitable level possible, had its headquarters in the maximum-security section of a large prison, and might have had its own reasons for getting rid of Villanueva.

The vulnerability of the mareros and the imperative of unity were apparent to at least some gang members. At the time of the 2003 transfers, leaders in MS-13 and M-18 signed a nonaggression pact that went into effect in prisons and reform centers throughout the country. Based on a Los Angles model and known as Southern United Raza, or Sur, in Guatemala it stipulated that MS-13 and M-18 would continue to fight outside, but not inside, the penitentiary system (see figure 4.2). During the two years Sur lasted, the intense fighting between MS-13 and M-18 inmates ceased. However, the pact suddenly and brutally broke down. It is unclear how hand grenades and others arms got inside El Hoyón in Escuintla, the most overcrowded and run-down prison, or by what means the news of the collapse of Sur so quickly spread throughout the country. According to reports, at 8:30 AM on August 16, 2005, young men in MS-13 threw grenades into a cell of members of M-18 and continued their assault with firearms.[36] Over the next three

FIGURE 4.2 Gang members from M-18 in El Hoyón Prison, Escuintla, walk by a wall inscribed with the words "Southern United Raza," in reference to the nonaggression pact between MS-13 and M-18 that prohibited rival clikas from fighting within penitentiary walls. It remained in effect from 2003 to 2005. Escuintla, 2005. Credit: Victor Blue.

hours, MS-13 attacked M-18 members with weapons that included knives, 9 mm pistols, revolvers, and Uzis at prisons at some distance from Escuintla, such as El Pavón; a prison in Quetzaltenango in the western highlands; one in Mazaltenango on the piedmont; and the male juvenile detention center Gaviotas in Guatemala City. Thirty youth between ages eighteen and twenty died, most of these inside El Hoyón, where sixty more were hospitalized with cuts and gunshot wounds.[37] Every news outlet covered the aftermath of this bloody national battle in detail. Images of the shirtless, tattooed wounded young men and the tattooed dead lying on floors patently slippery with blood, of bereft families, and of panicked neighbors in areas near the prisons circulated for weeks (see figures 4.3–4.5). President Óscar Berger, of the center-right Gran Alianza Nacional (Grand National Alliance, GANA), stated that he was relieved no one had escaped and called for a rapid completion of forty-nine cells that would expand Fraijanes 2, the high-security prison next to El Pavón.[38] His minister of the Interior, Carlos Vielmann, declared that this was not a "mutiny but a breakdown in the internal order of the penitentiary system."[39] There was no investigation of any aspect of this tragedy.[40]

Whoever propelled it, this war continued. On September 4, the National Police reported that MS-13 members managed to "force" their way into a detention center, open fire, blow off the heads of two members of M-18, and go on to kill ten more. Two weeks later this scenario repeated itself almost down to the last detail. On September 19, according to National Police, three MS-13 mareros between the ages of fourteen and seventeen walked into the juvenile reform center Etapa 2 in San José Pinula with an AK-47 and several pistols. They killed several members of M-18, two of whom they beheaded. The severed heads were placed in the outdoor space. Policemen and soldiers subsequently arrived, and the three were taken to Gaviotas. Later, however, one of the boys reported he had been picked up by the police and taken to the site of the crime; the second stated he had just been visiting; and the third, after declaring he knew his rights, remained silent. They were never charged. In a scenario that is hauntingly reminiscent of the war, and one in which the military was praised for its actions, all that clearly emerged about the events of the day was a televised video that showed two severed heads and the arrival of the armed forces, whose commander announced that the army had been called there in response to an "assault by a commando."[41] In this case, the criminals who were the "other" necessary to the definition of the good citizen that Michel Foucault describes in his classic work Discipline and Punish: The Birth of the Prison, might well have been invented, and the way

FIGURE 4.3 A mother waits for news of her incarcerated son in the aftermath of the August 2005 riots in El Hoyón Prison, Escuintla, that broke the nonaggression pact. Credit: Victor J. Blue.

FIGURE 4.4 Family members arrive at the morgue in Escuintla to look for their loved ones, 2005. Credit: Victor J. Blue.

FIGURE 4.5 Neighborhood boys search through the mess of discarded and ripped remains of the fighting, Escuintla, 2005. Credit: Victor J. Blue.

in which the prison system has become central to the national history is by facilitating the postwar reemergence of the Guatemalan military as a social force for the good of the good citizenry against, in this case, a few teenagers.

Yet more is going on than the creation of the "other." A year later, the state assaulted El Pavón. On September 25, 2006, Interior Minister Carlos Vielmann, National Police head Erwin Sperisen, and Alejandro Giammattei, the director of the national penitentiary system, personally led an attack force on the prison that consisted of three thousand members of the army and the National Civil Police, four tanks, and three helicopters, which flew over the heads of the fifteen hundred inmates. According to the official version, the troops marched forward against gunfire coming from the prison for thirty minutes, after which they entered, secured the prison in fifty minutes, and in the process killed seven "armed and combative prisoners." Vielmann, Giammattei, and Sperisen accompanied President Berger on an immediate tour of the captured grounds. The Berger government quickly produced a video titled TAKE CONTROL of a Territory Controlled by Criminals and subtitled TAKE CONTROL of a Paradise for Juvenile Delinquents. The film follows the soldiers as they occupied the prison premises, walked through the wreckage of shops and buildings, and peeked into elite inmate homes replete with Jacuzzis, refrigerators, and televisions. The assault was a public spectacle, had a name—Operación Pavo Real (Operation Peacock)—and made it into both national and international news.

What did not make the news was that a criminal ring controlled El Pavón. At the time of the assault the head of the COD was a drug lord named Luis Alfonso Zepeda, who had been sentenced in the early 1990s to twenty-six years for having committed multiple assassinations. Zepeda and his business partners administered an El Pavón prison town complex that included a school called Escuela de Arte Senderos de Libertad (The Paths of Liberty School of Arts); a cocaine-processing laboratory run by a well-known Colombian mafia inmate, Jorge "El Loco" Batres Pinto; and an auto repair shop where numbers were erased off the chassis of robbed cars before these vehicles were sent back to the street for sale.[42] Operación Pavo Real succeeded in destroying the COD. No gunfire was exchanged between prisoners and soldiers. A group of hooded men who entered with the soldiers and policemen went down a lineup of the fifteen hundred men with photos in their hands and pulled out Zepeda and five prisoners who were associates of El Loco. El Loco escaped the lineup and took refuge in his luxurious El Pavón residence, where he was soon discovered in his garden. The bodies of all seven turned up with signs of torture.[43] Four years later, Vielmann, Giammattei, and Sperisen would flee Guatemala when the UN Comisión Internacional contra la Impunidad en Guatemala (International Commission against Impunity in Guatemala, CICIG) revealed that this offensive against El Pavón settled a struggle about who controlled a large sector of the drug and stolen goods market.

In the twenty-first century the Guatemalan penitentiary system has become "a country within a country." It is one of no doubt several control centers of the growing illegal economy. The description here of the configuration of prison conflicts from 2003 to 2005 illustrates that these fights are between important business and political figures who operate across walls and use both the mareros and invisibility of what goes on inside prisons to their advantage. Though the conflict at El Pavón did not involve mareros, officials who were culprits in this drama had presented the pre-assault state of affairs in the prison as a "PARADISE FOR JUVENILE DELINQUENTS," despite this being a prison for adults, not minors. Even in their absence, the mareros have been dodging bullets.

In a subsequent fight between powerful adult criminals that again brought world attention to Guatemala's prison system, mareros tried to avoid the trap that they saw coming. This time, they demanded that legal authorities protect them. On February 19, 2007, three Salvadoran congressmen widely known to be connected to the drug trade were ambushed and murdered on their way to Guatemala City, along with their driver. Four members of the criminal investigation unit of the Guatemalan National Civil Police subsequently confessed to these murders, and they were confined in the maximum-security prison in El Boquerón, an MS-13 stronghold. A few days later, the four policemen were shot to death in their cells at close range. A riot immediately broke out in the prison. Aware that they might be blamed, members of MS-13 took a guard hostage and threatened to kill him unless authorities declared them innocent. They held their hostage at the very moment that the same officials involved at El Pavón—Vielmann, Sperisen, and Giammattei—were accusing the mareros of having slit the throats of the policemen—apparently they had not heard that the latter were gunned down—because, in their words, "mareros hate police." Alert to the utility of human rights discourse, the mareros insisted that the human rights ombudsman and television crews be brought inside the prisons to, as they put it, "protect their human rights." The ombudsman came, and the mareros released their hostage. Nonetheless, thirteen mareros were charged with the murder of the four policemen. Months later, the charges were dropped for lack of evidence, and the thirteen stayed in El Boquerón to complete their original sentences. The following month, "Small," one of the thirteen, was decapitated and his body burned in his cell.[44]

Making Youth Crazy

Who orchestrates this madness? Because a video from a closed-circuit camera fell into the hands of the human rights ombudsman in 2006, it is possible to see the degree to which authorities brutally manipulate youth. In June 2006, M-18 youth attacked MS-13 members in the juvenile center Etapa 2 in San José Pinula, murdered them, and mutilated their bodies. What the video picked up is that at 5 PM that day, the prison wardens threw blankets over the entrance to the section where M-18 youth were detained, and thus blocked the view of the camera and of a guard in a turret overlooking the wing. Over the next forty minutes, wardens went into the area under the blanket with objects not identifiable on the film. Ten minutes before the trouble started, the guard in the turret went on a dinner break, without being replaced. At 6:30 PM, three members of M-18 emerged from behind the blanket and entered the area where MS-13 youth lived, one that was presumably shut off by a locked door. During the next forty minutes, gang members attacked with sharp instruments, severed body limbs, and crushed skulls. A few minutes after the fight had started, someone had called the National Civil Police, which entered and left after two minutes. The policemen returned thirty-eight minutes later, the three boys from M-18 were back behind their blanket, and the policemen found three boys dead, with their limbs scattered, and six badly wounded boys, from whom no statements were taken. The human rights ombudsman presented the video to the UN special rapporteur, who brought accusations against Giammattei that have yet to be resolved.[45]

A contrast to the resulting chorus of "out of control" is at once obvious and startling: this was a tightly controlled sequence of events, right down to a stage manager who stopped the policemen from bungling the timing of their entrance and to the erasure of media publicity concerning the video. The venue for this manipulation was not an adult jail such as El Boquerón, where mareros have demonstrated some ability to hold their own, but a reform center for minors in an isolated setting in the countryside. This was the second terrifying and eerie news-making disaster at Etapa 2. It occurred a year following the incident, cited earlier, in which three boys were arrested for beheadings in which they probably had no involvement. It has been difficult to investigate what was at issue in these two episodes that resulted in the deaths of young mareros; however, the leadership given by police and prison personnel in the 2006 murders is evident.

It was in the same Etapa 2 in San José Pinula that youth murdered a schoolteacher three years later. On March 3, 2009, a few days following a search by authorities in which cell phones were seized from the resident youth and visitation rights taken away as a punishment, several boys took hostage two custodians, a cook, and two teachers, including forty-five-year-old Jorge Emilio Winter Vidaurre, who worked in one of the few programs at Etapa 2. The boys demanded that the cell phones be returned, that visiting privileges be restored, and that two youths recently transferred to another juvenile center be brought back. With the words "we aren't kidding," they shut the hostages in a room and waited to start negotiations; taking hostages had become the leverage common throughout the penal system. The Etapa 2 administrator did not negotiate. She called the National Civil Police, whose elite special forces encircled the prison. The boys responded by crushing Winter Vidaurre's skull and cutting out his heart. In view of the police and residents of San José de Pinula who by then surrounded Etapa 2, the boys came out into the central patio, danced, and yelled that Winter Vidaurre "had lived long enough." The police seized the youths, who held their fingers high in a gang sign, and took them out of the building to await trial in the adult Centro Preventivo, Zone 18, where they keep company with hundreds of mareros who were crammed into Section 11 of that prison.[46] The psychiatrist Rodolfo Kepfer, who worked at Etapa 2 at the time, said that when "the boys are upset, they get violent, obsessed, single-minded like addicts, almost glazed over. After something happens, you stay away until they are calmed down." Following the initial riot over the cell phones, Kepfer had unsuccessfully warned Winter Vidaurre and others to absent themselves for a few days after the youth rioted over their cell phones.

Winter Vidaurre's grotesque murder and the boys' disdainful boasting caused widespread horror and panic. State authorities had to act forcefully to project a vision of tenacious pursuit of mareros. Close on the heels of Winter Vidaurre's death, President Álvaro Colom, of the social democratic party Unidad Nacional de la Esperanza (National Unity of Hope, UNE), announced that "careful police intelligence and the cooperation of citizens over time" had led to the discovery of the identity of no less a persona than the shadowy figure behind the bus extortion rackets that have left hundreds of bus drivers and assistants dead in recent years and months. Colom's attorney general, Salvador Gándara, proclaimed Áxel Danilo Rodríguez, alias Smiley, a twenty-two-year-old leader of M-18, mastermind of these crimes and, in addition, the culprit in the recent murder of a well-to-do Korean couple.[47] Only weeks later, police captured this "public enemy number one" following a gun fight in Zone 10 of Mixco.

Smiley was already an urban legend, an example of what Foucault cited as the historic failure of the modern penal system to rehabilitate the criminal and its success "in producing delinquency, a specific type." A child of that system, Smiley was born in Colonia Primero de Julio in Zone 9, joined M-18 when he was ten, and soon thereafter was arrested for extortion and sent to the juvenile center Gaviotas, where he killed two young members of MS-13 during the large-scale multiprison battle between MS-13 and M-18 in August 2005. For that, the judge sentenced him to five additional years and moved him into the adult prison, even though he was a minor, from which he was released for "good behavior" shortly thereafter. He returned to the streets to become "public enemy number one."

His 2009 capture received wide publicity and high praise from and for President Colom. Upon his arrest, Smiley denied the charges. He stated that he was responsible for killing MS-13 rivals in August 2005 but not the bus drivers or the Korean couple. He called Gándara a "thief just like me, except he doesn't have tattoos." At an unusual press conference held in the police precinct following his arrest, Smiley spoke and looked like the marero who had been fantasized about for decades. Covered with tattoos, low voiced, and short on words, in answer to reporters' provocative and aggressive questions, he said that killing people satisfied him and that he was a thief. He was heard to have muttered, "The devil is my *jefe*." A few months later, the judge dropped the charges concerning the bus drivers and the Korean couple for lack of evidence and instead charged Smiley with "bearing weapons" to keep him in preventive custody in Zone 18's Centro Preventivo.[48]

Keeping up his momentum, Smiley held up his end as the perfect delinquent. One year later, he was part of an M-18 uprising coordinated by cell phone calls from the newly reinforced high-security cells at jail Fraijanes 2 and from the Centro Preventivo, Zone 18, at precisely noon on April 23, 2010. The mareros in both prisons took hostages and demanded the transfer of dozens of M-18 members from Fraijanes 2 to the Centro Preventivo in Zone 18. After days of a standoff, the human rights ombudsman negotiated a settlement to "protect the lives of the hostages." The hostages were released, and the M-18 members taken in heavily guarded trucks in middle of the night to the Centro Preventivo, Zone 18, where their presence increased the number of M-18 members from (according to the press) 272 to 366.[49]

On and on it goes. The "transition to democracy" cannot succeed without citizen security, which, because of these tattooed young gangsters, cannot happen without ironclad prisons. Yet the deep social changes that might root out the causes of misery and crime cannot happen because of well-dressed criminals in power who, as Smiley observed, do not have tattoos. These youth seem shackled into this sequence. Foucault frames the mas-

FIGURE 4.6 A member of MS-13 cries out as Guatemalan soldiers in downtown Guatemala City haul him and a woman away, to where is not known, 2005. The fate of both youth remains unclear. Credit: Victor J. Blue.

sive prison uprisings of the 1970s that inspired his thinking as "revolts, at the level of the body, against the very body of the prison." He writes that "at issue was not whether the prison environment was too harsh or too aseptic, too primitive or too efficient but its very materiality as an instrument and vector of power."[50] In sharp contrast to the revolts referred to by Foucault, such as the uprising in the Attica Correctional Facility in upstate New York in 1971, the conflicts in Guatemala's prisons and juvenile centers in the early 2000s have been the consequence of mareros and others fighting to buttress their places within the prison system. The prisons have sustained the delinquents and created the disorders that, however disruptive, also do not challenge the "vector of power" (see figure 4.6).

Clean and Dirty Bodies

Fighting crime has been central to political campaigns for decades.[51] Elected to the presidency in 2011, the ex-general and kaibil Otto Pérez Molina, member of the Partido Patriota (Patriotic Party, PP), has long fashioned himself as the tough guy, a man who once directed battles and now can stop "narcotraficantes, Maras and others."[52] His unsuccessful 2007 bid as well as the successful 2011 campaign focused on youth in televised advertisements in which every type of youth, and dozens of them—Maya, Ladino, male, female, clean shaven, neatly bearded, arty, middle class, worker, and student—cheerfully advocate and repeat over and over "mano dura," including in Maya languages. No matter whether hip or church-bound in their look, they contrast with those looming figures: the nonnational (LA), menacing, almost faceless because of tattoos, hypervisible, blue with ink mareros whose bodies call so much attention to themselves. The public cannot read the stories that the marking on the mareros' bodies tell. All the public seems to see is what is said about symbols of Satan. The clean bodies of the Guatemalan youth in the television videos represent a new Guatemala, one disassociated from the tattooed body's presumed representational schema of violence and chaos. Perhaps the images of the mareros' bodies are meant to replace or confuse memories of the kaibiles' blood-smeared faces.

OPEN ENDING 5

If something does not go well, you have to cover up the holes, like on the stage set. When an actor makes a mistake he goes on, like nothing happened. The public doesn't know the script. You don't have to go into all the mistakes.

—Fu (Juan Manuel Orozco Ambrosio), ex-marero, educator, and theater performer and producer, killed April 5, 2009; El Periódico, November 30, 2008

I want to say that I knew Fu and Chuky [a second assassinated actor and ex–gang member], and they were great people and their death hurts me and because of this same violence I had to leave and live outside in a foreign country, but I will never forget my brave friends. I send my condolences to the family of Fu and Chuky from North Carolina.

—Flakita de la Frutal, El Periódico, May 3, 2009

The political violence of the Guatemalan ruling elite is the result of calculated decisions about wealth and power, but mareros have no political power or wealth. Their violence is part of the unspoken story of subjectivities that have been created by the absence of positive means of power over life and by fear, terror, and the difficult material conditions that have been part of Guatemalan history. A tragic legacy of Guatemala's late twentieth-century history, the mareros of the twenty-first century are not rebels: sadly, they adhere to the standards set by Guatemala's ruling elites, drug lords, military leaders, and too many other influential people.

The backbone of this book has been the backstory of the current gangs. In the course of the decades since the 1980s, they have been vilified and victimized, and some of their members have responded in kind. Today clikas of the Maras with names such as Rokers, Los Locos, and Los Metalles, and young people who hang out and call themselves mareros are in the city and in most of the country's twenty-two departments. They have become central figures in the minds of many, and a political windfall for authoritarian political parties. As I have stressed, some of these youth may not be violent, but their preoccupation with violence and with death and their crimes against ordinary people alert us to a world in deep trouble. Young people who were once imagined as leading humanity into the great mythical future of the metanarrative of modernity, where "things are getting better, better all the time," are now shoved into corners by the past. This book has argued that capitalist modernity's promises have not borne fruit for youth, and it has traced the discourses and identities available to youth and the deeply violent and changing Guatemala in which these have arisen. "Youth" was once a temporal fix on capitalist development's failure to deliver in present time; it was the quintessential symbol of a bright national future on an always-distant and luminous horizon. "Youth" now seems to signal a marketing niche, the biggest in the world, and a horrific social problem.

Fortunately, girls and boys and young women and men are more than metaphors, symbols, objects, or images. They are subjects who transcend the frozen singular categories of identity such as delinquent and street child that obscure our vision (see figure 5.1). Young killers and thieves might also be overworked day laborers, artists on the side, and anxious parents; they are not simply wind-up toy soldiers without emotions. Many experience repulsion, yet feel immobilized inside of a persona named marero who must follow the lethal orders of others.

That youth abandon gangs gives hope, and so does the harrowing reality that they do so despite incalculable difficulties. The Maras MS-13 and M-18 "green-light" (give the death warrant to) youth who leave except, it has been claimed, in cases of conversion to Pentecostalism or of special permissions for "good behavior," which means that those who are requesting a "leave" have complied with orders and accomplished tasks that include homicide. It has been argued that youth who quit do so only in obedience to these Mara guidelines, and therefore only within the gang's regime of law.[1] But youth in fact do quit otherwise. Ex-mareros turn up in all kinds of places through the help of adults who have made no pacts with Mara leaders, or even without any adult support. Ex–gang members can be found working in jobs in the informal and formal economies; they can show up as artists such as Carlos Pérez (see figure 5.2), and as street educators and youth advocates. That they desert the Maras even at the risk of green-lighting brings to mind political activists of the early period who chose lives that they deemed meaningful despite knowing that they might die as a consequence.[2] Drawn into macabre gangs to which they can become faithful unto death, these children

FIGURE 5.1 A young man in the bustle of Guatemala City's Central Park, Zone 1, 1999. Youth are more complex than identifications such as "marero," "student," and "worker," or "Ladino," "mestizo," and "Maya" suggest. Credit: Andrea Aragón.

FIGURE 5.2 Artist Carlos Pérez, ex-marero, Guatemala, 2010. Credit: Copyright © Donna DeCesare, 2010.

and young women and men also can "decide for life"—certainly a kind of politics—though they might die for that.

Exiting through Pentecostalism

The Pentecostal ministry has had successes, and this is a topic on its own that is beyond the scope of this book. Based on interviews with ex-gang members, Robert Brenneman's *Homies and Hermanos: God and Gangs in Central America* offers a fine study of conversion. My own experiences in the early 2000s made clear to me that the Pentecostals' methods and rhetoric have changed over time, and these now vary from approaches centered on the hell-and-brimstone punishments such as those meted out in the reform centers by the brutal staff of REMAR, to the patience and kindliness given by individual pastors and particular ministries. In the best of the Pentecostal centers, youth join gentle communities, take the enormous step of entering detoxification programs, and do not necessarily have a relationship to the political affiliations of some of the megachurches, such as the ultraconservative El Shaddai Ministries.[3] Pentecostals have ministered to ex-mareros over the years through clubs such as Rescate Maras Para Cristo and encouraged them to open small cooperative businesses such as bakeries. Often with the assistance of the Guatemalan government, international groups and Guatemalan companies, these non-Catholic Christian groups have been involved in attempts to reform mareros since the 1980s, as chapter 4 notes. Moreover, because of the stated agreement between Pentecostals and some Mara leaders affirming that members who leave to convert will not be killed, in the minds of many young people the Pentecostals offer what seems to amount to a lifeboat. Youth sometimes join Pentecostal groups out of fear of the consequences of not joining (see figure 5.3). Ghastly public executions of mareros have added urgency to a safe passage out of the gangs. In 2005, a Pentecostal pastor recruited an entire clika of over thirty boys in the town of Palín, near the capital, after several men burned three mareros alive in a public "social cleansing."[4]

Conversion stories are profound and speak to the real agency of those who, in their words, "encounter Christ." Once saved, young people give emotional accounts of parental and other adult mistreatment, public testimonies that help them become more sympathetic to themselves and others. Many become activists for the ministries that guide them. Yet the notion that youth abandon the Maras only through Pentecostal conversion suggests that youth will not leave without the assurance that they will not be killed, and without strong religious persuasion and adult control over their every step.

FIGURE 5.3 Ex-members of MS-13 attending a Pentecostal service in
Palín, a town not far from Guatemala City, 2005. They renounced the
gang and joined the church after being frightened by the lynching of
three of their members. Credit: Victor J. Blue.

This account of "departure only through Pentecostal groups" is deceptive because gangs have sometimes green-lighted ex-members who converted. It is also misleading because it suggests that fear always paralyzes youth, or that they lack the internal and moral conviction necessary to make a radical break on their own without a group that gives them narratives, standards, and regulations to which they need to conform, and which are conformist.[5] These assumptions are belied by the fact that some youth just take a chance and desert, sometimes following the birth of their children, or in simple disgust.[6]

Just Quitting

The Guatemalan therapist Herbert Sánchez spent years working with young men who had abandoned the Maras. In his conversations with me in the late 1990s, he emphasized that youth he counseled had lived in conditions where "death and hatred" determine everyday life. In line with this, he sought out the writings of the Viennese psychotherapist Viktor E. Frankl, a survivor of the Nazi concentration camps, because Sánchez believed that these youth had to "survive the death camps." He drew on Frankl's argument that one can endure in situations that are constantly life threatening and soul deadening, as long as one gives life meaning, and that otherwise one cannot live.[7] He labored hard to create a therapeutic community where youth had to live at a "high level of consciousness" as he phrased it, and struggle to give meaning to their shattered lives through physical exertion, discussion, love, and positive deeds toward others. The meaning of meaning, he said in response to my asking, is catching a passion about and for life (see figure 5.4).[8] In his view this represents a conversion to one's own life.

Using a different vocabulary, ex-mareros expressed this resolution to make lives that made sense to them in defiance of death's apparent omnipotence. Alfredo got out after police killed his two brothers in a "social cleansing" operation in La Limonada. Still in La Limonada, Alfredo now works with an agency that involves neighborhood youth in sports and other recreational activities. Sitting inside a storefront drinking a beer, his eighteen-year-old friend and coworker José told me he left because he "got fed up. . . . The leaders thought they were tough but they got too tough, they would just say 'liquidate Fulano' [so-and-so]" and he simply did not want to murder people. In a different ambience, Luis, a young man in a Catholic group home, said with a smile that he quit because he "fell in love." Another, Rolando, explains his quitting as "I just decided to"; "I became a parent," he said, and did not "want my kid to have my life." When I asked Rolando

FIGURE 5.4 Street educators found these children living in the central bus terminal in Guatemala City and brought them to live in this group home, 1998. A number of former street children have developed organizations to alleviate the problems of homeless youth. Credit: Deborah T. Levenson.

whether he feared being killed by his old gang, he made the important observation that the probability of being killed while in the gang was higher: he said he would be "dead already anyway, in the clika, because of someone who would have jumped me."[9]

Rosa (see chapter 3) was suicidal because she took the life of an elderly woman — "I was ready to, I don't know, ready to kill myself. My heart ached, I went to live with an aunt." Rosa stayed out of sight for a while and then found a job. She put her reason for leaving as "I killed. . . . I really needed to get out of the Maras. . . . I didn't have friends. I hardly ever saw my sister, because she found out I've been in a Mara. She beat me. I didn't think much when I was younger, but now I know what is right and what is wrong. . . . When I grow up, I want to be a doctor. I want to have children, and I am going to give them lots of advice and all the love that I wasn't given." Rosa left without the protection of the Pentecostals to pursue her goals of being a loving parent and becoming a doctor who could help people who had been in her situation.

Not all youth who leave make it. Notwithstanding that some who abandon the Maras without playing by gang rules escape green-lighting, many others do not. Evidence indicates that getting away from gang life by leaving the country is particularly offensive to gang leaders, perhaps because in doing so youth remove themselves from the total control of "territory." One tragic example concerns Edgar Chocoy, who joined MS-13 at twelve in Guatemala City and left it two years later because, in his words, he "was not cut out for it" and he did not like the violence.

Years afterward, Edgar recounted to the U.S. immigration lawyer Kimberly Baker Medina that when he dropped out of MS-13 in 2002 at fourteen, the gang demanded that he pay three thousand quetzals a week to not be killed—a particularly horrific example of necroliving. He would have had to engage in continual big-time robbery to come up with such a large sum. Instead he hid in Guatemala City for a short period of time before he decided to leave the country and reunite with his mother, who had emigrated to Los Angeles almost a decade before, while he was still a toddler. Upon receiving news of his situation and his planned journey, she sent money to pay a *coyote* (the person paid to guide those without papers across borders). In kind with the hundreds of children who go north from Central America to search for or otherwise reunite with their mothers, he went through an uncertain and terrifying journey that involved crossing rivers; concealing himself; pretending to be Mexican; getting on buses in foreign lands; and defending himself from thieves, hunger, sickness, officials, and despair.[10] After he arrived in Los Angeles, life was hard. He had troubles with schoolmates because of gang rivalries there and his presumed inclusion in one of them. First his school kicked him out, and after a spell, so did his mother, who hardly knew him and did not want "problems" because she had other children (siblings Edgar barely knew) in her house. Afraid to stay homeless in the street, alone without real friends, Edgar went to the apartment of an older Spanish-speaking schoolmate, a gang member who proceeded to use Edgar as an armed drug runner. While he was there, and even while working for the gang—his resource for food and shelter—he found out about Homeboy Industries, a program founded by Jesuit Father Greg Boyle, which opens its arms to gang members. He went there for help, and there he decided to start the painful process of getting rid of his tattoos, tattoos that he saw as a major source of trouble because they identified him with gangs.

Then in 2003, the Los Angeles police arrested him for possession of cocaine base. The charge was adjudicated because of Edgar's age. However, because he had no papers, he was sent to an internment camp in Colorado to await deportation. In the camp he entered the loose weave of solidarity among detainees, and he learned about the possibility of applying for asylum, which he did through contacts he pursued while in detention. He met Kimberly Baker Medina, and together they built his case against deportation around the argument that he would be green-lighted by MS-13 if he returned to Guatemala, one the judge rejected despite letters and testimony from experts in Guatemala and in the United States who supported his claim, and in spite of an offer from an aunt in Virginia to care for him. In early 2004, two-and-one-half weeks following his deportation back to Guatemala City, he was shot the first time he dared leave what was essentially a hiding place in a relative's house in Villa Nueva, on the city's edge. He had stepped out into the doorway to watch a religious procession pass, and a few moments later, he was dead. He was sixteen (see figure 5.5).[11]

Edgar left Guatemala to save his life from the Mara, but U.S. laws and Los Angeles life made that impossible, and then a U.S. judge returned him to Guatemala marked to die because the judge ruled that Edgar did not "belong to a social group" that suffers persecution.[12] It is a tragedy that illustrates that the gangs do carry out their own laws when they want to. It also shows that U.S. judges are capable of ignoring facts put right in front of their eyes: ex-mareros are a persecuted group. But all that killed Edgar did not define him. He defined his own life by trying to find a way into a better one. His life is marked by his triumphs. Here is a youth of startling valor, one we must assume had a sense of self-worth. He abandoned MS-13 on his own and on his own tried to figure out a life for himself, a task that included crossing two borders, the entire length of Mexico and the Sonora Desert, and jour-

FIGURE 5.5 Edgar Chocoy, an ex-member of MS-13 who fled to the United States to escape gang life, Colorado, 2003. Edgar was deported by a U.S. judge who rejected Edgar's plea that he would be killed if returned to Guatemala. He was shot to death by MS-13 shortly after arriving back in Guatemala. Credit: Kimberly Baker Medina.

neying into a huge strange city, without papers, to a mother he hardly knew. In a new country, without speaking English, and through people he barely knew, he found resources in his Herculean effort to establish traction in his constantly falling-apart world. What more can we ask of a young person, stigmatized at every turn, alone, and without the named identities, signposts, and spaces given by citizenship, work, school, or family?

Fu's Story

Disidentifying: "The Public Doesn't Know the Script"

Eight years before he died, Juan Manuel Orozco Ambrosio, known as Fu, got out of M-18 when he joined a theater group that had arrived in the barrio where he lived. "At first," Fu told a friend, "I led a double life. During the day I would be at rehearsals and at night in the *rollo* [the gang activities]." Subsequently, at nineteen, he left M-18 for good because he had found a real passion, what Herbert Sánchez would call a meaning. Fu explained, "With theater I could leave who I was for a while and put myself in someone else's life. It was therapy. In these journeys I found myself." He pursued a career in performing arts through the organization Caja Lúdica, an artistic collective devoted to, in its own words, "promoting a culture of peace among people and demanding an end to violence and impunity."[13] Another ex-marero in Caja Lúdica described its work in an interview with a journalist in 2009. "We want to touch the human fiber in each person, to awaken that side that has been lost in the system. We have to look at ourselves, to recognize ourselves and see the power we have."[14]

Started in 2000 by theater people who had done similar work in Colombia, Caja Lúdica encourages youth to think about the history that generates the violent crucible of their "coming of age" so that they can emerge from subjugation (see figure 5.6). There exist other drama troupes in Guatemala City that also seek out gang members and other barrio youth to fashion true stories on a stage, whether that be a field or a street. These groups have helped generate skits based on the most gruesome truths about the war. In these, children reenact what happened to their parents and grandparents, and to that degree these young performers reclaim the "unclaimed experience" at the heart of trauma.[15]

A young woman in her teens in the Zone 12 settlement of Mezquital, which started in 1985, the same year the Maras came out in public, Estela is a street performer. She reminds one of Maritza (a member of the Maras in the 1980s; see chapter 3). She can tell it like it is: "We have the ability to change this country, and stop all this aggression that we're living through. The future is in our hands." "Mezquital" she explains to visitors, was created by people invading the land when they came here as refugees during the war. People fled here and raised their children here. The violence stems from that. . . . After the war there were a lot of traumatized young people with lots of violence in their heads and they kill each other. So it is dangerous.

It's important for everyone [to have the chance to express themselves], but we live in a culture that says we can't do anything. Through [theater] you find out that everyone has the same value. When you see others on stilts or juggling, you feel better straightaway because you see that it's possible.[16]

For Fu and other ex-mareros, the world of playing has offered a sensibility and mechanisms to develop themselves through the re-creation of life itself—settings, characters, scripts, plots, surprise endings, varied clothing, and new faces through makeup, dance, music, and—on stilts—a new height, literally. Fu flourished in it. He even traveled to Germany as part of a performing arts troupe, and M-18 had accepted this new life and ceased to brand him a traitor. But the old endless rivalry between M-18 with MS-13 gave him problems. In 2008, Fu was left paralyzed and confined to a wheelchair after an MS-13 member, who had participated in a workshop Fu ran, shot him. His response was to continue his theater work—"no reason to remain seated," he joked from his wheelchair—as a script writer and director of educational comedies, and he opened a business that ran parties for children to support himself and his family (see figure 5.7).[17]

Fu was shot to death as he sat in his wheelchair playing cards with a group of children outside his house on April 5, 2009, and a few weeks later, on May 23, two other members of Caja Lúdica were killed. These were ex-mareros Saulo Fernando Gómez Estrada, known as both "el Chuky" and Solo Estilos, who break danced and designed a line of clothes that he was about to trademark; and Nexus Pineda, an ex-marero nicknamed El Gordo who had established a community youth center in the Mario Alioto, a neighborhood in Guatemala City named after a student leader and political activist in the 1980s who was bludgeoned to death by police. Ten days later, shortly after a memorial for Fu, El Gordo, and Chuky, Caja Lúdica break dancers, actors, stilt walkers, and musicians Osmar Fernando Leiva Mejía, René Alexander Pérez Cruz, José Omar Pérez Cruz, Nelson Leonel Aguirre Tobar, and Juan María López were gunned down.[18]

Why? Although it is possible that mareros killed them because they had left their Maras, all these youth had been out of the gangs for years. What coincided with their deaths was the growing success of theatrical groups such

FIGURE 5.6 A parade performance presented by one of the several youth theater groups in downtown Guatemala City, 2007. Credit: Copyright © Donna DeCesare, 2007.

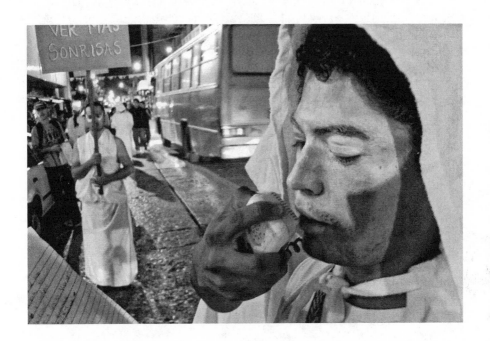

FIGURE 5.7 Ex-marero Juan Manuel Orozco Ambrosio, known as "Fu," photographed playing his part in an evening street performance by the theatre group Caja Lúdica. Courageous and determined, Fu helped create critical spaces and autonomous voices for youth. Credit: Copyright © Donna DeCesare, 2007.

as Caja Lúdica in barrios. Some see these killings in the light of that. Following a third memorial service, one young person in the theater group said that the dead youth "represented a threat to those who had economic interests in their neighborhoods, who exploit youth. Their murders were also a way to frighten others who might want to make change in these zones."[19]

According to the local official in the area, "various men who traveled in a vehicle and jumped out and opened fire" carried out the murders in May and April.[20] Youth who write their own scripts—young women such as Estela and young men turning into adults such as Fu—who leave the Mara and know that they can rewrite the play, and that they are authors behind the scenes, are politically dangerous. By animating life so, they pose a threat to the micropower of death used to run neighborhoods.

This short final chapter concludes the book but not the history. Movements against domination and injustice always appear at one point or another, and so will the counterparts of Edgar, Fu, Estela, and other young people who have their own thoughts and their own moments in time. These youths, and not the celebrated and the fictional obedient La Juventud of nineteenth- and twentieth-century national fantasies, need to be our heroes. However inconspicuous they are in the grand scale of things, they push against the grain of despondency and they delineate the possibility, once again, of a different Guatemala, with new lines.

NOTES

Introduction

The source of the introduction's first epigraph is *Primer Congreso Pedagógico Centroamericano*, 198. That of the second is Comisión para el Esclarecimiento Histórico (CEH), *Memoria del silencio*, 6:76.

1. By the middle of the 1970s, the Ejército Guerrillero de los Pobres (Guerrilla Army of the Poor, EGP) and the Organización Revolucionaria del Pueblo en Armas (Revolutionary Organization of the Armed People, ORPA) had replaced this traditional Marxist conception of the centrality of an educated elite who led urban workers with one that, at least in theory, placed the countryside and the Maya population at the heart of revolutionary charge. For the most part, the Partido Guatemalteco del Trabajo (Guatemalan Workers Party, PGT) and the Fuerzas Armadas Rebeldes (Rebel Armed Forces, FAR) retained their faith in the city and the citified.

2. The urban poor, the city's majority, depend on remittances from relatives abroad, the informal economy, the illegal economy of drugs and other goods, and a shrinking formal sector. Neoliberalism has meant lower wages, higher prices, fewer jobs, and dramatic cuts in state spending for social services. The portion of state funds spent on education, housing, and health decreased from 9 percent in 1980 to 2.9 percent in 1991. For a description of city life since the 1980s, see Instituto para la Superación de la Miseria Urbana de Centroamérica (ISMU), *Dinámica de las condiciones de la vida urbana*; Gellert and Palma C., *Precaridad urbana, desarrollo comunitario y mujeres en el área metropolitana de Guatemala*; AVANCSO, *El proceso de crecimiento metropolitano de la Ciudad de Guatemala*.

3. AVANCSO, *Más allá de la sobrevivencia.*

4. Author interview with Carlos López García, Guatemala City, 2000.

5. AVANCSO, *Por sí mismos.*

6. Reguillo Cruz, "La Mara."

7. Wolfe, "*Maras transnacionales.*"

8. García Noval, *Para entender la violencia,* 11.

9. Mbembe, "Necropolitics."

10. Mazariegos, *La guerra de los nombres,* 1–16.

11. Martín-Baró, *Writings for a Liberation Psychology,* 115.

12. Adorno, *Minima Moralia*, 50.

13. Taylor, *A Secular Age*, 171–72.

14. Demoscopía, *Maras y pandillas*.

15. *El Periódico*, March 5, 2009.

16. Author interview with Rodolfo Kepfer, Guatemala City, 2010.

17. Lira, "Violence, Fear and Impunity."

18. Davis, *Planet of Slums*.

19. According to most scholars, the English-language classic pacesetter is Frederic Thrasher's *The Gang*. Other well-known studies include Cohen, *Delinquent Boys*; Yablonsky, *The Violent Gang*; Cloward and Ohlin, *Delinquency and Opportunity*; Anderson, *Code of the Street*; Covey, *Street Gangs throughout the World*; Huff, *Gangs in America*; Vigil, *Barrio Gangs*; Schneider, *Vampires, Dragons and Egyptian Kings*; Bourgois, *In Search of Respect*; Hagedorn, *People and Folks*; Brotherton and Barrios, *Street Politics and the Transformation of a New York Gang*; and Hayden, *Street Wars*. There are a growing number of books about global gangs, such as Hazlehurst and Hazlehurst, *Gangs and Subcultures*; and Hagedorn, *Gangs in the Global City*.

    For studies of gang members and gangs in Latin America, see Rossana Reguillo Cruz's *En la calle otra vez*, as well as her fine essays about youth and culture, such as "La gestión del futuro." Among other important studies are Arce et al., *Las Maras*; Rubio, *De la pandilla a la Mara*; Rivera Solís, *Pandillas juveniles y gobernabilidad democracia*; Perea Restrepo, *Con el diablo adentro*; Strocka, "Youth Gangs in Latin America"; Centro Juana Azurduy, *Sin salida*; Lara Klahr, *Hoy te toca la muerte*; Fernández Menéndez and Ronquillo, *De los Maras a los zeta*; Cerbino, *Jóvenes en la calle*; and Jones and Rodgers, *Youth Violence in Latin America*.

20. Santos Anaya, *La vergüenza de los pandilleros*. John M. Hagedorn writes that "the gang has always been an arena for the acting out of gender." Hagedorn, "Gang," 329. Much attention has been paid to gangs and masculinity, from Bruce Davidson's photos of U.S. gang culture in the late 1950s to recent scholarly work, such as Paula Heinonen's *Youth Gangs and Street Children*.

21. Vigil, "Urban Violence and Street Gangs."

22. Cruz et al., *Exclusión social jóvenes y pandillas*; Brotherton and Barrios, *Street Politics and the Transformation of a New York Gang*; Hayden, *Street Wars*; Hagedorn, *A World of Gangs*.

23. Lara Klahr, *Hoy te toca la muerte*, 18. A famous figure in theater, Tito Estrada works with youth in Honduras.

24. Merino, "Las Maras en Guatemala," "Guatemala," and "Políticas juveniles y rehabilitación de mareros en Guatemala"; Núñez, *De la ciudad al barrio*; Tobar Estrada, *Entre mundos ajenos*; AVANCSO, *Heridas en la sombra*; AVANCSO, *Por sí mismos*; Cruz and Portilla, *Peña solidaridad y violencia*; Santacruz Giralt and Concha-Eastman, *Barrio adentro*; Trigueros Martel, "Las Maras salvadoreñas," 61; Rodríguez Rojas, *Cultura y contra-cultura*; Salomón, *La violencia en Honduras 1980–1993*; Smutt and Miranda, *El fenómeno de las pandillas*; José Luis Cruz Rocha's excellent articles on youth and gangs in *Envío Digital*, http://www.envio.org.ni; Wolseth, *Jesus and the Gang*; Rodgers, "Living in the Shadow of Death"; Rodgers, "Slum Wars of the 21st Century"; Savenije, *Maras y barras*; and Cruz et al., *Exclusión social jóvenes y pandillas*.

25. Reguillo Cruz, *Emergencia de culturas juveniles*, ii. In his thought-provoking book about

gangs in Ecuador, which are far less violent than those in Guatemala, Mauro Cerbino suggests we redefine symbols of violence in clothing and other items such as graffiti in order to envision these as life-confirming confrontations with cruelty and aggression that contradict "the logic of death, assault and rape." Cerbino, *Pandillas juveniles*, 94.

26. Koonings and Kruijt, *Armed Actors, Organized Violence and State Failure in Latin America*, 1.

27. Savenije, in *Maras y barras*, argues that the Central American wars are not a major factor in explaining the Maras, because Honduras has violent Maras and had no war.

28. Cruz, *Street Gangs in Central America*.

29. Zilberg, "'Fools Banished from the Kingdom'"; Narváez Gutiérrez, *Ruta transnacional*.

30. Taylor, "Between Global Process and Local Knowledge"; Abu-Lughod, "The Interpretation of Culture(s) after Television."

31. Wacquante, *Las cárceles de la miseria*.

32. Desjarlais and Kleinman, "Violence and Demoralization in the New World Order."

33. Ariès, *Centuries of Childhood*; Esteva, "Beyond Development and Modernity."

34. Ferguson, *Expectations of Modernity*, 138.

35. The influential sociologist Anthony Giddens describes modernity in the following terms: "At its simplest, modernity is a shorthand term for modern society or industrial civilization. Portrayed in more detail, it is associated with (1) a certain set of attitudes towards the world, the idea of the world as an open transformation by human intervention; (2) a complex of economic institutions, especially industrial production and a market economy; (3) a certain range of political institutions, including the nation-state and mass democracy. Largely as a result of these characteristics, modernity is vastly more dynamic than any previous type of social order. It is a society—more technically, a complex of institutions—which unlike any preceding cultures lives in the future rather than the past." Giddens, *Conversations*, 94. Scholars in studies that range from literature to history have implicitly responded to the blind eye that Giddens and many intellectuals turn to the relationship between violence and capitalism on the one hand and modernity and liberalism on the other. See, for example, Mehta, "Liberal Strategies of Exclusion." Candace Vogler and Pathchen Markell note that the distinction between liberalism's "mobility of abstraction and immobilizing grip of the concrete" is a false dilemma that sustains a "tired controversy between those who celebrate the power of liberalism's normative content to transcend its own historical limitations and those for whom the history of liberalism's concrete social forms merely revels the essential bankruptcy of liberal ideas." Vogler and Markell, "Introduction," 8.

That modernity is predicated on colonial violence is an old idea. For examples, see Dussel, "The Postmodernism Debate"; "Eric Williams and the Postcolonial Caribbean: A Special Issue," *Callaloo* 20 (1997): 12–34; and Rodney, *How Europe Underdeveloped Africa*; as well as Marable, *How Capitalism Underdeveloped Black America*.

36. Casal, *Reseña de la situación general de Guatemala, 1863*.

37. *Primer Congreso Pedagógico Centroamericano*, 391.

38. Ibid., 250–59.

39. González Orellana, *Historia de la educación*, 232.

40. Santos Chocano, *Minerva en América*.

41. Arévalo, "Las cuatro raíces del servilismo."

42. Levenson, *Hacer la juventud*.

43. In 2000, approximately 21 percent of boys and 11.1 percent of girls ages five to fourteen in Guatemala were working. The majority of working children were found in the agricultural sector (62.6 percent), followed by services (23.4 percent), manufacturing (10.7 percent), and other sectors (3.2 percent). The majority of children participating in the labor force are of indigenous heritage and from rural areas. On average, children in the labor force work 6.5 hours per day and five days per week. Child labor mostly occurs in the informal sector and in small family enterprises. ILO, "Ficha País: Guatemala"; see PAMI, *Menores trabajadores en labores de alto riesgo*; and Chapeton and Mazariegos, *Niñez trabajadora en la frontera del peligro*.

44. National Labor Committee and Center for the Studies and Support of Local Development, *Harvest of Shame*.

45. Hecht, *Minor Omissions*, 8.

46. On the trauma of the war, see Falla, *Masacres de la selva*; Melville and Lykes, "Guatemalan Indian Children"; Green, *Fear as a Way of Life*; Zur, "Remembering and Forgetting"; Lopes, "Factors Associated with Poor Mental Health."

47. Felman and Laub, *Testimony*. At age eleven, Dominga, the subject of the documentary *Discovering Dominga*, arrived in Iowa as an adopted child after having survived the massacre at Dos Erres. When she tried to talk about the massacre, people thought she was crazy. Her true stories were beyond the imagination of the people in Iowa to whom she spoke.

48. Connerton, *How Societies Remember*, 103.

49. La Capra, *Representing the Holocaust*; La Capra, *Writing Trauma, Writing History*; Khanna, *Dark Continents*.

50. Bourdieu, *Acts of Resistance*, 40.

51. Caruth, *Unclaimed Experience*, 3–4.

52. Caruth, "Violence and Time." See also La Capra, *Representing the Holocaust*.

53. Martín-Baró, *Writings for a Liberation Psychology*, 135.

54. Like all sources, oral histories are subjective ones generated by people in certain historical conjunctures. The debates about oral, and other, sources are many. Among other studies that discuss these are Thompson et al., "The Memory and Historical Debates"; Portelli, *The Order Has Been Carried Out*; Hodges and Radstone, *Contested Pasts*; Passerini, *Memory and Totalitarianism*; and Abrams, *Oral History Theory*.

55. Sassen, "The Global City," 111.

1. Death and Politics, 1950s–2000s

1. Author interviews with Victor, Guatemala City, 2002.

2. Sieder, *Guatemala after the Peace Accords*; Jonas, *Of Centaurs and Doves*; Jonas, "Democratization through Peace"; Stanley and Holiday, "Broad Participation, Diffuse Responsibility."

3. Scott, *Weapons of the Weak*, 44.

4. Author interview with Isabel Ruiz, Guatemala City, 2010.

5. The other genocide was against the Aché in Paraguay, 1968–72.

6. In the introduction to their edited volume *Violence in War and Peace, an Anthology*,

Nancy Scheper-Hughes and Phillip Bourgois give thoughtful consideration to the problems of defining violence.

7. Hannah Arendt, Frantz Fanon, and Georges Sorel—the three intellectuals commonly referenced on the topic "violence"—wrote about it in relationship to politics, without defining the word. Against a background of wars and revolutions, Arendt opposed violence in her aim to counter the notion that "political power flows out of a gun." She vigorously disputed the unification of power and violence. Within the specific context of colonialism, Fanon analyzed the sociocultural and psychological powers of violence and resistance. For Sorel, violence came down to a general strike, which he defended and contrasted with the uselessness of labor negotiations. See Arendt, "Reflections on Violence"; Sorel, *Reflections on Violence*; and Fanon, *Wretched of the Earth*.

Subsequent writers have emphasized the multiplicity of the structures, modes, uses, and meanings of violence. In "The Power of Violence in War and Peace," the anthropologist Philippe Bourgois draws on his research and that of scholars such as Bourdieu to classify four types of violence: direct political, structural, symbolic, and everyday. More recently, in his book *Empire of Sacrifice: The Religious Origins of American Violence*, Jon Pahl argues for a "maximalist approach" that defines violence to be "any harm to or destruction of life, whether intended by individuals or enacted by systems of language, policy and practice" because "people die just as surely from unjust systems as they do from a gunshot wound" (9). His point is particularly relevant in a world that mistakes peace for the lack of a war and defines nonviolence as nonphysical, yet it fails to capture the significance and immediacy of sharper physical and mental forms.

8. Brie, "Emancipation and the Left," 241.

9. Taussig, "Culture of Terror."

10. Toriello Garrido, *Guatemala*; McClintock, *The American Connection*; Gareau, *State Terrorism and the United States*; Doyle, "The Atrocity Files."

11. Aguilera Peralta et al., *Dialéctica del terror*.

12. Foucault, *Discipline and Punish*, 33–34.

13. Foucault, *The History of Sexuality*, 1:136.

14. Mbembe, "Necropolitics."

15. Foucault, *The History of Sexuality*, 1:138.

16. Foucault, *Discipline and Punish*, 33–34.

17. Ibid., 57–58.

18. Ibid., 49.

19. The various ways the war is dated in Guatemala suggests how much violence worsened. Many designate the war as the period from the early 1960s, when the conflict between an armed Left and the military started. Others refer to the military escalation of violence and the subsequent suspension of the Constitution in the 1980s as the war. *Memoria del silencio*, the twelve-volume study of war sponsored by the United Nations, dates it from 1960.

20. Agamben, *Means without End*, 154.

21. Koonz, *The Nazi Conscience*.

22. Aguilera Peralta et al., *Dialéctica del terror*; Kobrak, *State Violence in Guatemala*.

23. REMHI, *Informe*, 151.

24. The intensity of the Guatemalan Communist Party's influence from its 1949 founding until the late 1970s is documented in Grandin, *The Last Colonial Massacre*; and in Levenson-Estrada, *Trade Unionists against Terror*.

25. Berryman, *The Religious Roots of Revolution*; Melville and Melville, *Whose Heaven, Whose Earth?*

26. Gonzáles Orellana, *Historia de la educación*; Arévalo, *La pedagogía de la personalidad*.

27. Gutiérrez, *Sindicalistas y aparatos de control estatal*.

28. The assassinations in 1979 of well-known figures such as Manuel Colom Argueta, founder of the Frente Unido de la Revolución (United Revolutionary Front, FUR), and Alberto Fuertes Mohr, a Social Democrat, are two cases out of hundreds of "disappeared" and assassinated members of reformist electoral parties that sought change through legal means in the 1954–80 period.

29. The picture that can be drawn from Mario Payeras's *El trueno en la ciudad* that the urban Left was absolutely destroyed in 1981 is belied by the continued appearance of revolutionary literature, the participation of clandestine guerrilla members in any remaining social organizations, and the multiple kidnappings of active members of the revolutionary groups in the city throughout the 1980s and 1990s.

30. Author conversations with Miguel Ángel Albizures and with Guatemala City residents, 1983 through mid-1990s.

31. Levenson-Estrada, *Trade Unionists against Terror*, 49.

32. Fundación Madrid Paz y Solidaridad, "Operation Sofía."

33. Payeras, *El trueno en la ciudad*.

34. Konefal, *For Every Indio Who Falls*.

35. Commission for Historical Clarification, "Guatemala: Memory of Silence," 33. The war peaked in 1984 and it continued until the Peace Accords were signed in 1996, with the guerrillas formally laying down their arms. "State forces" refers to the machinery of repression's thousands of employees. This apparatus has been a large and flexible one, capable of changing methods and inventing new paramilitary units when necessary. It has included intelligence units in the National Defense Staff and in the Presidential General Staff, National Police (Criminal Investigations Department), Treasury Guard, and Mobile Military Police. During the war, military commissioners made the intelligence gathering of Civil Patrols one among many of their duties.

36. Mack Chang and Worby, *Política institucional*.

37. Falla, *Masacres de la selva*.

38. Zones marked red on military maps were considered guerrilla territory, and those colored pink and yellow had ties with the guerrillas.

39. Remijne, *Memorias de violencia*, 1–47.

40. Vela Castañeda, "Los peletones de la muerte." This genocide does not fit well into Foucault's formulation of twentieth-century wars and genocide as being "on behalf of the existence of everyone." "Entire populations," he continued, "are mobilized for the purpose of wholesale slaughter in the name of life necessity: massacres have become vital." Foucault, *The History of Sexuality*, 1:137.

41. Garrard-Burnett, *Terror in the Land of the Holy Spirit*, 65.

42. Porras Castejón, *Las huellas de Guatemala*, 68; author interviews with Guatemala City residents, 1984.

43. CEH, *Memoria del silencio*, vol. 1.

44. Ibid., 2:51–55, 169–71. "El testimonio del soldado," *El Periódico*, October 31, 2010.

45. Archdiocese of Guatemala, *Guatemala, Never Again!*, 131.

46. *Tribunal permanente de los pueblos indígenas*, 151.

47. There were 50,000 weapons for 900,000 patrollers. Authorities formed no patrols in Guatemala City; however, in a few large towns near the city, they initiated *patrullas escolares* (school patrols) composed of fourth-, fifth-, and sixth-graders. The PACs functioned to make hundreds of thousands of Guatemalans collaborators in the counterinsurgency war. They were first organized in 1981, and by 1983, 900,000 male Guatemalans were patrollers; their numbers declined to 200,000 by the time the 1996 Peace Accords dissolved them. For more on the patrols, see Americas Watch Report, *Civil Patrols in Guatemala*; and Remijne, *Memorias de violencia*.

48. CEH, *Memoria del silencio*, 2:188.

49. Ibid., 5:42.

50. Archdiocese of Guatemala, *Guatemala, Never Again!*, 30.

51. CEH, *Memoria del silencio*, 6:20.

52. Archdiocese of Guatemala, *Guatemala, Never Again!*, 137.

53. CEH, *Memoria del silencio*, 6:45–56.

54. Archdiocese of Guatemala, *Guatemala, Never Again!*, 75.

55. For the calculated nature of the military action, see the interviews with officers in the pathbreaking study by the lawyer Jennifer Schirmer, *Guatemala Military Project*, 44; see also Sanford, *Buried Secrets*.

56. *Tribunal permanente de los pueblos indígenas*, 147. In Finca San Francisco, six hundred soldiers, accompanied by a helicopter of military officials and supplies that landed in the aldea's soccer field, entered the hamlet on July 17, 1982, as part of La Victoria '82. They went house to house gathering women and children, whom they shut up in the local church before they pushed the men and elderly inside a small building and sacked the empty houses of their possessions, such as household wares, food, and radio/cassette players. At noon, a military official announced that they would "celebrate a fiesta" and told two villagers to get two bulls. At two o'clock, soldiers pulled the women out of the church in small groups. The women fled back into their houses, followed by soldiers, who raped them before setting fire to them and the houses. Then the soldiers took the boys and girls out of the church. A man who managed to escape testified that "after they killed our wives, they took out our children [from the church] by the feet like sacks. . . . Little ones, 10-, 8- and 5-year-olds and dashed them against poles, and their brains came out like pieces of corn dough. I had 6 children, they all died, and my wife too. Nobody stayed alive.

"The soldiers proceeded to kill the elderly by cutting their throats with dull knives. . . . Once the soldiers had concluded the massacre, they put the bulls over the fire and cooked them and ate and drank and danced to the music that they played out of the radio/cassette players they had taken out of the houses. They burned everything before they left." *Memoria*, 7:344–53. See also Falla, *Negreaba de Zopilotes*.

57. Either this is "true," or it is, as Theodor Adorno has suggested, an exaggeration as a means of reaching the truth. Adorno, *Negative Dialectics*.

58. McAllister, "An Indian Dawn."

59. Mack Chang et al., *Dónde está el futuro*; Mack Chang and Worby, *Política institucional*.

60. Gonzáles, *Se cambió el tiempo*, 283–91.

61. Echeverría, "Los niños y niñas sobrevivientes de las massacres en Guatemala."

62. Chinchilla and Hamilton, *Seeking Community in a Global City*; Chinchilla et al., "Central Americans and the Los Angeles Community."

63. Hagedorn, *People and Folks*.

64. Vigil, *Barrio Gangs*; Sanchez Jankowski, *Islands in the Street*; Rodriguez, *Always Running*; Álvarez, *The Power of the Zoot*; Kelley, *Black Rebels*.

65. Vigil, *Gangs and Non-gang Families*, 39–53.

66. Campo-Flores, "The Most Dangerous Gang in America," 4; Arana, "How the Street Gangs Took Central America."

67. Hayden, *Street Wars*. Patricia Foxen writes about the recontextualization of memory in *In Search of Providence*, 202–50.

68. Fritzsche, "Global History and the Bounded Subjects."

69. Vigil, *A Rainbow of Gangs*, 131–45; Hayden, *Street Wars*.

70. Narváez Gutiérrez, *Ruta transnacional*; Chinchilla and Hamilton, *Seeking Community in a Global City*.

71. Vigil, *A Rainbow of Gangs*, 41.

72. Dunn, *The Gangs of Los Angeles*, 217–18.

73. Quoted in Narváez Gutiérrez, *Ruta transnacional*, 87.

74. Ernesto Miranda, National Public Radio World News, March 17, 2005. Miranda was murdered when he was deported back to El Salvador after quitting MS-13 in Los Angeles.

75. Angel-face.com/tag/ (accessed January 2005).

76. United Nations Population Division, "World Urbanization Prospects: The 2001 Revision."

77. Gellert and Palma C., *Precaridad urbana*, 30; Moran Merida, *Condiciones de vida*.

78. Bastos and Camus, *Sombras de una batalla*; Gellert, "Migration and the Displaced."

79. Most of the discussion about war and memory in Guatemala has concerned collective memory: see Hinan, "To Remember or Forget?"; Sieder, "War, Peace, and the Politics of Memory"; Hale, "Consciousness, Violence, and the Politics of Memory"; Oglesby, "Educating Citizens"; Wilson, "Violent Truths"; Hamber and Wilson, "Symbolic Closure"; and Jelin, *State Repression and the Struggle for Memory*, 33.

80. I thank the writer Mary Jo McConahay for alerting me to the importance of unspecific fear.

81. Núñez, *De la ciudad al barrio*.

82. Gellert and Palma C., *Precaridad urbana*.

83. AVANCSO, *Aquí corre la bola*, 86.

84. Author interview with Juan Miguel Fuentes, Guatemala City, 2001.

85. Núñez, *De la ciudad al barrio*, 167.

86. United Nations Development Program, Human Development Report for Central America, 2010.

87. U.S. Department of State, 2009 *Human Rights Reports*.
88. Oficina de Derechos Humanos del Arzobispado de Guatemala, "Prevención y abordaje de tratos crueles, inhumanos o degradantes en las cárceles de Guatemala," 2005.
89. Ramírez and Paz, *Diagnóstico de conflictividad*.
90. Prophettei et al., "Violence in Guatemala."
91. Oglesby, "Historical Memory."
92. Sanford, *Guatemala*.
93. *El Periódico*, August 29, 2010.

2. 1980s: The Gangs to Live For

1. Palomo, *Efectos de un fenómeno natural en un país subdesarrollado*.
2. Morales, *Estudio comparativo de la estructura de dos comunidades*.
3. Interviews with the priest Padre Adrián Bastiaensen, cited in AVANCSO, *Aquí corre la bola*, 11–14.
4. Morales, *Estudio comparativo*, 55.
5. See Castoriadis, *Figures of the Unthinkable*.
6. Levenson-Estrada, *Trade Unionists against Terror*.
7. Bourdieu, *Outline of a Theory of Practice*.
8. Discussions with young people led me to think that they understood brek to be part of international youth, as well as African American, style.
9. Author interviews with Aníbal López, Guatemala City, 1993–94, 2000.
10. Death squad state terror continued following military urban counterinsurgency in 1981. On the first day of the 1984 Coca-Cola occupation, a factory worker who was a clandestine member of the communist Partido Guatemalteco de Trabajo (Guatemalan Party of Labor, PGT) was "disappeared." Over the coming months and years, leaders of the GAM were kidnapped and tortured.
11. Author interview with Guatemala City colegio student, 1987.
12. Author interview with Carlos Soto, Guatemala City, 1987; and Víctor, Guatemala City, 2002. The movie reference was to *The Naked Jungle*, a famous 1954 American thriller well known to Soto's generation. It told of the attack of the "Marabunta," an unforgettable horde of red ants who eat the flesh of human beings, on Charlton Heston and Eleanor Parker at a cacao plantation in Peru, which Soto had remembered as Brazil when we spoke.
13. *El Gráfico*, October 6, 1986.
14. *Prensa Libre*, October 8, 1986.
15. Author interview with Aura Marina Marcucci, Guatemala City, 1987.
16. Author interviews with Welfare Secretariat social workers, Guatemala City, 1987.
17. Author interview with Transgresión Juvenil official, National Police, 1987.
18. Garrard-Burnett, *Terror in the Land of the Holy Spirit*.
19. Author interview with Welfare Secretariat counselor, Guatemala City, 1987.
20. "La música roc y sus peligros," mimeo, Guatemala, 1987.
21. Author interview with Roberto Morales del Pinar, Guatemala City, 1987.
22. Plan Nacional de la Juventud, *Fenómeno de las Maras*.
23. AVANCSO, *Por sí mismos*.
24. Researchers' interviews with Silvio, Guatemala City, 1987.

25. Researchers' interviews with Lupe, Guatemala City, 1987.

26. Researchers' interviews with Yolanda, Guatemala City, 1987.

27. Researchers' interviews with Rafael, Guatemala City, 1987.

28. Researchers' interviews with Hernán, Guatemala City, 1987.

29. Researchers' interviews with Marvin, Guatemala City, 1987.

30. Researchers' interviews with Berlin, Guatemala City, 1987.

31. Researchers' interviews with Lucia, Guatemala City, 1987.

32. Author interviews with Welfare Secretariat social workers, Guatemala City, 1987.

33. Researchers' interviews with Tono, Guatemala City, 1987.

34. Researchers' interviews with Calixto, Guatemala City, 1987.

35. Researchers' interviews with Maritza, Guatemala City, 1987.

36. Researchers' interviews with Joel, Guatemala City.

37. Researchers' interviews with Rocío, Guatemala City, 1987.

38. Researchers' interviews with América, Guatemala City, 1987.

39. Researchers' interviews with Isabel, Guatemala City, 1987.

40. Author interviews with Coca-Cola workers, Guatemala City, 1987.

41. Núñez, De la ciudad al barrio, 176–77.

3. 1990s and Beyond: The Gangs to Die For

The source for this chapter's third epigraph is Colussi, "Entrevista a Rodolfo Kepfer."

1. Author interviews with Víctor, Guatemala City, 2002.

2. In terms of personnel and weapons, these companies form the largest security force in the nation, and it has been estimated that 30 percent of them have operated illegally, without any authorization or control of weapons. Banco Internacional de Desarrollo, Diagnóstico sobre la situación actual.

3. Ranum, "Diagnóstico Nacional Guatemala."

4. Prensa Libre, March 13, 2006.

5. Manwaring, Street Gangs.

6. Ramírez Heredia, La Mara.

7. Medina and Mateu-Gelabert, Maras y pandillas; Demoscopía, Maras y pandillas.

8. USAID, "Central America and Mexico Gang Assessment."

9. Author interview with Alberto, Guatemala City, 1997.

10. Ranum, "Diagnóstico Nacional Guatemala"; Moser and McIlwaine, Encounters with Violence in Latin America.

11. Rodgers, Dying for It; Smutt and Miranda, El fenómeno de las pandillas; Winton, "With Gangs and Violence."

12. Author interviews with residents, Guatemala City, 1997–2007; Aragón y Asociados, Encuesta de opinión pública; Pellicer, "La semilla de las Maras"; Núñez, De la ciudad al barrio. Some neighborhoods are called colonias and others are called barrios. Barrios are usually older. Colonias sometimes have their origins in a planned urban development.

13. AVANCSO, Heridas en la sombra; author interviews with residents and street workers, 2002.

14. Author interview with the anthropologist Julia González, Guatemala City, 2003;

AVANCSO, *Heridas en la sombra*; Merino, "Políticas juveniles y rehabilitación de mareros en Guatemala," 90–93.

15. AVANCSO, *Heridas en la sombra*.

16. Corsetti, "Marked for Death."

17. Estrada-Levenson, interviews with residents, Tapachula, Mexico, 2010.

18. *Prensa Libre*, August 5, 2002; author interviews, Guatemala City, 2002.

19. Author interview with anonymous, Baltimore, 2011.

20. Author interviews with Pentecostal gang minister, Guatemala City, 2008.

21. Camus, "Primero de Julio," 49–65.

22. Ibid., 60.

23. Author interviews with Coca-Cola union leaders, Guatemala City, 2008.

24. Author interviews with Coca-Cola salesman, Guatemala City, 2008.

25. *Siglo Veintiuno*, March 12, 2003, and June 14, 2003.

26. *Prensa Libre*, March 25, 2009.

27. *Prensa Libre*, December 10, 2008.

28. Colussi, "Entrevista a Rodolfo Kepfer."

29. Author interviews with Guatemala City residents, Zone 6, 1997, 2003.

30. Author interviews with street workers, Guatemala City, 2008; *El Periódico*, 2010.

31. Author interviews in a crisis shelter, Guatemala City, 1997.

32. Author interviews with Padre Manolo Maquieira, SJ, Guatemala City, 2003. Padre Manolo started a work-training program in conjunction with the maquiladora owner Manuel Fernández to give selected youth, two-thirds of whom were female, scholarships to work at one of the maquiladora owned by Fernández's Grupo Koramsa.

33. Maquieira, "Juventud marginal," 66–72.

34. Author interview with Herbert Sánchez, Guatemala, 1997.

35. *Prensa Libre*, March 13, 2009.

36. Author interview with Luis Arturo, Guatemala City, 1997.

37. Zubillaga, "Un testimonio reflexivo."

38. Author interviews with Short, Guatemala City, 2002.

39. Tobar Estrada, *Entre mundos ajenos*. Robert Brenneman's *Homies and Hermanos* is based exclusively on interviews with ex–gang members.

40. Author interview with Carrito, Guatemala City, 2002.

41. Author interviews with Lima, CC, and Gato, Guatemala City, 2002.

42. Author interviews with Orquídia and Junior, Guatemala City, 2002.

43. Author interviews with Abel, Guatemala City, 2002.

44. *El Periódico*, May 11, 2003.

45. Author interviews with Short and Jonny, Guatemala City, 2002.

46. Author interviews with anonymous mareros, 2002.

47. Kinnvall, "Globalization and Religious Nationalism," 759.

48. Gonzáles, "La comunidad a través del dolor."

49. Maquieira, "Juventud marginal."

50. Author interview with Z, Guatemala City, 2007.

51. Author interviews with Jonny, 2002.

52. Tobar Estrada, *Entre mundos ajenos*, 46.

53. Maquieira, "Juventud marginal," 71.

54. Personal communications with Padre Manolo Maquieira and members of the Equipo de Estudios Urbanos, AVANCSO; author interview with Victor, Guatemala City, 2002.

55. Social worker interview with Rosa, Guatemala City, 2006.

56. Author interviews with Carolina, Chata, and Carmen, Antigua, Guatemala, 2003.

57. Author interviews with Maquieira, Guatemala City, 2003.

58. Arendt, *The Origins of Totalitarianism*, 276–302.

59. Children and youth living and earning their keep in the streets have a long history in Guatemala City. Until the 1980s, the narratives about them were often romantic ones that emphasized their competence and portrayed them as young workers titled by their vocation—such as "the shoe shiners" who gave money to their mothers and siblings. One example is Oscar Valiente Rodríguez's novel *La historia de un lustrador*. They were "little men." This discourse shifted following the United Nations 1979 "Year of the Child" at the same time that the population of totally destitute homeless children who permanently live in the streets grew as a direct consequence of the war. Casa Alianza, *Torture of Guatemalan Street Children*; Human Rights Watch, *Guatemala's Forgotten Children*; Panter-Brick, "Street Children, Human Rights, and Public Health."

Thomas Offit points out that many youth in Guatemala City's streets successfully work there and give money to their kin. Sometimes called "children in the streets," they are distinguished from "children of the streets," the impoverished street children captured in Nancy Leigh Tierney's work and to whom I refer. Offit, *Conquistadores de la Calle*; Tierney, *Robbed of Humanity*.

60. Author interviews with Guillermo, Minor, and Carlos, Guatemala City, 1997.

61. Author interview with Guillermo, Guatemala City, 1997.

62. Files, crisis shelter, Guatemala City.

63. *Susto* means sickness from fright, an illness of low energy and depression. It has been described as a sickness in which the soul separates from the body, and it has been defined as "trauma." Rubel et al., *Susto*; Castillo, *Culture and Mental Illness*.

64. Bastos and Camus, *Sombras de una batalla*.

65. File "Estuardo Edwin Mendoza," crisis shelter, Guatemala City, 1998.

66. Ibid.

67. La Capra, "Trauma, Absence, Loss"; Hernandez, "Winnicott's 'Fear of Breakdown'"; Caruth, *Unclaimed Experience*.

68. Among the many discussions on how people handle trauma, see Becker et al., "Memory, Trauma, and Embodied Distress"; Henry, "Violence and the Body"; Jenkins, "The Impress of Extremity"; and Taquela, "Memoria sin tiempo."

69. Author conversations with Estuardo Edwin Mendoza, Guatemala City, 1997.

70. Bourdieu, *Outline of a Theory of Practice*, 82.

71. Of twenty files of children with indigenous surnames who had come from the countryside to the city in the late 1980s or early 1990s—or whose parents had— several mentioned or alluded to the war, for example, one report noted that Juan Aj

Tzoc (pseudonym) was born in 1980 inside a *finca* in Santo Tomás, Quiche. It goes on to say, "His family was massacred. An elderly couple adopted him but when he discovered that he was not their son, he ran away." The file also noted that Juan had a "problem with alcohol." Files, crisis shelter.

72. Caruth, *Unclaimed Experience*, 24.
73. Bourdieu, *Outline of a Theory of Practice*, 72–95.

4. Democracy and Lock-Up

1. Memoria del Seminario, "La situación actual y perspectivas del trabajo psico-social," 82.
2. Author interview with TOM official, Guatemala City, 1987.
3. Author interviews with Nora Figueroa, social workers, and TOM officials, Guatemala City, 1987.
4. Memoria del Seminario, "La situación actual y perspectivas del trabajo psico-social, 69–88.
5. Monzón, *La educación de los transgresores en Guatemala*.
6. Garrard-Burnett and Stoll, *Rethinking Protestantism in Latin America*.
7. Author interviews with Aura Marina Marcucci and Juventud para Cristo officials, Guatemala City, 1987.
8. Author interviews with Casa Mi Hogar director and with Panamá, Guatemala City, 1987; files, Casa Mi Hogar.
9. Human Rights Watch, *Guatemala's Forgotten Children*, 73–83; Merino, "Guatemala."
10. Ramírez and Cetina, *Alternativas a la justicia penal y la prisión*.
11. Vela, *La reforma procesal penal en Guatemala*, 82.
12. Among many others, see Díaz García, "Aplicación del sistema progresivo"; Tzún Ajxup, "Ejecución de sentencia en el proceso penal guatemalteco"; Guzmán Cermeño, "La necesidad de institucionalizar programas para hacer efectiva la reinserción social del recluso"; Instituto de Estudios Comparados en Ciencias Penales de Guatemala, *Prisiones*; and Oficina de Derechos Humanos del Arzobispado de Guatemala, "Prevención y abordaje de tratos crueles, inhumanos o degradantes en las cárceles de Guatemala."
13. Salvatore and Aguirre, *The Birth of the Penitentiary in Latin America*, x–xi.
14. Informe de Verificación, *La situación penitenciaria en Guatemala*, 3.
15. Ordóñez Jonama, *La cárceles en Guatemala*. According to this angry and sarcastic study written by the legal historian Ramiro Ordóñez Jonama, interest in modern prison reform preceded Independence, when Spanish jurists brought new ideas in the 1780s. Legislation passed before and after Independence reflected concerns for the mental rehabilitation and physical hygiene of inmates and stipulated the abolition of certain physical punishments in detail. Prisoners needed to be sorted out and separated according the crimes committed, and they needed sunlight, sufficient living space, medical care, moral instruction, and work that served to set them right, as well as opportunity to provide labor for public works. Ordóñez Jonama highlights the writings of José Mariano Méndez, a nineteenth-century Presbyterian minister and doctor who was a pioneer of prison reform and admirer of Jeremy Ben-

tham whose 1845 treatise "Idea sobre lo que pueden ser las cárceles, para presos, detenidos y declarados Reos" explicated Bentham's critiques of British prisons in detail. Ordóñez Jonama's point is that no one paid it much attention.

16. López Martín, *Cien años de historia penitenciaria en Guatemala*, 8–25; Ordóñez Jonama, *Las cárceles en Guatemala*, 114–20.

17. The presidents Jorge Ubico y Castañeda, Juan José Arévalo Bermejo, and Jacobo Árbenz Guzmán noted the need for reform, and Ubico made use of prisoners to express the state's power as social engineer; these were brief political gestures. In his annual parade at the Campo de Mars, Ubico had prisoners parade alongside schoolchildren with military precision and even had a film produced about manufacturing within La Penitencia Central. The two new constitutions of post–Second World War Guatemala—the October 1944 Revolution's 1945 Constitution and the 1954 counter-Revolution's Constitution of 1965—both affirm that "prisons are centers that secure and promote the reform of the incarcerated . . . and in no case can inflict tortures, or any form of cohesion"; they itemize the separation of prisoners, training of personnel, installation of schools and workshops, and so on. Estrada González, *Rehabilitación social del delincuente*.

18. Ordóñez Jonama, *La cárceles en Guatemala*, 168.

19. López Martín, *Cien años de historia penitenciaria en Guatemala*, 33.

20. Paiz Barrios, "Análisis jurídico de los grupos etarios," 58–68.

21. Alegría Hernández, "Análisis jurídico de los aspectos negativos."

22. Human Rights Watch, *Guatemala's Forgotten Children*, 32.

23. Álvarez López, "Realidad del sistema penitenciario guatemalteco," 85; Vega Romero, "Estudio de las clases sociales y su repercussión," 44.

24. Quex Mucia, "Derechos humanos y constitucionales," 7.

25. Díaz García, "Aplicación del sistema progresivo"; Guzmán Cermeño, "La necesidad de institucionalizar programas para hacer efectiva la reinserción social del recluso"; Alegría Hernández, "Análisis jurídico de los aspectos negativos."

26. *Prensa Libre*, September 4, 2006; *El Periódico*, September 13, 2006.

27. *Prensa Libre*, March 29, 2004; Álvarez López, "Realidad del sistema penitenciario guatemalteco," 57–84.

28. *Prensa Libre*, February 23, 2003.

29. Salazar Similox, *Una aproximación al fenómeno de las Maras y pandillas en Centroamérica*.

30. Tobar Estrada, *Entre mundos ajenos*.

31. Álvarez López, "Realidad del sistema penitenciario guatemalteco," 65.

32. Author conversations with Rodolfo Kepfer, Guatemala City, 2011; Cabrera Flores, "Cultura de castigo en Guatemala."

33. *Inforpress Centroamericano*, February 23, 2003.

34. *Inforpress Centroamericano*, February 13, 2003; *Prensa Libre*, April 14, 2003; Quex Mucia, "Derechos humanos y constitucionales," 28–35.

35. *El Periódico*, December 2, 2010.

36. *Prensa Libre*, August 16, 2005; *El Periódico*, August 16, 2005.

37. Echeverría et al., "Human Rights Violations in Guatemala," 84–86; there was no media that did not cover this outbreak.

38. *El Periódico*, August 17, 2005.

39. *Prensa Libre*, August 16, 2005.

40. *Prensa Libre*, September 7, 2005. The most vocal critic of the growing calls for mano dura came from the internationally known Pentecostal minister Nicky Cruz, once a leader of New York's Puerto Rican Mau Mau gang, who arrived in Guatemala City in late August to inaugurate the operations of the Nicky Cruz Foundation. He spoke publicly against Berger's lack of attention to youth, warned against iron fist policies, and called the mareros "innocents." Despite the fact that Cruz's eloquent book *¡Corre! Nicky ¡Corre!* has been widely read in the city since it was published in its Spanish edition in 1972, and in spite of Cruz's religious affinities, his remarks received almost no publicity.

41. *El Periódico*, September 23, 2005; *Prensa Libre*, September 23, 2005.

42. Castillo Chacón, "Un poco de historia," 44.

43. The Office of the Human Rights Ombudsman started to investigate the takeover three months later and had cited two brothers as part of an assassination team within the National Police. These two brothers were machine-gunned to death in June 2008. The UN Commission Internacional contra la Impunidad en Guatemala (CICIG) started to investigate in early 2009 and brought charges against Vielmann, and against others who were under suspicion for having taken part in the seizure. The wife of a prisoner who served as a witness to the CICIG investigation was assassinated in September 2009. *El Periódico*, *La Hora*, *Prensa Libre*, July–August 2010; *El Universal*, April 1, 2007.

44. *Guatemala Hoy*, February 2007; *Siglo Veintiuno*, February 27, 2007; *New York Times*, March 5, 2007. Crime is part of the highest offices of the government. A few examples among hundreds: President Alfonso Portillo (2000–2004) faces extradition to the United States for embezzling tens of millions of dollars' worth of public funds; two directors of the National Civil Police, the head of the Anti-narcotics Unit, and an attorney general have had to resign (though they have not been brought up on charges) because of their connections with drug trafficking.

Impunity is a guarantee. With one of the highest crime rates in the world, Guatemala has one of the lowest criminal conviction rates: less than 2 percent. In 2007, the United Nations established an international commission to investigate major cases of institutional corruption and organized crime that is deeply entrenched in the state. The 186-member CICIG works under the umbrella of the UN but operates under Guatemalan law to investigate criminal networks and assist local investigators and police in developing prosecutable cases. It has been responsible for removing hundreds of police officers and fifty police chiefs with links to organized crime. In 2010, the head of the CICIG in Guatemala, Carlos Castresana, resigned to protest President Álvaro Colom's appointment of a new attorney widely known for his connections with drugs rings.

45. Alston, "Civil and Political Rights"; *La Hora*, March 24, 2010.

46. Author interview with Kepfer, Guatemala City, 2010; *La Prensa*, March 4, 2009; *El Periódico*, March 4, 2009; *La Hora*, March 11, 2009.

47. *El Periódico*, March 14, 2009.

48. *El Periódico*, April 16, 2009; *Prensa Libre*, April 16, 2009; *La Hora*, April 19, 2009.

49. *El Periódico*, April 24, 2010; *Prensa Libre*, April 24, 2010; *La Hora*, May 5, 2010.

50. Foucault, *Discipline and Punish*, 30.

51. The story makes the rounds that the political campaigns of those claiming to fight crime are all funded by it.

52. Although he lost in the first round, Giammattei, director of the federal penitentiary system and hero of the 2005 El Pavón assault, ran as the presidential candidate in 2007 as a man who "took control" and could "take control."

5. Open Ending

1. Good behavior means having "served" well. According to a Mara leader, explaining that some leave, "You have to ask others and need to have your merits done, that is, what talks in your favor, like killing someone or having done this, or having done that." Quoted in Brenneman, "From Homie to *Hermano*," 114–59. See also O'Neill, "The Reckless Will."

2. Levenson-Estrada, *Trade Unionists against Terror*, 143–75.

3. El Shaddai Ministries is an ultraconservative group that provides a moral justification for free-market capitalism, using an argument that incorporates philosophies from Saint Augustine to Max Weber. El Shaddai Ministries launched its leader, Harold Caballeros, as a presidential candidate. The group has a huge membership among all social classes, which includes such important officials as the head of the National Civil Police. It may be one of the most active political organizations in the country.

4. *Prensa Libre*, August 17, 2005.

5. Vásquez, "Saving Souls Transnationally."

6. Author conversations with Guatemala City social workers, Guatemala City, 2007.

7. Viktor E. Frankl, author of the widely read *Man's Search for Meaning*, developed the so-called Third School of Psychotherapy in Vienna before the Second World War. His own subsequent spiritual survival in a concentration camp became the basis of a new kind of therapy called logotherapy.

8. Author conversations with Herbert Sánchez, San Juan, Sacatepéquez, 1997.

9. Author interviews with Luis, Rolando, Alfredo, and José, Guatemala City, 2003.

10. For a portrait of this extraordinary immigration of children in search of their relatives, see Sonia Nazario's award-winning book *Enrique's Journey*.

11. Campbell and Dryer, "Death by Deportation."

12. Proceedings of AS95619036 in Denver, Colorado, presided over by Judge James Vandello. *Edgar Chocoy Guzmán v. Immigration and Naturalization Service*, February 2004.

13. *El Periódico*, June 3, 2009.

14. *La Hora*, June 13, 2009.

15. Caruth, *Unclaimed Experience*.

16. Author interview with Estela, Guatemala City, 2011.

17. *El Periódico*, November 30, 2008.

18. *El Periódico*, April 6, April 18, May 24, June 3, 2009.

19. *El Periódico*, April 25, 2009.

20. *El Periódico*, May 28, 2010. In 2011 yet another artist, the twenty-four-year-old Caja Lúdica founder and performer Victor Arnoldo Levia Borrayo, was shot to death.

BIBLIOGRAPHY

Primary Documents

Comisión para el Esclarecimiento Histórico (CEH). *Memoria del silencio.* Guatemala City: United Nations Office of Project Services, 1999.

Commission for Historical Clarification. "Guatemala: Memory of Silence. Report of the Commission for Historical Clarification: Conclusions and Recommendations." Guatemala City, 2000.

Newspapers and Magazines

El Gráfico
El Periódico
El Universal
Inforpress Centroamericano
La Hora
Prensa Libre
Siglo Veintiuno

Interviews

Abel. Interview. Guatemala City. 2002.

Alberto. Interviews. Guatemala City. 1997.

Albizures, Miguel Ángel. Interviews. 1997.

Alfredo. Interview. Guatemala City. 2003.

América. Interview. Guatemala City. 1987.

Anonymous. Interview. Baltimore. 2011.

Augustín. Interview. Guatemala City. 2003.

Berlin. Researchers' interviews. Guatemala City. 1987.

Calixto. Researchers' interviews. Guatemala City. 1987.

Carolina, Chata, and Carmen. Interviews. Antigua, Guatemala. 2003.

Carrito. Interview. Guatemala City. 2002.

Casa Mi Hogar director. Interview. Guatemala City. 1987.

Ceta. Interview. Guatemala City. 2003.

Coca-Cola salesman. Interview. Guatemala City. 2008.

Coca-Cola union leaders. Interviews. Guatemala City. 2008.

Coca-Cola workers. Interviews. Guatemala City. 1987–2010.

Duarte. Interview. Guatemala City. 2003.

Enrique. Interview. Guatemala City. 2003.

Estela. Interview. Guatemala City. 2010.

Figueroa, Nora. Interview. Guatemala City. 1987.

Fuentes, Juan Miguel. Interviews. Guatemala City. 1997.

González Duras, Julia. Interview. Guatemala City. 2003.

Guatemala City colegio students. Interviews. Guatemala City. 1987.

Guatemala City Crisis Shelter. Interviews. 1997–98, 2003.

Guatemala City residents. Interviews. Various parts of the city. 1987–2011.

Guatemala City social workers. Interviews. Guatemala City. 1997, 2008.

Guatemala City street workers. Interviews. Guatemala City. 1996–97, 2002–3, 2008.

Guillermo, Minor, and Carlos. Interviews. Guatemala City. 1997.

Hernán. Researchers' interviews. Guatemala City. 1987.

Isabel. Interview. Guatemala City. 1987.

Joel. Researchers' interviews. Guatemala City. 1987.

Jonny and Short. Interviews. Guatemala City. 2002.

José. Interviews. Guatemala City. 1997, 2003.

Juventud para Cristo office worker. Interview. Guatemala City. 1987.

Kepfer, Rodolfo. Interviews. Guatemala City. 2002, 2010.

Lima, CC, and Gato. Interviews. Guatemala City. 2002.

Litegua. Interview. Guatemala City. 2003.

López, Aníbal. Interviews. Guatemala City. 1993–94, 2000.

López García, Carlos. Interview. Guatemala City. 2000.

Lucia. Interview. Guatemala City. 1987.

Lucky. Interview. Guatemala City. 2003.

Luis. Interview. Guatemala City. 2003.

Luis Arturo. Interview. Guatemala City. 1997.

Lupe. Researchers' interviews. Guatemala City. 1987.

Marcucci, Aura Marina. Interview. Guatemala City. 1987.

Maritza. Researchers' interviews. Guatemala City. 1987.

Marvin. Researchers' interviews. Guatemala City. 1987.

Maquieira, Padre Manolo, SJ. Interviews. Guatemala City. 2003.

Mendoza, Estuardo Edwin. Interview. Guatemala City. 1997.

Mixco street workers. Interviews. Mixco. 1997.

Morales del Pinar, Roberto. Interview. Guatemala City. 1987.

Noel. Interview. Guatemala City. 2003.

Orquídia and Junior. Interviews. Guatemala City. 2002.

Panamá. Interviews. Guatemala City. 1987.

Pentecostal gang minister. Interviews. Guatemala City. 2008.

Rafael. Researchers' interviews. Guatemala City. 1987.

Rocío. Researchers' interviews. Guatemala City. 1987.

Rolando. Interview. Guatemala City. 2003.

Rosa. Social worker's interview. Guatemala City. 2006.

Ruiz, Isabel. Interview. Guatemala City. 2010.

Sánchez, Herbert. Interview. San Juan, Sacatepéquez, Guatemala. 1997.

Short. Interviews. Guatemala City. 2002.

Silvio. Researchers' interview. Guatemala City. 1987.

Skinny. Interview. Guatemala City. 2002.

Soto, Carlos. Interviews. Guatemala City. 1987.

Tapachula, Mexico residents. Interviews conducted by Ana Estrada-Levenson. 2010.

TOM official. Interview. Guatemala City. 1987.

Tono. Personal interviews. Guatemala City. 1987.

Transgresión Juvenil police official. Interview. 1987.

Victor. Interviews. Guatemala City. 2002.

Welfare Secretariat counselor. Interview. Guatemala City. 1987.

Welfare Secretariat social workers. Interviews. Guatemala City. 1987.

Yolanda. Researchers' interviews. Guatemala City. 1987.

Z. Interview. Guatemala City. 2007.

Secondary Sources

Abrams, Lynn. *Oral History Theory*. London: Routledge, 2010.

Abu-Lughod, Lila. "The Interpretation of Culture(s) after Television." *Representations* 59 (1997): 109–34.

Adorno, Theodor. *Negative Dialectics*. New York: Routledge, 1990.

———. *Minima Moralia: Reflections on a Damaged Life*. London: Verso, 2006.

Agamben, Giorgio. *Means without End*. Minneapolis: University of Minnesota Press, 2000.

Aguilera Peralta, Gabriel, Jorge Romero Imery, Enrique Torres-Lezama, and Ricardo Galindo Gallardo. *Dialéctica del terror en Guatemala*. San José, Costa Rica: EDUCA, 1981.

Album de Minerva. Vol. 7. Guatemala City: Tipografía Nacional, 1907.

Alegría Hernández, Jeammy Corina. "Análisis jurídico de los aspectos negativos del internamiento de niños y adolescentes." Tesis de Maestría en Derecho Penal, Guatemala Universidad de San Carlos, 2008.

Alston, Philip. "Civil and Political Rights, including the Questions of Disappearances and Summary Executions, Report of the Special Rapporteur on Extrajudicial, Summary or Arbitrary Executions." Addendum "Mission to Guatemala." August 21–25, 2006.

Álvarez, Luis, *The Power of the Zoot: Youth Culture and Resistance in World War I*. Berkeley: University of California Press, 2008.

Álvarez López, Juan Alberto. "Realidad del sistema penitenciario guatemalteco en el Departamento de Guatemala y la falta de atención especial en los centros penitenciarios." Tesis de Licenciatura, Guatemala, Facultad de Ciencias Jurídicas y Sociales, Universidad Rafael Landívar, 2001.

Americas Watch Report. *Civil Patrols in Guatemala*. Washington, D.C.: Americas Watch Committee, 1986.

Anderson, Elijah. *Code of the Street: Decency, Violence, and the Moral Life of the Inner City*. New York: W. W. Norton, 1999.

Aragón y Asociados. *Encuesta de opinión pública sobre prevención de la violencia y delincuencia juvenil*. Guatemala City: Aragón y Asociados, 2003.

Arana, Ana. "How the Street Gangs Took Central America." *Foreign Affairs*, May/June 2005.

Arce, Manuel Valenzuela, et al., eds. *Las Maras: Identidades juveniles al límite*. Mexico City: Universidad Autónoma Metropolitana, 2007.

Archdiocese of Guatemala. *Guatemala, Never Again!* Marymount, N.Y.: Orbis Books, 1999.

Arendt, Hannah. *The Origins of Totalitarianism*. New York: Harcourt Brace Jovanovich, 1951.

———. "Reflections on Violence." *New York Review of Books*, February 27, 1969.

Arévalo, Juan José. *La pedagogía de la personalidad*. La Plata, Argentina: Biblioteca de las Humanidades, 1937.

———. "Las cuatro raíces del servilismo (Radiografía del ubiquismo y del hitlerismo)." In *Escritos políticos*, 29–52. Guatemala City: Tipografía Nacional, 1945.

Ariès, Philippe. *Centuries of Childhood: A Social History of Family Life*. New York: Vintage, 1962.

AVANCSO (Asociación para la Avance de las Ciencias Sociales en Guatemala). *Aquí corre la bola*. Guatemala City: AVANCSO, 1986.

———. *Por sí mismos: Un estudio preliminar de las "Maras" en la Ciudad de Guatemala*. Guatemala City: AVANCSO, 1988.

———. *Heridas en la sombra: Percepciones de la violencia en áreas pobres urbanos y perturbadas en la Ciudad de Guatemala*. Guatemala City: AVANCSO, 2000.

———. *El proceso de crecimiento metropolitano de la Ciudad de Guatemala*. Guatemala City: AVANCSO, 2003.

———. *Más allá de la sobrevivencia: La lucha ara una vida digna*. Guatemala City: AVANCSO, 2006.

Azpuru, Dinorah, and Mitchell A. Seligson, eds. *La cultura política y la democracia en Guatemala, 2004: Estudio acerca de la cultura democrática de los guatemaltecos*. Guatemala: ASIES, USAID, 2004.

Banco Internacional de Desarrollo. *Diagnóstico sobre la situación actual de las armas ligeras y la violencia en Guatemala*. Guatemala City: Banco Internacional de Desarrollo, 2002.

Bastos, Santiago, and Manuela Camus. *Sombras de una batalla: Los desplazados por la violencia en la Ciudad de Guatemala*. Guatemala City: FLACSO, 1994.

Becker, Gay, et al. "Memory, Trauma, and Embodied Distress: The Management of Disruption in the Stories of Cambodians in Exile." *Ethos* 28.3 (2000): 320–45.

Bender, Thomas. "The Boundaries and Constituencies of History." *American Literary History* 18 (2006): 267–82.

Berryman, Phillip. *The Religious Roots of Revolution: Christians in Central American Revolutions*. London: SCM Press, 1984.

Bourdieu, Pierre. *Outline of a Theory of Practice*. Cambridge: Cambridge University Press, 1977.

———. *Acts of Resistance: Against the Tyranny of the Market*. New York: New Press, 1998.

Bourgois, Philippe. "The Power of Violence in War and Peace: Post–Cold War Lessons from El Salvador." *Ethnography* 2.1 (2001): 5–34.

———. *In Search of Respect: Selling Crack in El Barrio*. Cambridge: Cambridge University Press, 2002.

Brenneman, Robert E. "From Homie to *Hermano*: Conversion and Gang Exit in Central America." PhD dissertation, University of Notre Dame, South Bend, 2009.

———. *Homies y Hermanos: God and Gangs in Central America*. New York: Oxford University Press, 2011.

Brie, Michael. "Emancipation and the Left: The Issue of Violence." In *Violence Today: Actually Existing Barbarism*. Edited by Leo Panitch and Colin Ley, 239–59. London: Merlin, 2009.

Brotherton, David C., and Luis Barrios. *Street Politics and the Transformation of a New York Gang*. New York: Columbia University Press, 2004.

Cabrera Flores, Diani Priscila. "Cultura de castigo en Guatemala: Reflexiones teórico-antropológicas sobre el castigo y su función social." Tesis de Licenciatura, Universidad de San Carlos, Guatemala City, 2008.

Campbell, Greg, and Joel Dryer. "Death by Deportation." *Boulder Weekly*, May 27, 2004.

Campo-Flores, Arian. "The Most Dangerous Gang in America." *Newsweek*, March 28, 2005.

Camus, Manuela. *La colonia Primero de Julio y "la class media emergente."* Guatemala: FLACSO, 2005.

———. "Primero de Julio: Urban Experiences of Class Decline and Violence." In *Securing the City: Neoliberalism, Space and Insecurity in Postwar Guatemala*. Edited by Kevin Lewis O'Neill and Kedron Thomas, 49–65. Durham: Duke University Press, 2011.

Caruth, Cathy. "Violence and Time: Traumatic Survivals." *Assemblage* 20 (April 1993): 24–25.

———. *Unclaimed Experience: Trauma, Narrative and History*. Baltimore: Johns Hopkins University Press, 1996.

Casa Alianza. *Torture of Guatemalan Street Children: Report to the United Nations Committee against Torture*. Guatemala City: Casa Alianza, 1995.

Casa Alianza et al. "Informe al Señor Philip Alston, Relator Ejecuciones Extrajudiciales de la ONU." Unpublished document. Guatemala City, 2006.

Casal, Pío (Enrique Palacios). *Reseña de la situación general de Guatemala, 1863*. Guatemala City: Academia de Geografía e Historia de Guatemala, 1981.

Castillo, Richard J. *Culture and Mental Illness: A Client-Centered Approach*. Florence: Wadsworth, 1996.

Castillo Chacón, Ana Margarita. "Un poco de historia: Pavón en manos de los propios reos." *Diálogo* 4.42 (August 2005).

Castoriadis, Cornelius. *Figures of the Unthinkable*. Stanford: Stanford University Press, 2007.

Centro de Estudios de Guatemala (CEG). "Las Maras . . . ¿Amenazas a la seguridad?" Informe especial. October 2005. http://www.c.net.gt/ceg/doctos/2005/maras.html.

Centro Juana Azurduy. *Sin salida: Pandillas infanto-juveniles en la Ciudad de Sucre*. Surce, Bolivia, 2000.

Cerbino, Mauro. *Pandillas juveniles: Cultura y conflicto de la calle*. Quito: Editorial El Conejo, 2004.

———. *Jóvenes en la calle: Cultura y conflicto*. Barcelona: Editorial Anthropos, 2006.

Chapeton, Carlos Enrique Peralta, and Williams Waldemar Mazariegos. *Niñez trabajadora en la frontera del peligro*. Guatemala City: PAMI, 1998.

Chinchilla, Norma Stoltz, and Nora Hamilton. *Seeking Community in a Global City: Guatemalans and Salvadorans in Los Angeles.* Philadelphia: Temple University Press, 2001.

Chinchilla, Norma, Nora Hamilton, and James Loucky. "Central Americans and the Los Angeles Community." In *In the Barrios, Latinos and the Underclass Debate.* Edited by Joan Moore and Raquel Pinderhughes, 51–69. New York: Sage, 1993.

Cloward, R. A., and L. E. Ohlin. *Delinquency and Opportunity: A Theory of Delinquent Gangs.* New York: Free Press, 1960.

Cohen, Albert K. *Delinquent Boys: The Culture of the Gang.* Glencoe, Ill.: Free Press, 1955.

Colussi, Marcelo. "Entrevista a Rodolfo Kepfer: Las sociedades tienen múltiples expresiones de la violencia." http://www.crhoy.com.

Connerton, Paul. *How Societies Remember.* Cambridge: Cambridge University Press, 1989.

Corsetti, Jeffrey D. "Marked for Death: The Maras of Central America and Those Who Flee Their Wrath." *Georgetown Immigration Law Journal* 20.3 (2006): 407–36.

Covey, H. C. *Street Gangs throughout the World.* Springfield: Charles C. Thomas, 2003.

Cruz, José Miguel, ed. *Maras y pandillas en Centroamérica.* Vol. 4: *Las respuestas de la sociedad civil organizada.* San Salvador: UCA Editores, 2006.

———. *Street Gangs in Central America.* El Salvador: Universidad Centroamericana, 2007.

Cruz, José Miguel, et al. *Exclusión social jóvenes y pandillas.* El Salvador: FLACSO, 2007.

Cruz, José Miguel, and Marlon Carranza. "Pandillas y políticas públicas: El caso de El Salvador." In *Juventudes, violencia y exclusión: Desafíos para las políticas públicas.* Edited by Javier Moro, 133–76. Guatemala City: IDB, Magna Torres Ediciones, 2006.

Cruz, José Miguel, and N. Portilla. *Peña solidaridad y violencia en las pandillas del Gran San Salvador: Más allá de la vida loca.* San Salvador: UCA Editores, 1998.

Davis, Mike. *Planet of Slums.* London: Verso, 2006.

Demoscopía. *Maras y pandillas: Comunidad y policía en Centroamérica. Hallazgos de un estudio integral.* San José, Costa Rica: Asdi, 2007.

Desjarlais, Robert, and Arthur Kleinman. "Violence and Demoralization in the New World Order." *Anthropology Today* 5 (1995): 9–12.

Diamond, Larry. *Developing Democracy: Toward Consolidation.* Baltimore: Johns Hopkins University Press, 1999.

Díaz García, Celeste. "Aplicación del sistema progresivo como una solución a la crisis del sistema penitenciario guatemalteco." Tesis de Maestría en Derecho Penal, Facultad de Ciencias Jurídicas y Sociales, Universidad de San Carlos, 2003.

Doyle, Kate. "The Atrocity Files: Deciphering the Archives of Guatemala's Dirty War." *Harpers,* December 2007.

Dunn, William. *The Gangs of Los Angeles.* Lincoln: Universe, 2007.

Dussel, Enrique. "The Postmodernism Debate in Latin America." *boundary 2* 20 (autumn 1993): 65–76.

Echeverría, Arturo. "Los niños y niñas sobrevivientes de las masacres en Guatemala." June 1999.

Echeverría, Arturo, et al. "Human Rights Violations in Guatemala: Alternative Report to the United Nations Committee against Torture." Geneva: World Organisation against Torture, 2006.

Esteva, Gustavo. "Beyond Development and Modernity." In *The Reordering of Culture:*

Latin America, the Caribbean and Canada in the Hood. Edited by Alvina Ruprecht and Cecilia Taian, 319–35. Montreal: McGill-Queen's University Press, 1995.

Estrada González, Miguel Ángel. *Rehabilitación social del delincuente*. Guatemala City: Tipografía Nacional, 1965.

Falla, Ricardo. *Masacres de la selva: Ixcán, Guatemala, 1975–1982*. Guatemala City: Editorial Universitaria, 1992.

—. *Juventud de una comunidad maya, Ixcán, Guatemala*. Guatemala City: AVANCSO, 2006.

—. *Negreaba de Zopilotes*. Guatemala City: AVANCSO, 2011.

Fanon, Frantz. *Wretched of the Earth*. New York: Grove, 1963.

Felman, Shoshana, and Dori Laub. *Testimony: Crises of Witnessing in Literature, Psychoanalysis and History*. New York: Routledge, 1992.

Ferguson, James. *Expectations of Modernity: Myths and Meanings of Urban Life on the Zambian Copperbelt*. Berkeley: University of California Press, 1999.

Fernández Menéndez, Jorge, and Victor Ronquillo. *De los Maras a los zeta*. Mexico City: Grijalbo/Mondadori, 2006.

Fernando García, Vilma Duque. *Guatemala: Trabajo infantil en los basureros*. Geneva: Organización Internacional de Trabajo, 2002.

Foro Ecuménico por la Paz y la Reconciliación (FEPAZ). "El fenómeno de las Maras desde la perspectiva socio-religiosa: Un desafío a las Iglesias, la sociedad y el Estado. Guatemala." FEPAZ, 2006.

Foucault, Michel. *Discipline and Punish: The Birth of the Prison*. New York: Vintage, 1978.

—. *The History of Sexuality*. Vol. 1: *An Introduction*. New York: Vintage, 1990.

Foxen, Patricia. *In Search of Providence*. Nashville: Vanderbilt University Press, 2007.

Frankl, Viktor E. *Man's Search for Meaning*. Boston: Beacon, 2006.

Fritzsche, Peter. "Global History and the Bounded Subjects: A Response to Thomas Bender." *American Literary History* 18 (2006):283–87.

Fundación Madrid Paz y Solidaridad. "Operation Sofía, Taking the Fish's Water Away." http://www.ccoomadrid.es/webmadrid (accessed September 27, 2011).

García Noval, José. *Para entender la violencia: Falsa rutas y caminos truncados*. Guatemala City: Editorial Universitaria, 2008.

Gareau, Frederick Henry. *State Terrorism and the United States*. London: Zed, 2004.

Garrard-Burnett, Virginia. *Terror in the Land of the Holy Spirit: Guatemala under General Efraín Ríos Montt*. New York: Oxford University Press, 2010.

Garrard-Burnett, Virginia, and David Stoll. *Rethinking Protestantism in Latin America*. Philadelphia: Temple University Press, 1993.

Gellert, Gisela. "Migration and the Displaced in Guatemala City in the Context of a Flawed National Transformation." In *Journeys of Fear: Refugee Return and National Transformation in Guatemala*. Edited by Lisa L. North and Alan B. Simmons, 112–29. Montreal: McGill-Queen's University Press, 1999.

Gellert, Gisela, and Silvia Irene Palma C. *Precaridad urbana, desarrollo comunitario y mujeres en el área metropolitana de Guatemala*. Guatemala City: FLACSO, 1999.

Giddens, Anthony. *Conversations with Anthony Giddens: Making Sense of Modernity*. Stanford: Stanford University Press, 1998.

Gonzáles, Mariano. "La comunidad a través del dolor." *Psico-red* 2 (2009): 4–5.

Gonzáles, Matilde. *Se cambió el tiempo*. Guatemala City: AVANCSO, 2004.

González Orellana, Carlos. *Historia de la educación en Guatemala*. Guatemala City: Editorial Universitaria, 1980.

Grandin, Greg. *The Last Colonial Massacre: Latin America in the Cold War*. Chicago: University of Chicago Press, 2004.

Green, Linda. *Fear as a Way of Life*. New York: Columbia University Press, 1999.

Gutiérrez, Marta. *Sindicalistas y aparatos de control estatal*. Guatemala City: FLACSO, 2011.

Guzmán Cermeño, Sindy Patricia. "La necesidad de institucionalizar programas para hacer efectiva la reinserción social del recluso." Tesis de Maestría en Derecho Penal Facultad de Ciencias Jurídicas y Sociales, Universidad Rafael Landívar, 2007.

Hagedorn, John M. *People and Folks: Gangs, Crime and the Underclass in a Rustbelt City*. With Perry Macon. 2nd ed. Chicago: Lake View, 1998.

———. "Gang." In *Encyclopedia of Masculinities*. Edited by Michael S. Kimmel and Amy M. Aronson, 329–31. New York: Sage, 2003.

———, ed. *Gangs in the Global City: Alternatives to Traditional Criminology*. Chicago: University of Illinois Press, 2007.

———. *A World of Gangs: Armed Young Men and Gangsta Culture*. Milwaukee: University of Minnesota Press, 2007.

Hale, Charles R. "Consciousness, Violence, and the Politics of Memory in Guatemala." *Current Anthropology* 38.5 (1997): 817–38.

Hamber, Brandon, and Richard A. Wilson. "Symbolic Closure through Memory, Reparation and Revenge in Post-conflict Societies." *Journal of Human Rights* 1.1 (2002): 35–53.

Hayden, Tom. *Street Wars*. New York: New Press, 2004.

Hazlehurst, K., and C. Hazlehurst, eds. *Gangs and Subcultures: International Explorations*. New Brunswick: Transaction, 1998.

Hecht, Tobias, ed. *Minor Omissions: Children in Latin American History and Society*. Madison: University of Wisconsin Press, 2002.

Heinonen, Paula. *Youth Gangs and Street Children: Culture, Nurture and Masculinity in Ethiopia*. New York: Berghahn Books, 2011.

Henry, Doug. "Violence and the Body: Somatic Expressions of Trauma and Vulnerability during War." *Medical Anthropology Quarterly* 20 (2006): 379–98.

Hernandez, Max. "Winnicott's 'Fear of Breakdown': On and Beyond Trauma." *Diacritics* 28.4 (1998): 134–41.

Hinan, Tamar. "To Remember or Forget? Collective Memory and Reconciliation in Guatemala and Rwanda." *Totem: The University of Western Ontario Journal of Anthropology* 18.1 (2010): 13–22.

Hodges, Katherine, and Susannah Radstone, eds. *Contested Pasts: The Politics of Memory*. London: Routledge, 2003.

Huff, C. H., ed. *Gangs in America*. London: Sage, 1996.

Human Rights Watch. *Guatemala's Forgotten Children: Police Violence and Abuses in Detention*. Washington, D.C.: Human Rights Watch, 1999.

ILO. "Ficha País: Guatemala." http://www.oit.org.pe/ipec/documentos/ficha_pais_gua .pd (accessed December 29, 2006).

Informe de Verificación. *La situación penitenciaria en Guatemala*. Guatemala City: Minugua, 2000.

Instituto de Estudios Comparados en Ciencias Penales de Guatemala. *Prisiones, el desafío del nuevo milenio*. Guatemala City: IECCP, 2000.

Instituto para la Superación de la Miseria Urbana de Centroamérica (ISMU). *Dinámica de las condiciones de la vida urbana: El caso específico del área metropolitano de la Ciudad de Guatemala*. Guatemala City: ISMU, 1998.

Jelin, Elizabeth. *State Repression and the Struggle for Memory*. London: Latin American Bureau, 2003.

Jenkins, Janis. "The Impress of Extremity: Women's Experiences of Trauma and Political Violence." In *Gender and Health: An International Perspective*. Edited by Caroline Brettell and Carolyne Sargent, 278–91. Upper Saddle River, N.J.: Prentice Hall, 1996.

Jonas, Susanne. *Of Centaurs and Doves: Guatemala's Peace Process*. Boulder: Westview, 2000.

———. "Democratization through Peace: The Difficult Case of Guatemala." *Journal of Interamerican Studies and World Affairs* 42.4 (2001): 9–37.

Jones, Gareth A., and Dennis Rodgers. *Youth Violence in Latin America: Gangs and Juvenile Justice in Perspective*. New York: Palgrave Macmillan, 2009.

Kelley, Robin. *Black Rebels: Culture, Politics and the Black Working Class*. New York: Free Press, 1996.

Khanna, Ranjana. *Dark Continents: Psychoanalysis and Colonialism*. Durham: Duke University Press, 2003.

Kinnvall, Catarina. "Globalization and Religious Nationalism: Self, Identity, and the Search for Ontological Security." *Political Psychology* 25 (2004): 741–67.

Kobrak, Paul. *State Violence in Guatemala, 1960–1996: A Quantitative Reflection*. New York: American Association for the Advancement of Science, 1999.

Konefal, Betsy. *For Every Indio Who Falls: A History of Maya Activism in Guatemala, 1960–1990*. Albuquerque: University of New Mexico Press, 2010.

Koonings, Kees, and Dirk Kruijt. *Armed Actors, Organized Violence and State Failure in Latin America*. London: Zed Books, 2004.

Koonz, Claudia. *The Nazi Conscience*. Cambridge, Mass.: Harvard University Press, 2003.

La Capra, Dominick. *Representing the Holocaust: History, Theory, and Trauma*. Ithaca: Cornell University Press, 1994.

———. "Trauma, Absence, Loss." *Critical Inquiry* 25 (1999): 696–727.

———. *Writing Trauma, Writing History*. Baltimore: Johns Hopkins University Press, 2001.

Lara Klahr, Marco. *Hoy te toca la muerte: El imperio de las Mara visto desde dentro*. Mexico City: Editorial Plantea Mexicana, 2006.

Levenson, Deborah. *Hacer la juventud: Jóvenes de tres generaciones de una familia trabajadora en la Ciudad de Guatemala*. Guatemala City: AVANCSO, 2005.

Levenson-Estrada, Deborah. *Trade Unionists against Terror: Guatemala City, 1954–1985*. Chapel Hill: University of North Carolina Press, 1994.

Lira, Elizabeth. "Violence, Fear and Impunity: Reflections on Subjective and Political Obstacles for Peace." *Peace and Conflict: Journal of Peace Psychology* 2 (2001): 109–18.

Lopes, Sabine M., et al. "Factors Associated with Poor Mental Health among Guatemalan Refugees Living in Mexico 20 Years after Civil Conflict." *Public Health* 19 (2006): 132–70.

López Martín, Antonio. *Cien años de historia penitenciaria en Guatemala: De la Penitenciaria Central a la Granja Penal de Pavón*. Guatemala City: Tipografía Nacional, 1978.

Mack Chang, Myrna, et al. *Dónde está el futuro*. Guatemala City: AVANCSO, 1992.

Mack Chang, Myrna, and Paula Worby. *Política institucional hacia el desplazado interno en Guatemala*. Guatemala City: AVANCSO, 1990.

Manwaring, Max G. *Street Gangs: The New Urban Insurgency*. Washington, D.C.: Strategic Studies Institute, 2005.

Maquieira, Padre Manolo, SJ. "Juventud marginal, necesitada de jubileo." *Voces del Tiempo: Revista de Religión y Sociedad* 30 (2000): 66–72.

Marable, Manning. *How Capitalism Underdeveloped Black America*. Boston: South End, 1999.

Martín-Baró, Ignacio, SJ. *Writings for a Liberation Psychology*. Cambridge, Mass.: Harvard University Press, 1994.

Mazariegos, Juan Carlos. *La guerra de los nombres: Una historia de la rebelión, el genocidio y el ojo del poder soberano en Guatemala*. Guatemala City: AVANCSO, 2010.

Mbembe, Achille. "Necropolitics." *Public Culture* 15 (winter 2003): 110–40.

McAllister, Carlota. "An Indian Dawn." In *The Guatemala Reader: History, Culture, Politics*. Edited by Greg Grandin, Deborah T. Levenson, and Elizabeth Oglesby, 352–59. Durham: Duke University Press, 2011.

McClintock, Michael. *The American Connection: State Terror and Popular Resistance in Guatemala*. London: Zed Books, 1985.

Medina, Juan José, and Pedro Mateu-Gelabert. *Maras y pandillas: Comunidad y policía en Centroamérica. Hallazgos de un estudio*. San José, Costa Rica: Asdi, 2007.

Mehta, Urday S. "Liberal Strategies of Exclusion." In *Tensions of Empire*. Edited by F. Cooper and A. Stoler, 59–86. Berkeley: University of California Press, 1997.

Melville, Margaret, and Brinton Lykes. "Guatemalan Indian Children and the Sociocultural Effects of Government-Sponsored Terror." *Social Science Medicine* 34 (1992): 533–48.

Melville, Tom, and Marjorie Melville. *Whose Heaven, Whose Earth?* New York: Knopf, 1971.

Memoria del Seminario. "La situación actual y perspectivas del trabajo psico-social en la Secretaría de Bienestar." *Secretaría de Bienestar* 82 (June 1987): 69–88.

Merino, Juan. "Las Maras en Guatemala." In *Maras y pandillas en Centroamérica*. Vol. 1. Edited by ERIC, IDESO, IUDOP, and IDIES, 112–95. Managua: UCA publicaciones, 2001.

———. "Guatemala: Variables de capital social asociadas a la presencia de Maras." In *Maras y pandillas en Centroamérica*. Vol. 2: *Pandillas y capital social*. Edited by ERIC, IDESO, IDIES, and IUDOP, 89–177. San Salvador: UCA editores, 2004.

———. "Políticas juveniles y rehabilitación de mareros en Guatemala." In *Maras y pandillas en Centroamérica*. Vol. 3: *Políticas juveniles y rehabilitación*. Edited by ERIC, IDIES, IUDOP, NITLAPAN, and DIRINPRO, 133–72. San Salvador: UCA editores, 2004.

Monzón, Samuel Alfredo. *La educación de los transgresores en Guatemala*. Guatemala City: Universidad de San Carlos, 1986.

Morales, Hilda. *Estudio comparativo de la estructura de dos comunidades: Tierra Nueva y aldea Lo de Fuentes*. Guatemala City: Mimeo, 1981.

Morán Mérida, Amanda. *Condiciones de vida y tenencia de la tierra en asentamientos precarios de la Ciudad de Guatemala*. Guatemala City: CEUR, University of San Carlos, 1997.

Moser, Caroline, and Cathy McIlwaine. *Encounters with Violence in Latin America: Urban Poor Perceptions from Colombia and Guatemala*. New York: Routledge, 2004.

Münzel, Mark. *The Aché: Genocide Continues in Paraguay*. Copenhagen: International Work Group for Indigenous Affairs, 1974.

National Labor Committee and Center for the Studies and Support of Local Development. *Harvest of Shame*. Chicago, March 2000.

Narváez Gutiérrez, Juan Carlos. *Ruta transnacional: A San Salvador por Los Ángeles*. Mexico City: Universidad Autónomo de Zacatecas, 2007.

Nazario, Sonia. *Enrique's Journey*. New York: Random House, 2007.

Núñez, Juan Carlos, SJ. *De la ciudad al barrio: Redes y tejidos urbanos. Guatemala, El Salvador y Nicaragua*. Guatemala City: Universidad Rafael Landívar, 1996.

Offit, Thomas. *Conquistadores de la Calle: Child Street Labor in Guatemala City*. Austin: University of Texas Press, 2008.

Oficina de Derechos Humanos del Arzobispado de Guatemala. "Prevención y abordaje de tratos crueles, inhumanos o degradantes en las cárceles de Guatemala." *Informe* (Report). 2005.

Oglesby, Elizabeth. "Historical Memory and the Limits of Peace Education: Examining Guatemala's Memory of Silence and the Limits of Peace Education." Carnegie Council on Ethics and International Affairs, 2004.

———. "Educating Citizens in Postwar Guatemala: Historical Memory, Genocide, and the Culture of Peace." *Radical History Review* 97 (2007): 77–98.

O'Neill, Kevin Lewis. "The Reckless Will: Prison Chaplaincy and the Problem of Mara Salvatrucha." *Public Culture* 22 (2010): 67–87.

Ordóñez Jonama, Ramiro. *La cárceles en Guatemala (visión histórico-legal)*. Guatemala City: Universidad Rafael Landívar, 1970.

Pahl, Jon. *Empire of Sacrifice: The Religious Origins of American Violence*. New York: New York University Press, 2010.

Paiz Barrios, Blanca Esther. "Análisis jurídico de los grupos etarios y efectos negativos de su internamiento en el Centro Juvenil y de Privación de Libertad." Tesis de Licenciatura, Guatemala, Universidad de San Carlos, 2008.

Panter-Brick, Catherine. "Street Children, Human Rights, and Public Health: A Critique and Future Directions." *Annual Review of Anthropology* 31 (2002): 147–71.

Palomo, H. C. *Efectos de un fenómeno natural en un país subdesarrollado: Tierra Nueva a consecuencia del terremoto de 1976*. Guatemala City: Universidad de San Carlos, 1977.

PAMI. *Menores trabajadores en labores de alto riesgo*. Guatemala City: PAMI, 1997.

Passerini, Luisa. *Memory and Totalitarianism*. New Brunswick, N.J.: Transaction Publishers, 2005.

Payeras, Mario. *El trueno en la ciudad: Episodios de la lucha armada urbana de 1981 en Guatemala*. Mexico City: J. Pablos Editor, 1987.

Peacock, Susan C., and Adriana Beltrán. *Poderes ocultos: Grupos ilegales armados en la Guatemala post conflicto y las fuerzas detrás de ellos*. Washington, D.C.: Washington Office on Latin America, 2003.

Pellicer, Liliana. "La semilla de las Maras." *Revista D. La Prensa Libre*, April 3, 2005.

Perea Restrepo, Carlos Mario. *Con el diablo adentro: Pandillas, tiempo paralelo y poder*. Mexico City: Siglo XXI, 2007.

Plan Nacional de la Juventud. *Fenómeno de las Maras*. Guatemala City, 1987.

Porras Castejón, Gustavo. *Las huellas de Guatemala*. Guatemala: F y G Editores, 2009.

Portelli, Alessandro. *The Order Has Been Carried Out: History, Memory and the Meaning of a Nazi Massacre in Rome*. New York: Palgrave Macmillan, 2003.

Primer Congreso Pedagógico Centroamericano 1893. Guatemala City, 1894.

Procurador de los Derechos Humanos (PDH). *Muertes violentas de niñez, adolescencia y jóvenes y propuestas para su prevención*. Guatemala City: PDH, 2004.

———. *Primer Informe del Observatorio Guatemalteco de Cárceles 2004*. Guatemala City: PDH, 2005.

Prophettei, Albane, Claudia Paz, José Garcia Noval, and Nieves Gómez. "Violence in Guatemala after the Armed Conflict." Unpublished paper, June 2003.

Quex Mucia, Nilda Ileana. "Derechos humanos y constitucionales de los reclusos en el Centro de Detención Preventiva de Fraijanes." Tesis de Maestría en Derecho Penal, Universidad de San Carlos, 2006.

Ramírez, Luis Rodolfo, and Gustavo Cetina. *Alternativas a la justicia penal y la prisión*. Guatemala City: ECCP, 1998.

Ramírez, S., and Claudia Paz. *Diagnóstico de conflictividad local en la pos-guerra*. Guatemala City: Instituto de Estudios Comparados en Ciencias Penales de Guatemala, 2002.

Ramírez Heredia, Rafael. *La Mara*. Mexico City: Alfaguara, 2004.

Ranum, Elin Cecilie. "Diagnóstico Nacional Guatemala." Proyecto "Pandillas juveniles transnacionales en Centroamérica, México y Estados Unidos." Centro de Estudios y Programas Interamericanos (CEPI) del Instituto Tecnológico Autónomo de México (ITAM), 2006. http://interamericanos.itam.mx/maras/docs/Diagnostico_Guatemala.pdf (accessed October 16, 2012).

Reguillo Cruz, Rossana. *En la calle otra vez: Las bandas juveniles, identidad urbana y usos de la comunicación*. Guadalajara: ITESO, 1995.

———. *Emergencia de culturas juveniles*. Bogotá: Grupo Editorial Norma, 2000.

———. "La gestión del futuro." *Revista de Estudios sobre la Juventud* 5 (2001): 6–25.

———. "La Mara: Contingencia y afiliación con el exceso." *Nueva Sociedad* 20 (2005): 70–84.

REMHI (Recuperación de la Memoria Histórica). *Inforrme: Nunca Mas*. Guatemala: Oficina de Derechos Humanos del Arzobispado de Guatemala, 1998.

Remijne, Simon. *Memorias de violencia, patrullas de autodefensa civil y la herencia del conflicto en Joyabaj, Quiche*. Guatemala City: AVANCSO, 2005.

Rivera Solis, Luis Guillermo, ed. *Pandillas juveniles y gobernabilidad democracia en América Latina y el Caribe*. Buenos Aires: FLACSO, 2004.

Rodgers, Dennis. *Dying for It: Gangs, Violence and Social Change in Urban Nicaragua*. London: DESTIN, 2003.

————. "Living in the Shadow of Death: Gangs, Violence and Social Order in Urban Nicaragua, 1996–2002." PhD dissertation, University of Cambridge, 2004.

————. "The Gangs of Central America: Major Players and Scapegoats." *Revista Envío* 317 (December 2007). http://www.envio.org.ni/articulo/3704.

————. "Slum Wars of the 21st Century: Gangs, Mano Dura, and the New Urban Geography of Conflict in Central America." *Development and Change* 40.5 (2009): 949–76.

Rodney, Walter. *How Europe Underdeveloped Africa.* Rev. ed. Atlanta: Howard University Press, 1981.

Rodriguez, Luis J. *Always Running: La Vida Loca, Gang Days in LA.* New York: Touchstone, 2005.

Rodríguez Rojas, María Eugenia. *Cultura y contra-cultura en la posmodernidad: El lenguaje en las Maras centroamericanas.* San José, Costa Rica: Editorial, Librería y Centro de Foto-copiado Alma Mater, 2008.

Rodríguez Valiente, Oscar. *La historia de un lustrador.* Guatemala City: P. Amenabar, 1989.

Rubel, Arthur J., et al. *Susto: A Folk Illness.* Berkeley: University of California Press, 1984.

Rubio, Mauricio. *De la pandilla a la Mara: Pobreza, educación, mujeres y violencia juvenil.* Bogotá: Universidad Externado de Colombia, 2007.

Salazar Similox, Vitalino. *Una aproximación al fenómeno de las Maras y pandillas en Centro-américa: Punto de partida para la reflexión y acción de la comunidad cristiana mesoamericana.* Tegucigalpa: Comunidad Cristiana Mesoamericana, 2006.

Salomón, Leticia. *La violencia en Honduras 1980–1993.* Tegucigalpa: CEDOH, 1993.

Salvatore, Ricardo D., and Carlos Aguirre. *The Birth of the Penitentiary in Latin America: Essays on Criminology, Prison Reform and Social Control, 1830–1940.* Austin: University of Texas Press, 1996.

Sanchez Jankowski, Martin. *Islands in the Street: Gangs and American Urban Society.* Berkeley: University of California Press, 1991.

Sanford, Victoria. *Buried Secrets: Truth and Human Rights in Guatemala.* New York: Palgrave Macmillan, 2003.

————. *Guatemala: Del genocidio al feminicidio.* Guatemala City: F y G Editores, 2008.

Santacruz Giralt, María L., and Alberto Concha-Eastman. *Barrio adentro: La solidaridad violenta de las pandillas en El Salvador.* San Salvador: IUDOP, OPS, and Homies Unidos, 2001.

Santos Anaya, Martín Christian. *La vergüenza de los pandilleros: Masculinidad, emociones y conflictos en esquineros del cercado de Lima.* Lima: Centro de Estudio y Acción para la Paz, 2002.

Santos Chocano, José. *Minerva en América.* Guatemala City: Tipografía Nacional, 1909.

Sassen, Saskia. "The Global City: One Setting for New Types of Gang Work and Politi-cal Culture." In *Gangs in the Global City: Alternatives to Traditional Criminology.* Edited by John M. Hagedorn, 97–119. Chicago: University of Illinois Press, 2007.

Savenije, Wim. *Maras y barras: Pandillas y violencia juvenil en los barrios marginales de Centro-américa.* El Salvador: FLACSO, 2006.

Scheper-Hughes, Nancy, and Phillip Bourgois. *Violence in War and Peace, an Anthology.* Oxford: Blackwell, 2003.

Schirmer, Jennifer. *Guatemala Military Project: A Violence Called Democracy*. Philadelphia: University of Pennsylvania Press, 1999.

Schneider, Eric C. *Vampires, Dragons and Egyptian Kings: Youth Gangs in Postwar New York*. Princeton, N.J.: Princeton University Press, 2001.

Scott, James. *Weapons of the Weak: Everyday Forms of Peasant Resistance*. New Haven: Yale University Press, 1985.

Sieder, Rachel. *Guatemala after the Peace Accords*. London: Institute of Latin American Studies, 1999.

————, ed. "War, Peace, and the Politics of Memory in Guatemala." In *Burying the Past: Making Peace and Doing Justice after Civil Conflict*. Edited by Nigel Biggar, 184–206. Washington, D.C.: Georgetown University Press, 2001.

Sieder, Rachel, Megan Thomas, George Vickers, and Jack Spence. *Who Governs? Guatemala Five Years after the Peace Accords*. Cambridge, Mass.: Hemisphere Initiative, 2002.

Smutt, Marcela, and Jenny Lissette E. Miranda. *El fenómeno de las pandillas en El Salvador*. El Salvador: FLACSO, 1998.

Sorel, Georges. *Reflections on Violence*. Cambridge: Cambridge University Press, 1999.

Stanley, William, and David Holiday. "Broad Participation, Diffuse Responsibility: Peace Implementation in Guatemala." In *Ending Civil Wars: The Implementation of Peace Agreements*. Edited by Stephen John Stedman et al., 421–62. Boulder: Lynne Rienner, 2002.

Strocka, Cordula. "Youth Gangs in Latin America." *SAIS Review of International Affairs* 36.2 (summer–fall 2006): 133–46.

Taquela, Graciela María. "Memoria sin tiempo." In *La impunidad: Una perspectiva psicosocial y clínica*. Edited by Diana Kordon et al., 80–83. Buenos Aires: Editorial Sudamericana, 1995.

Taussig, Michael. "Culture of Terror—Space of Death: Roger Casement's Putumayo Report and the Explanation of Torture." *Comparative Studies in Society and History* 26.3 (1984): 467–97.

Taylor, Charles. *A Secular Age*. Cambridge, Mass.: Harvard University Press, 2007.

Taylor, William B. "Between Global Process and Local Knowledge: An Inquiry into Early Latin American Social History, 1500–1900." *Journal of Latin American Studies* 38 (2006): 267–92.

Thompson, Alistair, Michael Frisch, and Paula Hamilton. "The Memory and Historical Debates: Some International Perspectives." *Oral History* 22 (1994): 33–43.

Thrasher, Frederic. *The Gang: A Study of 1,313 Gangs in Chicago*. Chicago: University of Chicago Press, 1927.

Tierney, Nancy Leigh. *Robbed of Humanity: Lives of Guatemalan Street Children*. New York: Pangaea Press, 1997.

Tobar Estrada, Anneliza. *Entre mundos ajenos: Encuentro de percepciones de jóvenes pandilleros, ex pandilleros y acompañantes sobre la sociedad guatemalteca*. Guatemala City: FLACSO, 2006.

Toriello Garrido, Guillermo. *Guatemala: Más de veinte años de traición, 1954–1979*. Guatemala City: Editorial Universitaria, 1981.

Tribunal permanente de los pueblos indígenas. Madrid: Mimeo, 1983.

Trigueros Martel, Roxana. "Las Maras salvadoreñas: Nuevas formas de espanto y control social." In *Estudios Centroamericanos*, 957–79. El Salvador: 2004.

Tzún Ajxup, Herbert Macario. "Ejecución de sentencia en el proceso penal guatemalteco: Granja de Rehabilitación Cantel, Quetzaltenango." Tesis de Licenciatura, Universidad Rafael Landívar, 2005.

United Nations Population Division. "World Urbanization Prospects: The 2001 Revision." http://www.un.org/esa/population/publications/wup2001/wup2001dh.pdf (accessed November 1, 2010).

USAID. "Central America and Mexico Gang Assessment." Washington, D.C.: USAID, 2006. http://transition.usaid.gov/locations/latin_america_caribbean/democracy /gangs.html.

U.S. Department of State. *2009 Human Rights Reports: Guatemala*. http://www.state.gov /g/drl/rls/hrrpt/2009/wha/136114.htm.

Vásquez, Manuel A. "Saving Souls Transnationally: Pentacostalism and Gangs in El Salvador." In *Globalizing the Sacred*. Edited by Manuel A. Vásquez and Marie F. Marquandt, 199–243. New Brunswick, N.J.: Rutgers University Press, 2003.

Vega Romero, Edgar. "Estudio de las clases sociales y su repercusión en los delitos y en el número de personas recluidas en el centro de detención preventivo para Hombre, Fraijanes, Guatemala." Tesis de Licenciatura, Facultad de Ciencias Jurídicas y Sociales de la Universidad de San Carlos, Guatemala, 2007.

Vela, José Francisco de Mata. *La reforma procesal penal en Guatemala*. Barcelona: Universidad Autónoma de Barcelona, 2007.

Vela, Manolo, Alexander Sequén-Mónchez, and Hugo Antonio Solares. *El lado oscuro de la eterna primavera: Violencia, criminalidad y delincuencia de post-guerra*. Guatemala City: FLACSO, 2001.

Vela Castañeda, Manolo. "Los pelotones de la muerte: La construcción de los perpetradores del genocidio guatemalteco." PhD dissertation, El Colegio de México, Mexico City, 2009.

Vigil, James Diego. *Barrio Gangs: Street Life and Identity in Southern California*. Austin: University of Texas Press, 1988.

———. *A Rainbow of Gangs: Street Cultures in the Mega-city*. Austin: University of Texas Press, 2002.

———. "Urban Violence and Street Gangs." *Annual Review of Anthropology* 32 (2003): 225–42.

———. *Gangs and Non-gang Families in East Los Angeles*. Austin: University of Texas Press, 2007.

Vogler, Candace, and Pathchen Markell. "Introduction: Violence, Redemption, and the Liberal Imagination." *Public Culture* 15.1 (winter 2003): 1–10.

Wacquante, Loic. *Las cárceles de la miseria*. Madrid: Alianza Editorial, 2000.

Wilson, Richard. "Violent Truths: The Politics of Memory in Guatemala." In *Negotiating Rights: The Guatemalan Peace Process*, 18–28. London: International Review of Peace Initiatives, 1997.

Winton, Alisa. "With Gangs and Violence: Analyzing the Social and Spatial Mobility of Young People in Guatemala City." *Children's Geographies* 3 (2005): 167–84.

Wolfe, Sonja. "*Maras transnacionales*: Origin and Transformations of Central American Street Gangs." *Latin American Research Review* 1 (2010): 256–65.

Wolseth, Jon. *Jesus and the Gang: Youth Violence and Christianity in Urban Honduras*. Tucson: University of Arizona Press, 2011.

Yablonsky, Lewis. *The Violent Gang*. New York: Macmillan, 1966.

Zilberg, Elana. "'Fools Banished from the Kingdom': Remapping Geographies of Gang Violence between the Americas (Los Angeles and El Salvador)." *American Quarterly* 56 (2004): 759–79.

Zubillaga, Verónica. "Un testimonio reflexivo sobre la experiencia de construir historias de vida con jóvenes de vida violenta." *Revista Mexicana de Sociología* 65 (2003): 305–38.

Zur, Judith. "Remembering and Forgetting: Guatemalan War Widows' Forbidden Memories." In *Trauma: Life Stories of Survivors*. Edited by Kim Lacy Rogers et al., 43–58. New York: Routledge, 1999.

INDEX

Note: Page numbers followed by "f" indicate figures.

political vs. apolitical violence, 8–9; politics and, 8–9; wars and, 9. *See also* Maras; *pandillas*

Garavito, Marco, 52, 89

Garrard-Burnett, Virginia, 58

gender roles, 7, 57, 96–97. *See also* machismo

genocide, 3, 23, 34, 150n40. *See also* massacres; Mayas: persecution of; scorched-earth campaigns

Giammattei, Alejandro, 122–24

Giddens, Anthony, 147n35

Gómez Estrada, Saulo Fernando ("el Chuky"/Solo Estilos), 129, 141

Gonzáles, Mariano, 93

graffiti, 81f, 82f, 85f

Grandin, Greg, 33

"green-lighting" (giving death warrant), 130, 135, 137, 138

group homes, 39, 91, 108, 136f

Grupo de Apoyo Mutuo (GAM), 55

Guarchaj, Edgar, 39

Guatemala City, 54; problems in, 1–2, 78; "shadows of war" in, 43–52. *See also* specific topics

Guatemalan Army, 35, 38–39; abusive training of recruits, 35–36; persons forced to join, 35, 37f; violence against civilians, 2, 16, 33–34, 39 (*see also* massacres)

Guatemalan Civil War, 22, 35; growth of violence following, 49; in 1980s–90s, 32–35

Guatemalan Liberal Party, 1

Guerrilla Army of the Poor. *See* Ejército Guerrillero de los Pobres

Guevara, Che, 68

Guillermo, 98, 101

Hamilton, Nora, 40

Hayden, Tom, 41

Heredia, Rafael Ramírez, 79

Hernán (Mara 33 member), 63–67, 72

history and violence, 16–17

Holocaust, 26

homosexuality, 58, 65, 72

hopelessness, accepting, 93

Huelga de Dolores (Strike of Sorrows), 31

Imery, Jorge Romero, 26

immigration to Los Angeles, 40–43, 137–38

imperialism, opposition to, 27–28

impunity, 17, 49, 83, 86–88, 123, 140, 159n44

"Indian Problem," 13

indigenous populations. *See* genocide; Mayas

"indios," 13–14

industrial development, 43

Instituto de Varones, student review parade at, 29f

International Workers' Day march and rally, 32

Ixpancoc, Rodrigo Sic, 35

jails. *See* penitentiary system; prisons

Joel (Mara Belén member), 65–66

Julio, 40, 41

juvenile delinquency, causes of, 57–58

juvenile detention centers. *See* Etapa 2; penitentiary system

Kepfer, Rodolfo, 7, 77, 87, 125

kidnappings, 26, 31, 33, 42. *See also* "disappeared" persons

killing, 91–93, 95–98; "green-lighting" of (giving death warrant), 130, 135, 137, 138; methods of, 36, 49; motivations for, 49; statistics, 49, 50, 97. *See also* genocide; massacres; necroliving

labor activists, 20

labor market, 43

labor strikes, 31, 54, 86–87

Ladinos, 26, 73

La Eme (Mexican drug ring), 21, 40, 42

"LA gangs," 9

La Juventud (Youth), 1, 2; social construction of, 12–13

La Liga de Higiene Mental, 52

Latin Kings (gang). *See* Almighty Latin King and Queen Nation

lesbians, 72

liberalism, 147n35

liberation theology, 32, 47, 53

life, power of, 27–32

Lima Oliva, Bryan, 115, 116
López, Aíibal, 53–55, 73, 74f
Los Angeles, immigration to and gangs in, 40–43, 137–38
Los Locos, 43, 85f, 92
love and Maras, 72
Luis Arturo, 89
Lupe (Mara Pirañas member), 61, 65, 67

machismo, 72
Maldonado Castillo, Marta Yolanda, 60–61
mano dura (iron fist) politics, calls for, 4, 88, 128, 159n40
Manolo, Padre. *See* Maquieira, Manolo
Manwaring, Max G., 78
Maquieira, Manolo, 88, 93, 95–97
Mara de la 4, 65
Mara-18 (M-18), 41, 83, 87, 88, 90, 103, 113, 114f, 117f; conflict with MS-13, 116, 118, 124
Mara FIVE, 69
Mara Nene, 47, 55
Mara Plaza Vivar Capitol, 21, 77
Maras (gangs), 34, 43, 71, 73; characterizations of, 53, 88–89; children in, 98, 101–4; city residents' perspectives on and perceptions of, 80–89; economics of, 72; exiting, 89, 133, 135–40; families and, 61, 63, 95; formation and early history of, 2, 3, 16, 22, 34; internal life of, 91; members of (*see* mareros); names of, 55; offering clues to the world around them, 3; origin of the name, 57; overview of, 55–56; politics and, 4, 6, 8–10; prisons and, 5f, 113, 115; psychology and sociology of, 59–61, 63–73, 98; reasons for joining, 53, 91, 96–98; religious, 59 (*see also* Pentecostalism and Pentecostal groups); as Satanic, 58–59; transformation of, 3–4, 7–8, 17; "us vs. them" mentality, 3–4; violent deaths and, 4, 6–7. *See also* gangs; *specific topics*
Mara Salvatrucha. *See* MS-13
Maras Las Cobras, 47, 55
Mara 33, 57, 69
mareros: characterizations of, 92–93, 97–98; as foot soldiers, 97–98; research

about, 59–75; skilled and professional manipulation of, 87; "Why should I talk?," 89–97. *See also* Maras; *specific topics*
marginalization, 7
Maritza (Mara de la 4 member), 53, 65, 66, 68, 70–71, 140
Markell, Pathchen, 147n35
Martín-Baró, Ignacio, 6, 18, 77
Marvin (Mara Garañones member), 63, 66
masculinity, 7; machismo, 72. *See also* gender roles
massacres, 16, 21; 1980–83, 1, 34–36, 38, 39, 50; at Cuarto Pueblo, 36; at Dos Erres, 148n47; Efraín Ríos Montt and, 35, 107; fear of speaking about, 39, 43; at Finca San Francisco, 38, 151n56; "high-intensity" and "low-intensity," 52; at Panzós, 3, 33; reactions to and memories of, 16, 102–4; religion and, 35, 107, 108; at Río Pixcayá, 1; in rural areas, 34–36, 38, 101–4, 108, 151n56; statistics, 22, 34; writings about, 16
Mayas, 13; barbarized and made into cruel soldiers, 35–36; and ethnic and class structure and hierarchy, 73, 74f; forced into army, 35, 37f; persecution of, 26, 27, 32–35, 39; racism against, 26
media, 27
Medina, Kimberly Baker, 138
Memoria del silencio, 1, 35, 50
memories, 75; "collective war memory," 46, 152n79; of massacres, 16, 102–4
Menchú, Rigoberta, 68
Mendoza, Estuardo Edwin, 20, 39, 101–4
Mexican Americans, 40, 41
Mexican border, 10, 15, 39
Mexicans, 42
Mexico, 33
Mezquital, 48f
migration, 39
Miguel (Mara FIVE member), 62f
military massacres, 23
Miranda, Ernesto, 41–42
modernity, 12, 147n35; childhood, adolescence, violence, and, in Guatemala, 11–16
Montenegro, Julio César Méndez, reformist government of, 24

growth of, following Civil War, 49; in Guatemala's dumpy modernity, 11–16; historical perspective on, 49–50; history and, 16–17; internalization of, 52; law of conservation of, 16–18; statistics, 34; terminology, 50. *See also specific topics*

"violencia, la," 49, 50, 93, 96

Vogler, Candace, 147n35

Winter Vidaurre, Jorge Emilio, 89, 125

Yolanda (Mara Belén member), 61, 63, 64

Young Catholic Worker movement, 32

Zepeda, Luis Alfonso, 122

zones, 12, 34, 54; Zone 1, 54, 57; Zone 6, 88, 89; Zone 18, 124